India at a Glance

India at a Glance

Jaya S. Nagendra

KALPAZ

India at a Glance

Jaya S. Nagendra

ISBN : 978-81-7835-935-9

Published in 2013 in India by
Kalpaz Publications
C-30, Satyawati Nagar,
Delhi - 110052
E-mail: kalpaz@hotmail.com

Laser Type Setting : Sanya Computers, Delhi
Printed at : Chawla Offset Printers, Delhi

Contents

Preface (xi)

1. India at a Glance **1**

About India
Geological Formation of India
(a) Surface Features
(b) Climate
(c) People
(d) Languages – Sanskrit and Linguistics Science, Hindi Language Dialectics

2. Ancient India and Origin of Hindu Civilisation **12**

Early Habitation in India
300,000-250,000 B.C.-Narmada Man
7000-2600 B.C.-Mehrgarh Site
7000-5500 B.C.-Period I: Neolithic (New Stone Age)
5500-4500 B.C.-Period II: Burj Basket Marked Phase
4500-4000 B.C.-Period III: Togau
4000-3800 B.C.-Period IV: Togau/Kechi Beg
3800-3500 B.C.-Period V: Kechi Beg
3500-3200 B.C.-Period VI: Kechi Beg/ Damb Sadaat
3200-2600 B.C.-Period VII: Damb Sadaat
3000 B.C.-Harappa and Mohenjo-Daro (Indus-Valley Civilisation)
1700 B.C.-Aryan Civilisation
(a) Aryan Invasion Theory
(b) Non-Aryan Invasion Theory
(c) The New Model
1500-600 B.C.-Vedic Period
(a) Rig Veda

(b) Yajur Veda
(c) Sama Veda
(d) Atharva Veda
(e) Vedic Cosmology
800-400 B.C. – Upanishads
List of 108 Upanishads
700-300 B.C.-Mahajanapadas
600 B.C.-200 A.D.-Epic Period
Ramayana
Outline of the Story, Versions, Buddhist Version of Ramayana, and Jain Version of Ramayana
Mahabharata
Outline of the Story, Kurukshetra war, Pandava Army, Kaurava Army, Army Division and Weaponry Used, Military Formations, Rules of War, Course of War, Akshauhini, Jain Version of Mahabharata
Bhagavad Gita
From 200 A.D.-Sutra Period
300-1200 A.D.-Puranas/Mythology
Purpose of Puranas, Functions of Mythology as per Joseph Campbell,
Evolution of Puranas/Mythology, List of Puranas
From 200 A.D.-Scholastic Period
Indian Music **64**
Indian Philosophers **160**
3000 B.C. – Hinduism
900 B.C. and 600 B.C. – Jainism
Structure of Jain Universe and Time Cycles, Karma Theory,
Customs and Practices, Major sects, Contributions
600 B.C. – Buddhism
Hinayana (Theravada), Mahayana, The Noble Eightfold Path
Magadha Empire **83**
684-550 A.D.-Magadha Empire
684–320 B.C.-Magadha Dynasties
1700-799 B.C.-Brihadratha dynasty

799-684 B.C.-Pradyota dynasty
684-413 B.C.-Haryanka dynasty
413-345 B.C. B.C. Shishunaga dynasty
345-321 B.C.-Nanda dynasty
324-184 B.C.-Maurya dynasty–Chandragupta Maurya
Chanukya's Arthashasthra
Megasthanese' Indica
304-232 B.C.-Ashoka the Great
185-73 B.C. Shunga dynasty
73-43 B.C. Kanva dynasty
240-550 A.D. Gupta Dynasty
240-280 A.D. Srigupta and Ghatotkacha
280-319 A.D.Chandragupta I
335-390 A.D. Samudragupta
Ramagupta
380-413 A.D. Chandragupta II
415-455 A.D. Kumaragupta I
455-467 A.D. – Skandagupta
Gupta administration
Huna invasion and the decline of the Empire
Middle Kingdoms of India **118**
230 B.C.–1279 A.D. Middle Kingdoms
600 B.C. Gandhara
600-500 B.C. Persian and Greek Conquests
200 B.C.-10A.D. The Indo-Greeks
200 B.C.-400 A.D. The Indo-Scythian Sakas
100 B.C.–400 A.D.-The Yavanas
12 B.C–100 AD-The Indo-Parthians (Pahlavas)
35-405 AD-The Western Satraps
100-300 A.D.-The Kushans
240-410 A.D.-The Indo-Sassanid Kushanshahs
500-600 A.D.-The Hephthalite Huns
489-632 A.D.-The Rais
300-900 A.D.-The Shahis
Gangetic Plains and Deccan **123**
Gangetic Plains and Deccan
230 B.C.–220 A.D.-The Satavahanas
193 B.C.–170 B.C.-The Kharavela

North-East India 125
350-650 A.D.-The Varman dynasty
650-900 A.D.-The Mlechcha dynasty
900-1100 A.D.-The Pala dynasty of Kamarupa
250-500 A.D.-The Vakatakas
606-647 A.D.-Harsha Vardhana
550-1018 A.D-The Gurjaras
420-624 A.D.-The Vishnukundinas
475-767 A.D.-The Maitrakas
600-1036 A.D.-The Gurjara Pratiharas
600-1956 A.D.-The Rajputs
942-1244 A.D.-The Solankis
800-1327 A.D.-The Paramaras
800-1200 A.D.-The Tanwars (Tomara)
800-1200 A.D.-The Chauhans
750-1174 A.D.-The Palas
1070-1230 A.D.-The Senas
900-1050 A.D.-The Candras
1028-1434 A.D.-The Eastern Gangas
Southern India 135
The South
300 B.C.-200 A.D.-The Sangam Era Kingdoms
500 B.C.–1345 A.D.-The Pandyan Dynasty
300 B.C.–600 A.D.-The Cheras
300 B.C-1300 A.D.-The Cholas
250-600 A.D.-The Kalabhras
345-525 A.D.-The Kadambas
350-1000 A.D.-The Western Gangas
600-1200 A.D.-Badami Chalukyas
400-800 A.D.-The Pallavas
700-1100 A.D.-The Eastern Chalukyas
800-1500 A.D.-The Pandyan Dynasty (later Pandyas)
600-1000 A.D.-The Rashtrakutas
1000-1200 A.D.-The Western Chalukyas
850-1334 A.D.-Yadavas
1083-1323 A.D.-The Kakatiyas
1000-1200 A.D.-The Kalachuris
1130-1184 A.D.-Southern Kalachuris
1026-1343 A.D.-The Hoysalas

1336-1646 A.D.-Vijayanagara Empire
Indian Philosophers 160
788-820 A.D.-Shankaracharya
1017-1137 A.D.-Ramanujacharya
1238-1317 A.D.-Madhvacharya
1132-1196 A.D.-Basaveshwara

3. Mughal Empire 170

Mughal Empire
971-1030 A.D.-Mahmud of Ghazni Alberuni
1175-1206 A.D.-Muhammad of Ghur
1221-1327 A.D.-Mongol invasion
The Sultanates 182
1210-1526 A.D.-The Delhi Sultanates
1206-1290 A.D.-Mamluk (Slave) Dynasty
1290-1320 A.D.-Khilji Dynasty
1320-1413 A.D.-Tughlaq Dynasty
1414-1451 A.D.-Sayyid Dynasty
1451-1526 A.D.-Lodi Dynasty
1347-1527 A.D.-Bahamani Sultanates
The Deccan Sultanates 186
1490-1687 A.D.-The Deccan Sultanates
1490-1636 A.D.-Ahmadnagar Sultanate
1490-1574 A.D.-Berar Sultanate
1492-1619 A.D.-Bidar Sultanate
1490-1686 A.D.-Bijapur Sultanate
1518-1687 A.D.-Golkonda Sultanate
Sultanates Cultural contributions
1526-1530 A.D.-Babur
1530-1556 A.D.-Humayun
1556-1605 A.D.-Akbar
1605-1627 A.D.-Jahangir
1592-1666 A.D.-Shah Jahan
1618-1707 A.D.-Aurangzeb
1720-1782 A.D.-Hyder Ali
1750-1799 A.D.-Tippu Sultan
List of Mughal Emperors from 1526 A.D., Influence of Mughal Rule, Urdu Language, Astronomy, Technology

Sikh Empire 209
1799-1849 A.D.-Sikh Empire
Maratha Empire 213
1674-1818 A.D.-Maratha Empire
1642-1680 A.D.-Chhatrapati Shivaji

4. Colonial India 216

1510-1947 A.D.-Colonial India
1510 to 1961 A.D.-Portuguese
1605 to 1825 A.D.-Dutch
1620 to 1869 A.D.-Danish
1674-1954 A.D.-French
British India 220
1612-1947 A.D.-British India
British India and the Native States, Major Provinces, Minor Provinces, Princely States, Governors-General and Viceroys/Events and accomplishments, British Life, Awakening the Consciousness of Indian people, The Plan for Partition
English Education
Social Reformers
(a) 1772-1833 A.D.-Raja Rammohan Roy
(b) 1836-1886 A.D.-Ramakrishna Paramahamsa
(c) 1863-1902 A.D.-Swami Vivekananda
(d) 1828 A.D.-The Brahmo Samaj
(e) 1869 A.D.-The Arya Samaj
(f) 1824-1883 A.D.-Dayanand Saraswati
(g) 1838-1884 A.D.-Keshab Chandra Sen
(h) 1850-1885 A.D.-Bharatendu Harishchandra
(i) 1861-1941 A.D.-Rabindranath Tagore
(j) 1872-1950 A.D.-Aurobindo
(k) 1820-1891 A.D.-Ishwar Chandra Vidyasagar
(l) 1838-1894 A.D.-Bankim Chandra Chattopadhyay
(m) 1866-1915 A.D.-Gopal Krishna Gokhale
(n) 1856-1950 A.D.-Balagangadhar Tilak

(o) 1897-1945 A.D.-Subhash Chandra Bose
(p) 1869-1948 A.D.-Mohandas Karamchand Gandhi
(q) 1889-1964 A.D.-Jawarharlal Nehru
(r) 1878-1972 A.D.-Chakravarthi Rajagopalachari

5. Independent India **276**

1947 – Independent India
Objectives of Five-Year Plans
Excerpts from the Constitution of India

Appendices **313**

1. List of Prime Ministers
2. National Parties
3. Indian States and Union Territories
4. List of Indian Languages
5. Number of Official Languages of India

Index **325**

Preface

India at a glance emerged out of the desire to integrate chronologically the events, facts, and happenings in India since ancient days and to understand the history of India.

When we think of history, we always think about wars, kings, human suffering, etc. But studying history is more than wars and human suffering. History teaches us about ancient people, their culture, art, music, literature, technological development, industrial development and scientific developments. To understand how our cultures are developed is important for critical thinking. It is a unique contribution that history can make to civic life.

History helps us to understand how the world works, and how human beings behave. Knowledge of the past is required for understanding the present realities. It shows us what it means to be a human and makes us better thinkers.

The origins of modern Indian society lie in the ancient and medieval past. Scholars trace the roots of the Indian culture to Harappa and Mohenjo-Daro in the north, between Indus plains and Gangetic plains in the north-east, and the southern peninsula of Vindhya mountains. The ancient world provided several cultural elements that the modern world has inherited. First came the vedic teachings or sacred writings that embodied the Hindu law, history, philosophy and culture. Sanskrit language became the instrument of verbal and written communication for the Vedic people.

Ancient cities Gandhara and Magadha created a brilliant culture that greatly influenced the Indian civilisation. The classic Vedic period witnessed an incredible pinnacle of philosophical ideas. The Bhagavad Gita is an excellent holy book of questioning and investigating the secrets of universe. It held that human beings and their environments represent the essential subject for philosophical inquiry. The Bhagvad Gita taught that excellence could be learned, and by seeking excellence through knowledge, human beings could find the highest good and ultimately true happiness.

The long and bitter struggle between the Indians and invaders were a severe blow to the Indian civilisation. No single state was strong enough to dominate others. Taking advantage of the situation, Mughal's invaded India in the mid of 10th century. Even though the earlier invaders adapted the Indian religion, culture and languages gradually. The Mughal's invasion destroyed the social fabric of India. Unable to resolve their domestic quarrels, Indians lost their freedom by the Mughals first and later to the British.

The idea of reform is as old as Buddhism itself. Social reformers and humanists in the 18the century and 19th century urged to reform Indian mind on the pattern of early India. Educated, informed and intelligent people, especially in the cities, condemned the superstitions and casteism, which were plaguing India. Brahma Samaj and Arya Samaj were established insisting on the necessity of religious unity for political order and social stability.

Despite history's vitality as a discipline, it seems both the public and intelligentsia are losing interest in the past. A young woman who wanted to pursue her future career in politics asked, "Why we must study history? Past is past. We have to think about the future"—as if history is dead and has no use at present.

How do we understand present realities? On what ground we should make decisions about the future? Should we act blindly out of passion and ignorance, or should we attempt to act rationally based on prior knowledge? If the option is knowledge, there is only one place to find it. The great philosopher of education, John Dewey, wrote, "...the achievements of the past provide the only means at command for understanding the present."

History provides instructive examples. The use of historical examples is ancient and undoubtedly predates written language. We can imagine cave dwellers sitting around the evening campfire sharing stories of admired ancestors worthy of excellence. People need models, and historical examples are especially powerful models because they actually happened. Raja Rammohun Roy demonstrated the upliftment of women and education; Gandhi demonstrated non-violence; Basaveshwara represented the equality for all human beings; Joan of Arc demonstrated the power of individual belief and action; Galileo symbolised the fight against authority for freedom of thought; Hitler personifie the evil.

The common-sense outlook is supported by a report from the National Research Council referring to studies on the reasoning proficiency of experts. Such research is important, says the report, "Because it provides insights into the nature of thinking and problem solving." It is not simply general abilities such as memory or intelligence, or the use of general strategies that differentiate experts from novices. Instead, experts demonstrate extensive knowledge that influences what they notice and how they organise, represent, and understand information in their environments. This, in turn, shapes citizens' abilities to remember, reason, and solve current social, political and economical problems.

In this book, I intend to give great attention to India's economic, political, intellectual, literary, architectural, religious and cultural developments that they indisputably deserve. In preparing this book, I have worked hard to provide complete picture of India as judicious as possible. It starts from the period when India was attached to supercontinent of Pangaea 225 million years ago, and continues to cover geological formation of India, the origin of Hindu civilisation, Vedic, Epic and Puranas period, rise and spread of the Indian philosophies such as cosmic questions of Hinduism, non-violence of Jainism, act of compassion towards humanity of Buddhism, Indian philosophers and social reformers. It also covers Neolithic agricultural revolution, political and economic growth in the ancient India, earlier Mehrgarh, Harappa and Mohenjo-Daro cultures, Mahajanapadas, great empires of Magadha, Mauryas and Guptas, southern kingdoms Cheras, Cholas and Pandyas, later Mughal period and British rule, social reformers who awakened India from its miserable state, and life in India after independence. The incorporation of all major events happened in the Indian subcontinent where economy, art, culture, science and language flourished in its golden period and modern Independent revolutionary period is a noteworthy subject in this book.

Moreover, I have classified each part chronologically as much as possible for organisation and clarity. Part I is organized to demonstrate India's geological description, its climate, people, languages, etc., Part II is organised to exemplify Ancient India and Origin of the Hindu Civilisation, Part III is organised to illustrate Mughal Empire, Part IV is organised to show Colonial India and Part V is organised to describe India after Independence.

To keep the book fresh and appealing, I have also added religious developments with special emphasis on their popular and social aspects, extending from ancient to modern times. The reader will also find material on many topics, notably the Greek, Persian, Huns, Sakas, Mughal and Colonial invasions on India, ancient empires, dynasties and rulers, their contributions to India in science, mathematics, literature and architecture.

The maps presented in the book are intended to assist the reader to know India's geography, rise and fall of its empires. The physical features of India have shaped its history in the fundamental way.

Besides, the book also discusses the illustrative component including maps containing geological formation of India since Pangaea, seismic zone, rivers, ancient empires and present India are included. Illustrations of ancient coins, architecture and paintings of earlier times come alive.

I have also tried to mention how early intellectual people actually worked and thought. I have quoted extensively from a wide variety of primary sources, and have demonstrated by quotations how historians filter and evaluate evidences. It is my hope that the primary quotations, carefully fitted into their historical context, will give the reader a sense that even in the earliest and most remote periods of human experience, history has been shaped by individual man and woman some of them were great aristocrats and other ordinary folks.

At the end, some extracts from constitution of India. Its purpose is to educate Indian people to get acquainted with citizen's fundamental rights, and citizen's duties and responsibilities to the country.

Honest attempt has been made hoping this book helps to understand Indian history, geography, culture, philosophy and every aspect of India and its related subjects.

1

India at a Glance

About India

On Friday, the 15th of August, 1947, India obtained independence from British Rule and Jawaharlal Nehru was sworn in as the Prime Minister of India. Outcome of the independence was remarkable: India's thousands of territories were united and became one India, and democracy was restored.

In writing about any topic of social importance, we have to deal with the past, present, and future. There are lessons to be learned from the past; the present is where we are and needs careful descriptions; we want guidance for the future. The future hides behind clouds of uncertainty, and its description must be carefully analysed with warning.

In the past, India faced numerous challenges and overcame with changes in various fields.

Most people are not philosophers, but nevertheless they have a basic outlook of life, a more or less rational perception. The perception of early India was primarily religious and theological. Not only did Hindu, Buddhist or Jain teachings form the core of people's religious and philosophical beliefs, but religious teachings also permeated in all human thought and activity. In the course of nineteenth century, this religious and theological perception of the educated classes of India, mainly in the north, underwent fundamental transformations. Many educated people came to see the world primarily in secular and scientific terms. While few established new way of organisations like Brahma Samaj and Arya Samaj, many became openly hostile toward practices like sati, untouchability and superstitions. Among many in the upper-middle class educated people, a new critical and secular perception took shape.

Development of radical concepts of politics and society were accompanied by comparable changes in literature and other arts during the independence movement. The early nineteenth century marked the peak of the literary movement, which profoundly influenced and enriched Indian culture immeasurably. Of these, Ravindranath Tagore and Bankim Chandra Chattopadhyay are noteworthy. Tagore—a passionate advocate of feeling, freedom, and natural goodness was the most influential.

Now, India is no more economically underdeveloped or developing country. It has a great potential to become a successful nation by synthesising its past and present.

Geological Formation of India

The geology of India started with the geological evolution with other parts of the Earth 4.57 billion years ago. Initially the subcontinent of Indian region was a part of the supercontinent of Pangaea. At that time, it was attached to Madagascar and southern Africa on the south west coast and Australia along the east coast.

In the early Mesozoic period, 248.2 million years ago, all the major landmasses were connected into Pangaea. At the end of the Mesozoic period, one of the greatest volcanic eruptions in earth's history occurred causing the Deccan lava flow and finally Gondwana broke apart. This land mass split into a northern Laurasia and a southern Gondwana early in the Cretaceous period. The southern land mass also split further and the part of India started to float towards the Asian plate. The present northern part of India was still submerged. Rajasthan and Kucch zones contain oceanic fossils dating back to the Jurassic period. The Himalayan zone shows aquatic fossils until the end of Mesozoic period. The Indian peninsula presents dinosaur fossils dating back to 98 million years.

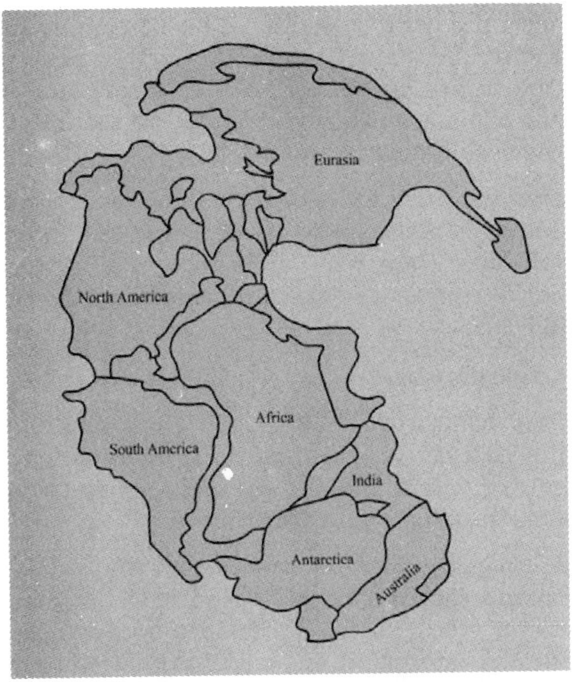

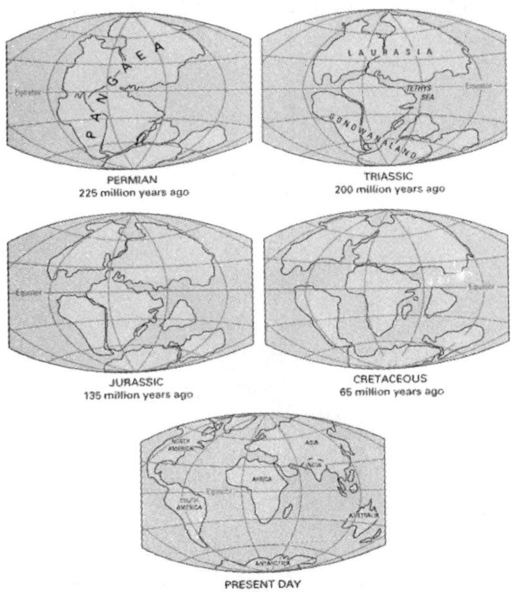

Pangaea Supercontinent

All over the peninsula, huge lava flows were found on the boundary between Cretaceous and Tertiary periods. During the transition between the Oligocene and Miocene period, the Himalayas started rising at the southern edge of the northern Angaraland plate.

During the early ice age, the Himalayan snowline was several hundred metres down to sea level, and even the sea level was lower than what it is today connecting all of Andamans into one island and also connecting the Ceylonese Island to India.

Surface Features

Spread over an area of 32,87,2631 sq. km., India is the seventh largest country in the world. India is divided into six major zones: East India, West India, North India, South India, Northeast India and Central India.

Three major geologic divisions exist in India: (1) the huge northern mountain belt of folded rock known as the Himalayan system; (2) the solid massif of rock that forms the south-central upland plateau of the Deccan peninsula; and (3) the fertile, alluvial plain formed by the Indo-Gangetic riverine system.

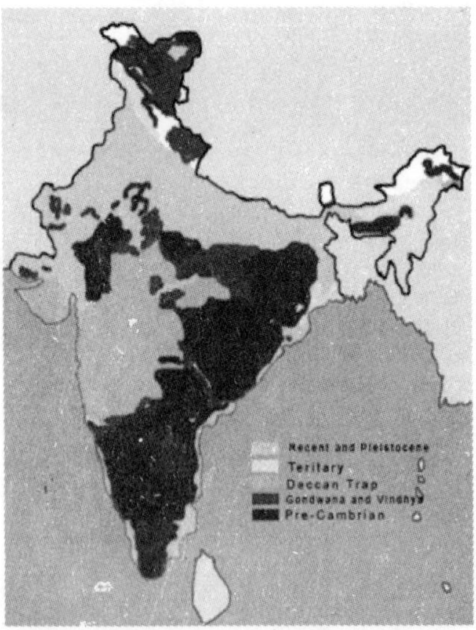

The great mountain walls of the Himalayas rise sharply along the northern, eastern, and western borders of the subcontinent and shield South Asia from the icy air of central Asia. The whole chain is scattered with magnificent, snow-capped peaks, among which at least 40 peaks rise to heights of 25,000 ft. or more. In total, the Himalayan system spreads 1,500 miles from the source of the Brahmaputra River in the east to the origin of the Indus River in the west.

The Himalayan system safeguards northern India shielding it from the climate and the people of central Asia. Also the Himalayan system defends northern India in another respect because it is the source of the major rivers which flow southward into the subcontinent. These rivers have created the life-giving Indo-Gangetic plain by carrying rich soil down from the mountain of their origin. In addition, they provide water for irrigation. Though the Indo-Gangetic plain appears to be uniformly leveled, there are minor local variations in grade and drainage. A major difference in surface causes the Gangetic and Brahmaputra systems to flow southeastward from the Himalaya and the Indus and tributaries to flow southwestward.

Climate

In most of South Asia three separate seasons are recognised. The first of these is the hot season (March through May), the second is the rainy season (June through October), and the third is the cool season (November through February). During the hot season, the highest daytime temperature of approximately 100°F. (38°C.) is found in the interior of Deccan during March, in April the temperature climbs to 110 F. (43°C) in the daytime in central India, and in May daytime temperature in northern India climbs to the 120 F. (49°C) mark. By this time the earth is baked hard and dry, and life comes to a halt awaiting the restorative rains.

Indian subcontinent's monsoon weather created a combination of eastern wet evergreen forests and western moist deciduous regions. The wet or summer monsoon crosses India from the Indian Ocean and from the southwest.

When the rain-bearing air reaches the Tropic of Cancer, it curves toward the north and northwest along the Gangetic plain in the direction of the Indus plain. The mass of rain-bearing air usually drops its moisture by the time it reaches the southern side of the Himalayas, often with special force along the Himalayan foothills. However, part of the monsoon air system mixes with dry continental air coming southward toward the Indus from Central Asia. When this happens suddenly, the result will be the dissemination of the rain-bearing air and a consequent failure of the certainly needed rainfall.

People

India presents a larger variety of ethnic population than contemporary Europe. A majority of population in South Asia are of Caucasoid racial stock. Many of the Caucasoid inhabitants of India exhibit distinct similarities with the Mediterranean and Alpine subraces among the Europeans. However, the Indian Caucasians are normally of darker colour than the European Caucasians. Alpine Caucasians, characterised by broad rather than long heads, are found in the interior of the peninsula, along the coast in the vicinity of Bombay, and in the northeast of Bengal and in the northwest of Sindh. There are also sections of a Nordic element with tall frames, light hair colour, and blue-gray eye color. It seems that the darker pigmentation of the Caucasians in India is the result of ancient intermingling with prehistoric black-skinned inhabitants: Australoids and Negritos. Today the evident traces of the Negrito type are found among the forest tribes of the highlands. Along the Himalayan frontiers of India, various genetic admixtures of Mongoloid peoples are found.

Languages

Though the number of languages in India is more than 1652, 22 of these are spoken by 90% of the people. Fifteen of the 22 are descended from Sanskrit, and are members of the Indo-Aryan branch of the Indo-European family of languages. They are: Assamese, Bengali, Dogri, Gujarati, Hindi, Kashmiri, Konkani, Maithili, Marathi, Nepali, Oriya,

Punjabi, Sanskrit, Sindhi, and Urdu. Five languages spoken in the southern part of India are members of the Dravidian family of languages. They are: Kannada, Malayalam, Telugu, Tamil, and Tulu.

Sanskrit and Linguistics Science

Linguistics Science is a field in which India held unique position in the ancient world. The discovery of this science by Europeans at the end of the 18th century led to the development of modern linguistic science in the 19th century in Europe.

Panini
Courtesy: Indianetzone

Records indicate that a great work in Sanskrit grammar of Panini (5th century B.C.) consists of eight lessons, containing 3,873 grammar rules. These are lists of roots and table of sounds. The rules are definitions of technical terms, of principles followed in the formulation of grammar and grammatical operations. Sir Charles Wilkins introduced Panini's analysis of word form to Europe through western Sanskrit grammar (1808) following Panini's principles, but remodelling his expression for the benefit of European scholars.

Sanskrit, denoting refined, purified, perfected, is one of the ancient languages and oldest member of the Indo-Aryan language family and the basis of several important language in the world.

The enormous amount of Sanskrit literature, the largest collection of literature from the ancient world, offers a unique access to several aspects of Indian culture. The earliest Sanskrit literature is conserved in the Vedas and in the compilation of ancient hymns. Sophisticated scientific literature dealing with linguistics, mathematics, and astronomy evolved to preserve Vedic culture. Gradually this literature expanded to include works of many other areas.

The wonderful epics and Puranas present an inexhaustible source of linguistic works for the study of Indian mythology as well as law and politics. Classical Sanskrit authors composed a rich literature of poetry and drama. Emergence of Buddhism and Jainism created an enormous number of religious and philosophical works together with works on logic and philosophy of language.

Sanskrit holds the rank of a classical language, including other languages such as Classical Greek, Latin, Persian, Arabic, and Hebrew. Awarding of the title of a "classical" needs to fulfill certain requirements from the language in question:

(a) Its origins must be recognised as having taken place over a long period of time.

(b) It should possess a sovereign tradition that arose virtually on its own and not as a derivative of another tradition.

(c) It must have a huge and extremely rich accumulation of ancient literature.

Sanskrit satisfies all these requirements having a tradition going back more than 3,000 years and is the language in which every ancient Hindu text is written in.

Eventually Sanskrit enabled to emerge the Prakrit (natural) languages, which are contemporary Indian languages of today such as Hindi, Bengali, Marathi, Gujarati, Nepali and Singhalese. Sanskrit is the source language for all of the Indian subcontinent's regional languages. Considered to be the oldest language in human history, Sanskrit is the forefather and inspiration for virtually every language spoken in India.

Prakrit dialects were spread and mixed with other various regional languages. Buddhists selected one of these dialects roughly in the 6th century B.C. and developed it into Pali. The simplification of the dialects continued concluding in the Apabhramsha phase in 600 A.D. Further modification of the regional Apabhramshas during 600-1000 A.D. culminated to the New Indo-Aryan languages of today.

Apabhramsha is a term used by Sanskrit grammarians to refer to dialects that deviate from the standard or rules of Sanskrit grammar. The term apabhramsha literally means "corrupt" or non-standard language. This term is used for the dialects that developed the transition period between the 6th and the 13th centuries.

Apabhramshas evolved into modern languages, which are spoken by millions of people today. Languages such as Hindi, Bengali, Urdu, and Gujarati are all representative languages of contemporary states.

Hindi Language

Hindi is a national language of India. Without mentioning the Sanskrit, Hindi cannot be understood with its completeness. A straight descendant of Sanskrit via Prakrit and Apabhramsha, Hindi pertains to the Indo-Aryan division of languages, a group of the Indo-European family. Hindi not only acquired its writing system from Sanskrit, but also borrowed large amount of vocabulary. It has been influenced and enriched by Arabic, Dravidian, Turkish, Farsi, Portuguese, Persian, and English languages. Hindi is largely identical to Urdu, and is related to Bengali, Gujarati, and Punjabi. Hindi acquired its writing system from Sanskrit.

Hindi started to emerge as Aprabhramsha in the 7th century and by 10th century it became stable. Several dialects of Hindi have been used in literature. Braj was the popular literary dialect until it was replaced by Khari Boli in the

19th century. A number of former literary languages with massive number of literature, such as Braj, Avadhi, and Maithili, have been effectively merged into the fabric of Hindi. Maithili, spoken in northern Bihar, has huge literature and its own grammar. Advocates of its use maintain that it is a language related closely to eastern Indo-Aryan languages than to Hindi. Other regional languages, such as Marwari in Rajasthan and Magadhi in southern Bihar are considered variants of Hindi.

Hindi is spoken in northern and central India. Linguists think of Hindi and Urdu as the same language, the difference being that Hindi is written in the Devanagari (Sanskrit) script and derives much of its vocabulary from Sanskrit, while Urdu is written in the Persian script and derives much of its vocabulary from Persian and Arabic.

Hindi shares the same ancestral roots as with other European languages. They evolved from a language considered to have been spoken in Central Asia around 5,000 B.C., called by linguists the Indo-European parent language. For this reason, many basic words in Hindi are the same as or similar to their correspondent in English.

Hindi became the official national language of India on January 26, 1965, although the Constitution of India recognizes English and 21 other languages as official languages. After the Independence of India from Britain in 1947, the Government of India started the work on standardisation of the Hindi language. As a result, the following changes took place:

- Standardisation of Hindi grammar: In 1954, the Government of India set up a Committee for preparing a grammar of Hindi. The committee's report was later released as "A Basic Grammar of Modern Hindi" in 1958.
- Standardisation of Devanagari script by Central Hindi Directorate, Ministry of Education and Culture to bring about uniformity in writing and improve the shape of some of its characters.

- Additionally, Hindi spelling was standardised and a system of transcribing the Devanagari alphabet was designed.
- The general appearance of the Devanagari script is that letters "hanging from a line". The script has no capital letters.

Due to the influence of Hinduism, Hindi derives most of its high-level vocabulary from Sanskrit. Due to the Moslem influence in Northern India, it also has many Persian, Arabic and Turkish loanwords.

Interesting characteristic is a three levels of reverence, with great sensitivity to match "formal", "familiar" and "intimate" conversational situation. Thus, the polite communication of respect and gratitude is an integral part of the language itself and does not require separate words for Please and Thank You.

Dialects

Hindi has several dialects like Marwari, Braj, Bundeli, Kanauji, Urdu, Chattisgarhi, Bagheli, Avadhi, Bhojpuri, Bundeli, Awadhi, and Marwari, Maithili, Bhojpuri, and many others.

Hindi is the main language in the states and union territories of India such as Himachal Pradesh, Delhi, Haryana, Uttar Pradesh, Madhya Pradesh, Bihar, Uttaranchal, Jharkhand, Rajasthan and Chhattisgarh. Linguistic scholars refer to this area as Hindi belt. Outside these areas, Hindi is widely spoken in cities like Mumbai, Chandigarh, Ahmedabad, Kolkata, and Hyderabad, although they have their own native languages.

2

Ancient India and Origin of Hindu Civilisation

Early Habitation in India

The study of distribution pattern of Paleolithic sites in different parts of India has shown that there was habitational preference for certain regions. The region characterised by semi-arid monsoonal climate with suitable physiographic setting in the form of fertile upland, flat surface by riverside, and sparsely forested savanna type of vegetation was preferred for settlements.

A group of Indo-French researchers has discovered that the prehistoric Indians were skilled at crafting stone tools like hand-axes, cleavers and flakes, which they used for digging roots and tubers. They also knew wood-working besides butchering and skinning large animals.

The team recovered 3528 stone tools from excavations at Attirampakkam, an open-air Paleolithic site situated near a tributary of the river Kortallaiyar, northwest of Chennai. Known as Acheulian tools, they indicate the ancient stone tool making industry of early humans in India. Analysis of Tamil tools suggests that they were made between 1.07 and 1.5 million years ago.

300,000 -250,000 B.C. Narmada Man

The discovery of a fossilised human skull was noticed first by the villagers of Hathnora of Madhya Pradesh on the bank of the Narmada. The find which consists of nearly right half of and a part of left half of the skull cap was found in the flood plain of the river Narmada. It was found in association with fossils of extinct Pleistocene mammals, like Stegodon (an extinct animal), Box, Curves and Equus (kind of animals including horses, donkeys, zebras and onagers) are indisputable proof that man existed in India during the Pleistocene epoch. Stone implements, like choppers, scrappers, hand-axe and cleaver, made on flint, chert were found in abundance with the skullcap. It appears that Narmada homo was responsible for the earliest hand-axe industry in this region. On the basis of geological calculations it appears that Narmada Man lived around 3,00,000 to 2,50,000 years before from the present day and belonged to Early Stone Age.

A study conducted on these subjects indicate that the Narmada *Homo* was lesser than 135 cm (4′ 4″) in stature and had about 30 cm broad shoulder, and a moderate chest depth. These dimensions correspond to a modern day pygmy body frame with a very robust body build. The study documents a robust, short and stocky archaic *Homo* in the Narmada Valley as the maker of the Acheulian tools, found along with the hominid fossils.

The Bhimbetka rock shelters are located in Madhya Pradesh. The Bhimbetka shelters illustrate the primitive marks of human life in India. Studies indicate that these shelters were inhabited by humans for more than 1,00,000 years. Some of the Stone Age paintings found at the Bhimbetka rock shelters are approximately 30,000 years old.

Bhimbetka rock paints in Madhya Pradesh. 30,000 years old.

Molar teeth of Australopithecus and pebble stone tools of 2 million years old were located near Chandigarh. Late Pliocene stone artifacts of 2 million years old were reported from the Conglomerate deposit at Riwat in Sohan valley near Rawalpindi in Pakistan area.

Pebble stone tools were found mostly in northwest and northeast India. Abundant Paleolithic tools were found in Rajasthan, Gujarat, Bhimbetka, Adamagarh, Belan, Sithwal, Central Asia, and Attampakaram in Deccan, Eastern Ghats, south east coast and many other places.

Archeological survey has discovered numerous ancient habitation sites in Karnataka. Some Middle Paleolithic sites have been found in different parts of North Karnataka like Hotgal, Kalagi, and Bommanahalli.

7000-2600 B.C.-Mehrgarh Site

The site of Mehrgarh, which is in present day Pakistan area on the Kachi Plain of the Indus Valley, is a major archaeological discovery about India. It is an area over 495 acre. The site was discovered by a team of French archaeologists headed by Jean-Francois Jarrige together with the Pakistan Department of Archaeology. Excavations have shown that the area was never totally settled at any one time. There are seven periods within the boundaries of the site, dated by a series of radiocarbon dates. The projected chronology is :

Period I: Neolithic (7000-5500 B.C.);
Period II: Burj Basket Marked Phase (5500–4500 B.C.);
Period III: Togau (4500–4000 B.C.);
Period IV: Togau/Kechi Beg (4000–3800 B.C.);
Period V: Kechi Beg (3800–3500 B.C.);
Period VI: Kechi Beg/Damb Sadaat (3500–3200 B.C.);
Period VII: Damb Sadaat (3200–2600 B.C.);

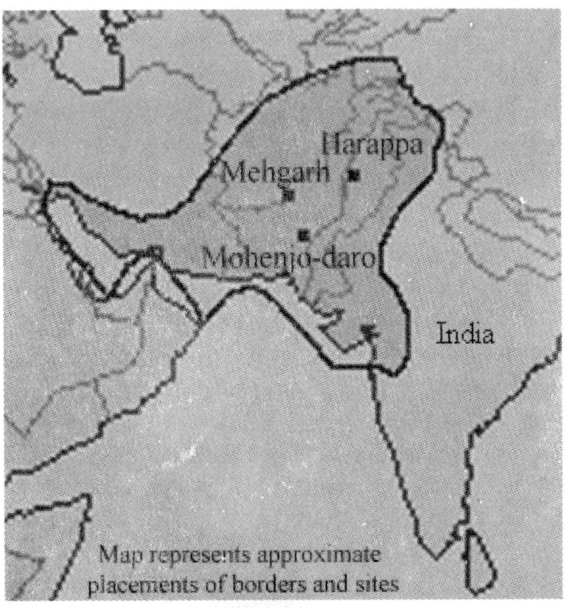

7000–5500 B.C.-Period I: Neolithic (New Stone Age)

Mehrgarh I was a small village consisting of farmers and herders covering the area of 7 to 10 acres. Houses and cubicle buildings and granaries were found in the area. Storage facilities of this type began in Period I. As agricultural production increased, their number and sophistication was also developed. The houses were simple and built by mud-brick structures. Ovens and hearths were commonly found in the corners of rooms, and signs of their use are revealed in marks of smoke on the walls. The technology of Mehrgarh I was simple. A small amount of copper (not smelted) appears to be of the native variety. The bed of the Bolan River holds cobbles of light brown flint from which tools were shaped and some sickle blades were occasionally polished. For food processing ground-stone tools were also found. Slabs of bitumen with basket impressions, a small amount of pottery, unbaked clay figurines appear toward the end of Period I.

There was a rich bone industry: awls, spatulas, a bone needle, and two highly polished bone pendants with round hole were found in the area.

The animal economy was dominated by twelve species of large game animals. Richard Meadow refers that the first inhabitants of a ceramic Mehrgarh I exploited not only the surrounding hills but the Kachi Plain also. The chaff-temper (separating outer seed cover from grain) technology appears between 6000 and 5500 B.C.

5500–4500 B.C.-Period II: Burj Basket Marked Phase

Evidence of manufacturing activity, more advanced techniques, terracotta beads and images were found in this period. Images of females were decorated with paint and had varied hairstyles and ornaments. Two flexed burials with a covering of red ochre on the body were found. The button seals, geometric designs from terracotta and bone were produced. Technologies included stone and copper drills, upward ovens, large pit ovens, and copper melting crucibles. The discovery of several semi precious stones such as blue beads of lapis originally from Badkshan shows that there was a long-distance trade in period II. Mehrgarh Periods II and III are also contemporaneous with an expansion of the settled populations.

4500–4000 B.C.-Period III: Togau

Period III Togau remnants cover an estimated 170 acres. The distinguishing feature in this period is further development of craft activities. Evidence of use of metallurgy appears first at this time. The other noticeable feature is the evolution of the ceramic industry in Mehrgarh. It is dominated by fine red ware and wheel-made vessels.

A shell industry using conch shells existed in Period II shows a bangle fragment decorated with carving parallel lines. Evidence for melting, refining, and smelting copper came from a domestic structure. Ceramics are the most ubiquitous evidence for craft production at Mehrgarh.

Craft production expanded significantly in Period III at Mehrgarh. Development of pyrotechnics and pottery production, copper and gold metallurgy occurred in this period and the basic bead-drilling technology was invented. By the end of Mehrgarh III, the technology used by the Harappan civilisation as well as long-distance trade was already existed on the plains of the Indus River.

4000–3800 B.C.-Period IV: Togau/Kechi Beg

In Togau/Kechi Beg period farmers cleared and leveled their sites to enhance their agricultural fields.

3800–3500 B.C.-Period V: Kechi Beg

Information is not available.

3500–3200 B.C.-Period VI: Kechi Beg/ Damb Sadaat

Information is not available.

3200–2600 B.C.-Period VII: Damb Sadaat

Sometime during the Period VII, occupation of another major settlement was established at Nausharo, next to Mehrgarh. Mehrgarh was gradually abandoned and new settlement of Nausharo was occupied paving the way to more mature urban phase of Harappan civilisation when the Indus Valley Civilisation was in the development stage.

The elephants roamed free from Assam to the western reaches of Mehrgarh. It has been recorded that in the Pleistocene period, there were seventeen varieties of Indian elephants.

Early farming village in Mehrgarh, 7000 B.C. with houses built with mud bricks

3000 B.C.-Harappa and Mohenjo-Daro (Indus-Valley Civilization)

A matured civilisation was settled in the broad plains of Indus Valley. In pre-Harappan period, there existed small peasant states, each self-contained. There is no evidence of any uniform arbitrary standards accepted or imposed throughout the territory. But, later the Harappan civilisation developed a system to build Empires. Diversity is replaced by uniformity. A sophisticated and technologically advanced urban culture was formed in the Indus Valley Civilisation making them the first urban centres in the region.

A figurine from Mehrgarh, 3000 BCE Musée Guimet, Paris

A first major civilisation of the subcontinent India was located in the valley of the Indus River and flourished between 2500 B.C. and 1500 B.C. It was centered about two great cities, Harappa and Mohenjo Daro. The Harappa civilisation was highly developed. Excavated remains indicate connections with the ancient culture of Mesopotamia and Harappa influence on Indian culture persists today. Harappa's major cities were carefully laid out on a rectangular pattern. They had elaborate municipal drainage system, great granaries, and public buildings of impressive size. Tools of bronze and copper were used, and clay seals and bronze images of high artistic quality were produced. There was an active trade with the ancient Near East. Presumably the Harappa people were predecessors of the Dravidian people of southern India.

Amaury de Reincourt, a French Historian, writes about the glory of Harappan civilisation:

"Archeological evidence shows that a huge irregular triangle area with the sides measuring 950 by 700 by 550 miles. From end to end of this region, some forty settlement sites containing pottery vessels of identical mass-produced types have been excavated; houses are built from baked bricks of standard dimensions; stamp seals are used, and a uniform script, as yet unread; a standard system of weights is recognisable. While some sites are villages, others are small towns. Two cities, probably twin capitals of an Empire, stand 350 miles apart each covering at least a square mile of ground. To a British archeologist the inevitable parallel is the Roman Empire.

"The gigantic Empire, twice the size of Old Kingdom Egypt, had two enormous metropolises: Harappa in the North and Mohenjo-Daro in the South. Towns were no longer laid out for military defense as in the old pre-imperial days because a universal type of peace prevailed throughout the "civilised" world of those times. The extremely advanced stage of standardisation indicates the existence of a universally accepted commercial code and uniform technique of production controlling the sizes of bricks, the capacity of pots, and so on. Agricultural output was under municipal control, and huge granaries similar to those of the contemporary Egyptian Civilisation dotted the landscape. For centuries street-frontage regulations were strictly observed.

"The amazing efficiency of the Harappa Civilisation was linked to a remarkable cultural stagnation. Its uniformity was expressed in time as well as in space. There were at least nine phases of rebuilding at Mohenjo-Daro, and all indications are that there was no change in the people's way of life. The script, with its 270 characters, essentially hieroglyphic as in contemporary Egypt, remained identical throughout the entire period. This urban and literate Civilisation, known to us only in its mature form, was undoubtedly the heir to the Culture whose scattered remnants are strewn over Sind and Baluchistan.

"Who were the people dwelling in the Harappa Empire? There are evidence of two main racial strains: the first, belonged to the long-headed "Mediterranean" type which spreads from Spain to India. The second belonged to the "Australoid" group with their thick lips and coarse noses, probably the original natives of the land. If we include brachycephalic (flat head) and the Mongoloid hill people of the Himalayan foothills, we have a complex ethnic situation where white, brown, dark and yellow races lived side by side within the compass of a great cosmopolitan Civilisation. But the majority must have belonged to a stock very similar to the modern dark-skinned Dravidians of southern India.

"The colossal size of the capital cities reminds one of Imperial Rome. The sheer size of the Citadel, the impressive Great Bath, the Collegiate Building, the Pillared Hall, all these great monuments indicate that Mohenjo-Daro was a center of religious and administrative life on a grand scale. The city itself, with its countless shops and residential districts, was laid out like a gridiron of large avenues cutting each other at right angles, dividing the city into large rectangular blocs. The large houses of the wealthy people were provided with doormen, elaborate bathrooms, and rubbish chutes running through the outside walls into bins probably cleared by the municipal authorities. A complex drainage system under the streets was connected with the house drains. There seems to be no doubt that the general standard of health and sanitation were remarkably high. Large sections of the town were laid out for the workers; depressingly uniform rows of cottages lined narrow streets. Massive wooden mortars, large granaries, metal worker's furnaces, everything suggests a high degree of semi-industrialisation. In fact, archeology claims that the Harappa Civilisation attributes the first really organised industry in Western Asia.

"Little is known about the Harappa religion, although archaeological research suggest the widespread cult of a Mother Goddess—undoubtedly the direct ancestor o the Grama-Devatas who are still worshipped in countless Indian villages to this day and whose priests are outcastes, remnants of the pre-Aryan population of India. Archaeological excavations have also found prototypes of the future god Siva seated in the position of a yogi, as well as evidence of phallic worship. And, the important of all, the Harappa people buried their dead, the symbolic gesture of men concerned with duration in sharp contrast to the succeeding Aryans.

"From 2700 B.C. to 1700 B.C., this great Civilisation flourished in relative peace. But like all Civilisations, it seems to have become completely sterile and ossified as time streamed by. Even technologically, it became backward. Although Harappa men were at the time the sole inventors and users of saws with undulating teeth, although they made ample use of copper and bronze, they did not know iron; and whereas from the millennium onward Mesopotamians knew how to fashion tools with sockets for handles, Harappa ignored this technical revolution. Harappa, it seems, had not domesticated the horse. Inevitably, this great Civilisation was the mercy of barbarians who were technologically more advanced. When those barbarians appeared, sometime in the first half of the second millennium B.C. on the north-west passes of Lak Phusi, the Bolan and the Gaj Valley, the great Civilisation of Harappa collapsed for all time and faded from the memory of man until archaeology began to unearth its impressive remains in the 20th century A.D."

Indus Valley cities also maintained an active commerce, and probably had close cultural contacts with Sumerian and Persian Gulf region.

In the Gangetic Plain there were settlements of people who made a crude ocher colored pottery and perhaps combined hunting with primitive agriculture. In the Deccan the flint tools were in use side by side with artifacts of bronze and copper. In the far south there was a complex megalithic culture that may have had links with Mediterranean megalithic culture.

1700 B.C.-Aryan Civilisation

There are two theories about Aryan Civilisation in India.

Aryan Invasion Theory

Around 2000 B.C. when a huge migration period was occuring, a large number of Aryan tribesmen started travelling from Central Asian home town to Mesopotamia and up to the Iranian highlands. Some of these Aryan tribesmen proceeded down to the vast plains of Indus Valley where its great cities, accumulated wealth, fertile lands, warm climate and large populations of sophisticated city dwellers were living peacefully. They were totally unprepared for military defence. Aryans were more effective because they knew iron tools and weapons. They defeated original people easily. Consequently, Harappan Civilisation came to an end.

Aryans first great literary work, Rig-Vida, is a unique source of information. It gives us the atmosphere of this period with a wealth of hymns, chants, prayers, songs and magic spells sometimes sublime and sometime childish. It is a colorful and invaluable document on the wars between Aryan invaders and native dwellers of the Indus Valley region. The hymns reflect the feelings of victorious and warlike masters of a huge fertile land and a scared local population. The picture which emerges from a careful scrutiny of the Rig-Veda is as follows:

> "The tall, fair-skinned Aryan appeared into the broad plains of the Indus Valley mounted on horses, dressed in heavy coats, with weapons made of iron and military equipment which the men of Harappa did not possess. Looking down at dark-skinned, flat-nosed Dasyus, the victorious Aryans (Bharatas, Yadus, Anus, Purus, etc.) gradually occupied a large part of India. There was a fierce struggle between the Aryan chieftain Divodasa and the Dasyu ruler Sambara. The Indra, the prominent god of Rig-Veda, was a destroyer of "forts" (purandara), a wrecker of cities."

The Rig-Veda provides many glimpses of the social life of those times. Life was exclusively rural; the great cities of the Harappan period had completely disappeared. The word "city" (nagara) is never mentioned in the Rig-Veda. In the most powerful military-based society, the feudal lords lived in their purs (forts) which were used as refuse for the surrounding population. War and agriculture were the chief occupations of the times even though there was a certain amount of trade. The art of writing, fully developed in the Harappa Civilisation, have become completely lost after the Aryan invasions. The early literature of the Aryans was not written down but transmitted orally. Nevertheless, those ages were also ages of youth and hope, of dynamic vigor, the childhood of a new Culture. The early Vedas are full of this enthusiasm for life which is the privilege of youth, new outlook on life, and rebirth.

Vedic India was split into an unknown number of independent states (Rashtras) and by kings (Rajas). In the early days, the Aryan leaders checked the power of the rajas through their assemblies (samiti or sabha) and, gradually these assemblies discontinued when the power of the royal rulers became more autocratic.

Non-Aryan Invasion Theory

The Aryan invasion theory is one of the most controversial historical topics for over a century. The Aryan invasion theory is based upon the idea that the name Aryan represents a specific group of people. In the traditional view of the Aryan invasion, the Aryans are a particular ethnic group, speaking a particular language. However, in Vedic literature Aryan is not the name of the Vedic people or their descendants. It is a title of honor and respect given to certain groups for good or dignified manners. In this regard even the Buddha calls his teaching Aryan or Arya Dharma. The Jains also call themselves Aryans, as did the ancient Persians.

Another vital point in this regard is that nomadic people do not use chariots. An invasion of India from Central Asia required crossing mountains and deserts. A chariot is useless for such an exercise. Therefore, the Aryan invasion theory is false. Much later, further excavations in the Indus Valley revealed horses and evidence of the wheel on the form of a seal showing a spiked wheel was used on chariots.

According to Bal Gangadhar Tilak's theory, North Pole was the original home of Aryans during pre-glacial period. They had to leave their place due to the ice surge around 8000 B.C. and had to migrate to the Northern parts of Europe and Asia looking for lands and for new settlements. Supporting this theory, Tilak has given certain Vedic hymns, Avestic passages, Vedic chronology, and Vedic calendars with interpretations in detail in his book, :The Arctic Home in the Vedas."

The New Model

The New Model of ancient India has surfaced from the collapse of the Aryan invasion theory. This new model suggests that an indigenous civilisation existed in ancient India at Mehrgarh site during 6500 BC. The people in this tradition were the same ethnic groups as in India today, with their basic form of languages: Indo-European and Dravidian. Later Harappan civilization 3100-1900 BC shows massive cities, complex agriculture and metallurgy, sophistication of arts and crafts, and precision in weights and measures. Post-Harappan civilisation 1900-1000 BC shows the abandonment of the Harappan towns due to ecological and river changes without a break in the continuity of the culture.

Therefore, the new model declares throughout these changes, traditions, culture and languages continued without a break.

1500-600 B.C.-Vedic Period

Initially, in ancient Indian cities, people worshipped a mother goddess like any other civilisation; they also had a male divinity, represented in one of the typical attitudes of yoni, surrounded by animals. For Aryans, most important divinities were male. They had an important class of priests who were very skilled in composing hymns for use at the sacrifices and in memorising the hymns composed by others.

The word Veda is derived from the Aryan root "vid", that is, "seeing" vision (in Latin, video). The early Vedic poets, the rishis, called themselves the seers of the hymns. They looked upon the universe and thought it is absolute, indisputable, and having existed for all eternity. The Vedas were the brilliant product of instinctive insight, though it may not be of the logical intellect. It was passed on orally by word of mouth from master to disciple.

The Vedic Period deals with the age of the settlement of the Aryans and the steady development and spread of the Aryan culture and civilisation. It was the time which witnessed the growth of the forest universities, where the sublime idealism of India was evolved. They described their thoughts through Mantras or the hymns, the Brahmins and the Upanishads. Their views presented in this process are not philosophical in the technical sense of the term. It was the time of probing, examining and investigating the nature of the universe, where superstition and thoughts were contradictory.

The oldest Vedic deities were the Dyaus, the glittering God of Heaven and Prithvi, the Earth Goddess. Later appeared innumerable Gods: Varuna, (god of sky, of water), Vayu (god of wind, air or atmosphere), Agni (god of fire), and Surya (the sun God). Stars, mountains, rivers, human qualities and faults, all had their controlling deity.

Some scholars implicate the Vedic hymns to 3000 B.C., and some others to 4500 B.C., 6000 B.C. and so on. Dr. S. Radhakrishnan assigns 1500 B.C. so that the date will not be challenged as being too early.

Rig-Veda

The Rig-Veda is the oldest noteworthy existing text of India. It is a collection of 1028 Vedic Sanskrit hymns and 10,600 verses, organised into ten books. The hymns are dedicated to Rigvedic gods. The books were composed by sages and poets from different priestly groups over a period about 500 years. The ten rishis or the composers of Rig-Veda: Angirasa, Kanva, Vasishta, Vishvamitra, Atri, Bhrgu, Kashyapa, Grtsamada, Agasthya, Bharata.

There are strong linguistic and cultural similarities between the Rig-Veda and the early Iranian Avesta, obtaining from the Proto-Indo-Iranian times, frequently associated with the Andronovo[1] culture. The earliest horse-drawn chariots were found at Andronovo sites near the Ural Mountains which date to 2000 BC.

1. The Andronovo culture is a collection of similar local Bronze Age cultures that thrived during 2300-1000 BC in western Siberia and the west Asiatic grassland.

Rig-Veda means the Veda of Adoration and contains verses adoring deities. It also deals with other subjects, like the procedure of wedding, the foolishness of gambling, etc. About two-thirds of Rigveda is about the gods Agni (Fire) and Indra (King of gods). Other Rigvedic gods include Rudra (destroyer), the two Ashvins (two horsemen, who are sons of cloud and sun), Savitar (solar power) and Surya (sun), Varuna (water), the Maruts (winds) and the Ribhus (rays of the sun). There are references to a divine creeper, the Soma, whose juice was an energiser. Some animals, rivers, and even implements (like mortar and pestle) were sanctified. Rigveda contains a sense of intimate communion between Nature and the Rishis or visionaries.

In this period, new deities began to join the Vedic gods: Vishnu and Shiva became powerful deities but the most metamorphosis among the gods was that of Brahman (from the root Brh, to swell or to grow). Brahman was regarded as the creative principle of the universe.

Yajur Veda

The Yajur-Veda (Veda of sacrificial formulas) consists of ancient mantras. In this Veda some parts of verses are borrowed from the Rig-Veda. Yajurveda refers the acts of worship like sacrifice made to Agni or Fire. It has two branches: Krishna or Black and Shukla or White. The recensions of Black Yajurveda are Taittirya, Katthaka, Maitrayani and Kapishtthala. Those of White Yajurveda are Madhyanadina and Kanva. The literary value of Yajurveda is mostly for its prose, which consists of short concise sentences full of meaning and intonation.

Sama Veda

The Sama Veda is the Veda of chants or knowledge of melodies. It consists of 1549 stanzas, taken from the Rig-Veda except 78 stanzas. Its purpose is liturgical and practical, and a priest who sings hymns from the Sama-Veda during a ritual is called an *udgat.* The methods of chanting are important to the liturgical use of the verses. Therefore, hymns should be sung according to certain fixed melodies.

It has two parts: Purva-Archika (First Adoration) and Uttar-Archika (Later Adoration), containing verses addressed to the three gods Agni (Fire), Indra (King of Gods) and Soma (Energizing Herb). The verses need to be sung in specifically indicated melodies using the seven svaras or notes. Such songs are called Samagana and in this sense Samaveda is really a book of hymns.

Atharva Veda

Atharva Veda means the Veda of the wise. It is related to the name of the ancient poet Atharvan. According to the tradition, the Atharva Veda was composed by two groups of rishis: Atharvana and the Angirasa. Atharvaveda contains about 6000 verses forming 731 poems and a little portion in prose. About one seventh of the Atharvaveda text is similar to the Rig-Veda. Atharvaveda contains unique poetry coming from visionary poets, much of it being glorification of the curative powers of herbs and waters. Many poems are related to diseases like cough and jaundice, to male and female demons that cause diseases, to sweet-smelling herbs and magic things, which drive diseases away. There are poems relating to sins and their punishments, errors in performing rituals and their penalty acts, political and philosophical issues, and a magnificent hymn to Prithvi or Mother Earth.

Vedic Cosmology

The authors of the hymns are greatly concerned with the origin of the universe. They suggested that the world emerged from a golden embryo at the beginning of time. They concluded that really nobody, not even the gods themselves, knows certainly how the creation came out. Among the most significant of these cosmogonic hymns in the Rig Veda is the "Hymn of the Primeval Man" (Purusha-sukta), where it is described that the whole universe appeared as a result of a great sacrifice performed at the beginning of time, when a mighty primeval person was sacrificed by the lesser gods. Then the Primeval Man mystically surviving his own dismemberment produced from the different parts of his body the various features of the universe, including the four great classes of society.

In fact, the sacrifices are now conceived as repetitions of the first great sacrifice due to which the universe was created, and the creative process is symbolically repeated again and again, and the universe is being renewed.

It is assumed that the caste concept started in Rig Vedic period. In those days, caste was the expression of the talent of Indian Civilisation: Once it was like a labor union, enforcing certain rigid social security and the extreme and social expression of Civilisation's specialisation. Every member of a given caste was trained for a particular function from the day the child is born. It enforced democratic equality with the group, provided a particular religious framework according to their psychological nature for the particular caste members, and yet instilled respect to all Indians for multitudes of other forms of worship. Unfortunately, it became a national menace and causing wide problems of discrimination and prejudice.

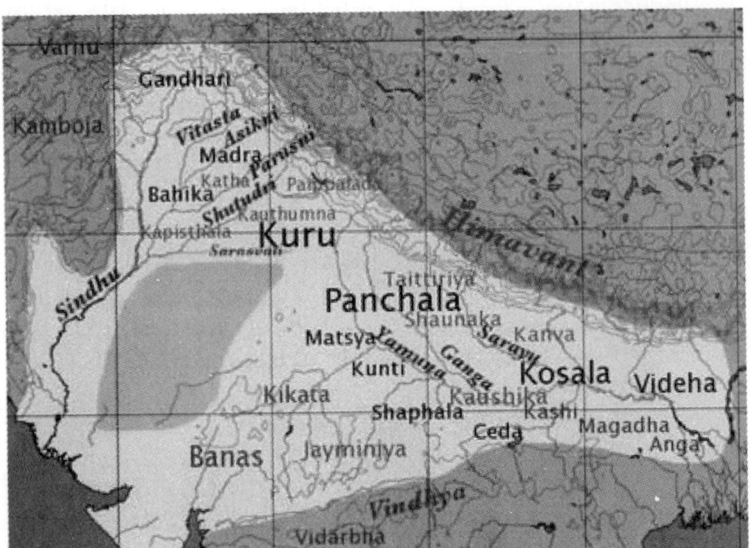

Map of northern India in the late Vedic period

800-400 B.C.—Upanishads

The word Upanishad comes from the Sanskrit verb *sad* (to sit) and the two prepositions *upa* (near) and *ni* (below), sitting below near the teacher to obtain Vedic knowledge. Upanishads are sacred texts of spiritual and philosophical nature. Vedic literature is divided into Karmakanda containing *Samhitas* (hymns) and *Brahmins* (commentaries); and Gyanakanda containing knowledge in the form of the *Aranyakas* and *Upanishads*. Thus each Upanishad is associated with a Veda, Isha-upanishad with Shukla Yajurveda, Kena-upanishad with Samaveda, and so on.

The earliest Upanishads have been composed between 800 and 400 B.C. There have been several later additions leading to 112 Upanishads available today. But the major Upanishads are ten: Isha, Kena, Kattha, Prashna, Mundaka, Mandukya, Taittiriya, Aitareya, Shwetashwatara, Chhandogya and Brihadaryanyaka.

The Isha-upanishad emphasises the identity of the human soul with the divine soul. The Kena-upanishad discusses the qualities of the divine essence (Brahman) and the relationship of the gods to the divine essence. The Katha-upanishad, through the story of Nachiketa, discusses death and the permanence of the soul (Atman). The relatively long Chhandogya-upanishad develops the idea of transmigration of souls. The Brihadaryanaka Upanishad, the longest of the Upanishads, carries the message of the completeness of the divine essence, and associated peace. As literary pieces of the ancient past, the Upanishads - both cogent and elegant have great literary values.

In India, complete freedom of thought was observed as Indians were free to contemplate upon all the great spiritual and metaphysical problems in unconditional liberty. No Indian was put to death because his opinions did not meet with fellow thinker, nor was there any investigation or examination of their thinking. Impressed by Upanishads, Schopenhauer called them, "the production of the highest human wisdom."

There are 11 main old Upanishads and around 108 smaller Upanishads which came later. They include:

1. Brahadharanyaka Upanishad
2. Kathopanishad
3. Isa Vasya Upanishad.
4. Mandukya Upanishad
5. Thaitriya Upanishad
6. Aithreyapanishad
7. Kenopanishad
8. Mundaka Upanishad
9. Chandogya Upanishad
10. Prashnopanishad
11. Shwethaswarthopanishad

List of 108 Upanishads

Rig Veda : (10)
Aitareya Upanishad
Atmabodha Upanishad
Kaushitaki Upanishad
Mudgala Upanishad
Nirvana Upanishad
Nadabindu Upanishad
Akshamalika Upanishad
Tripura Upanishad
Bahvricha Upanishad
Saubhagyalakshmi Upanishad

Yajur Veda : (50)
Katha Upanishad
Taittiriya Upanishad
Ishavasya Upanishad
Brihadaranyaka Upanishad
Akshi Upanishad
Ekakshara Upanishad
Garbha Upanishad
Pranagnihotra Upanishad
Svetasvatara Upanishad
Sariraka Upanishad

Sukarahasya Upanishad
Skanda Upanishad
Sarvasara Upanishad
Adhyatma Upanishad
Niralamba Upanishad
Paingala Upanishad
Mantrika Upanishad
Muktika Upanishad
Subala Upanishad
Avadhuta Upanishad
Katharudra Upanishad
Brahma Upanishad
Jabala Upanishad.
Turiyatita Upanishad
Paramahamsa Upanishad
Bhikshuka Upanishad
Yajnavalkya Upanishad
Satyayani Upanishad
Amritanada Upanishad
Amritabindu Upanishad
Kshurika Upanishad
Tejobindu Upanishad
Dhyanabindu Upanishad
Brahmavidya Upanishad
Yogakundali Upanishad
Yogatattva Upanishad
Yogasikha Upanishad
Varaha Upanishad
Advayataraka Upanishad
Trisikhibrahmana Upanishad
Mandalabrahmana Upanishad
Hansa Upanishad
Kalisantaraa Upanishad
Mahanarayana Upanishad
Tarasara Upanishad
Kalagnirudra Upanishad
Dakshinamurti Upanishad
Pancabrahma Upanishad
Rudrahrdaya Upanishad
Sarasvatirahasya Upanishad

Sama Veda : (16)
Kena Upanishad
Chandogya Upanishad
Maha Upanishad
Maitrayani Upanishad
Vajrasuci Upanishad
Savitri Upanishad
Aruneya Upanishad
Kundika Upanishad
Maitreyi Upanishad
Sanyasa Upanishad
Jabaladarsana Upanishad
Yogachudamani Upanishad
Avyakta Upanishad.
Vasudeva Upanishad
Jabali Upanishad
Rudrakshajabala Upanishad

Atharva Veda : (32)
Prasna Upanishad
Mandukya Upanishad
Mundaka Upanishad
Atma Upanishad
Surya Upanishad
Narada-Parivrajakas Upanishad
Parabrahma Upanishad
Paramahamsa-Parivrajakas Upanishad
Pasupatha-Brahma Upanishad
Mahavakya Upanishad
Sandilya Upanishad
Krishna Upanishad
Garuda Upanishad
Gopalatapani Upanishad
Tripadavibhuti-mahnarayana Upanishad
Dattatreya Upanishad
Kaivalya Upanishad
Narsinhatapini Upanishad
Ramatapani Upanishad
Ramarahasya Upanishad
Hayagriva Upanishad

Atharvasikha Upanishad
Atharvasira Upanishad
Ganapati Upanishad
Brihajjabala Upanishad
Bhasmajabala Upanishad
Sarabha Upanishad
Annapurna Upanishad
Tripuratapani Devi Upanishad
Bhava Upanishad
Sita Upanishad

700-300 B.C.-Maha Janapadas (Indo-Aryan kingdoms)

Early Vedic texts indicate several Janas or clans of the Indo-Aryans living in a semi-nomadic tribal state and fighting among themselves, and with other Non-Aryan tribes for cows, sheep and green pastures. These early Vedic Janas later came together into the Janapadas of the Epic Age.

The Pre-Buddhist north-west area of the Indian sub-continent was divided into several Janapadas distinguished from each other by borders. According to Panini's interpretation, *Janapada* means country and *Janapadin* for its citizenry. Each of these Janapadas was named after the Kshatriya tribe, who had settled therein.

The Buddhist and other texts occasionally refer to the following sixteen great nations of Mahajanapadas, which were in existence before the time of Buddha:

1. Anga (East Bihar)
2. Kosala (Oudh)
3. Kashi (Benares)
4. Magadha
5. Vajji/Vriji (Near Bihar)
6. Malla (Gorakhpur)
7. Chedi (On the Jamuna)
8. Vatsa (Allahabad)
9. Kuru (Delhi)
10. Panchala (Bareily)

11. Machcha/Matsya (Jaipur)
12. Surasena (Mathura)
13. Asmaka (Godavari)
14. Avanti (Malwa)
15. Gandhara (Peshawar)
16. Kamboja (South Kashmir and Kafristan)

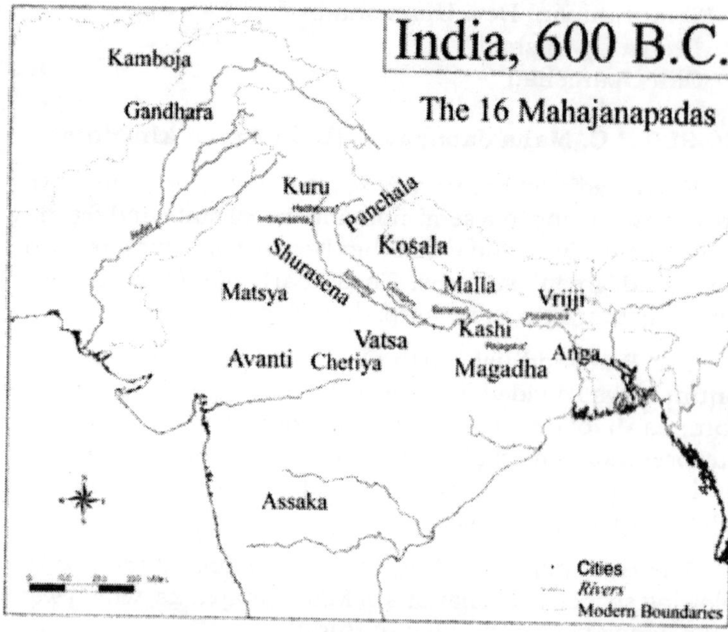

600 B.C.-200 A.D-Epic Period

The Epic Period extends between the early Upanishads and the Darshanas (a sense of seeing or beholding), a metaphysical system of Indian philosophy. The epics of the Ramayana and Mahabharata conveyed the new message of the heroic and the pious nature in human relations. The religious systems of Buddhism, Jainism, Saivism, and Vaishnavism belong to this age. The development of abstract thought in the schools of Indian philosophy, the darsanas, also belongs to this period. Most of the systems took shape early in this period, and they expanded side by side through many centuries.

Mahabharata

The Mahabharata, which means, "The Great Story of Bharata Dynasty", is one of the two major Sanskrit epics of India. Apart from narrative stories of Kauravas, Pandavas, and Kurukshetra War, Mahabharata contains philosophical and devotional material.

The authorship of the Mahabharata is attributed to Vyasa. Scholars have made attempts to determine its historical growth and compositional stages. The text most likely reached its final form by the early Gupta periods, 400 A.D. The original form of Mahabharata consisted 24,000 verses and called Bharata. Later, it is extended up to one hundred thousand verses. According to Howard Spodek and Amartya Sen, the Mahabharata is roughly ten times the length of the Iliad and Odyssey combined. W.J. Johnson has compared the importance of the Mahabharata to world civilization to Bible, the works of Homer, Greek dramas, the Quran, and the works of Shakespeare. He writes, "It is this universal quality that prompted a recent western theatrical adaptation to characterise it as the "poetical history of mankind". The Mahabharata has acquired an iconic and culturally talismanic significance that is reflected in its assessment of itself: "what is here may be found elsewhere, what is not here is nowhere at all."

The epic consist a story within a story structure, and it is recited by Vaisampayana to the King Janamejaya who is the great-grandson of Arjuna. Many years later the story recited again by Ugrasrava Sauti to an assembly of sages performing the twelve year long sacrifice for King Saunaka Kulapati in the Naimisharanya (Naimisha forest).

Research on the Mahabharata has put an enormous effort to recognize and date of various stages within the text. Some incidents of the present Mahabharata can be traced back to Vedic times. The background to the Mahabharata suggests the origin of the epic occurs after the very early Vedic period and before the first Indian Empire was to rise in the third century B.C. Unlike the Vedas, which have to be preserved letter-perfect, the epic reciters would inevitably conform to changes in language and style. It is estimated that the Sanskrit text probably reached a final form by the early Gupta period around the 4th century A.D.

Several stories within the Mahabharata took separate identities in classical Sanskrit literature. For example, Abhijnana Shakuntala by Kalidasa (400 AD), which is believed to have lived in the period of the Gupta Dynasty, is based on a story in Mahabharata. Urubhanga, a Sanskrit play written by Bhasa who is believed to have lived before Kâlidâsa, is based on the slaying of Duryodhana by splitting his thighs by Bhima.

The copper-plate inscription of the Maharaja Sharvanatha (533-534 AD) from Khoh (Satna District, Madhya Pradesh) describes the Mahabharata is a collection of 100,000 verses (Shatasahasri Samhita). The book Mahabharata is divided into 18 parvas (sections) as follows:

1. Adi Parva
2. Sabha Parva
3. Vana Parva
4. Virata Parva
5. Udyoga Parva
6. Bhishma Parva
7. Drona Parva
8. Karna Parva
9. Shalya Parva
10. Sauptika Parva
11. Stri Parva
12. Shanthi Parva
13. Anushasana Parva
14. Ashvamedhika Parva
15. Ashramavasika Parva
16. Mausala Parva
17. Mahaprasthanika Parva
18. Svargarohana Parva

Outline of the Story

The centre of the story of Mahabharata is a dynastic struggle for the throne of Hastinapura, the kingdom ruled by the Kuru clan. The Kurus were an Indo-Aryan tribe. Their kingdom existed in the Vedic period of India and later became a republican part of Mahajanapada. Kurus formed the first political center of the Indo-Aryans in Punjab after the Rigvedic period. It was there that the codification and revision of the Vedic texts began. Archaeologically, they correspond to the Black and Red Ware Culture of the 12th to 9th centuries B.C. At this time, iron first appears in western India. Panchala was the second urban center of Vedic civilization due to its focus moved to east from Punjab.

The two divisions of the family that fought for the throne were the Kauravas and Pandavas. Although the Kaurava was the senior branch of the family, Duryodhana, the eldest Kaurava was younger than Yudhisthira, the eldest Pandava. Both Duryodhana and Yudhisthira claim to be first in line to inherit the throne.

The struggle concludes with the war between Kauravas and Pandavas in the battlefield of Kurukshetra, and ultimately Pandavas turn out to be victorious. The battle creates complex conflicts between kinship and friendship, family loyalty and duty, right and wrong.

The Kurukshetra War

Pandava Army

The Pandavas gathered seven Akshauhinis or divisions of army with the help of their allies. Kingdoms from all over ancient India supplied troops and provided logistic support to the Pandavas side. Some of these were Kekaya, Pandya, Cholas, Keralas, Magadha, and others.

Kaurava Army

The Kaurava army consisted of eleven Akshauhinis. Besides, one hundred Kaurava brothers, they were assisted on the battlefield by Drona (Teacher of advanced Military arts) and his son Ashwathama and many kings who were bound by their loyalty towards Hastinapura and Dhritarashtra.

Army Divisions and Weaponry

According to calculations, an Akshauhini (division) includes 21,870 chariots and chariot-riders, 21,870 elephants and riders, 65,610 horses and riders, and 109,350 foot-soldiers (in the ratio of 1:1:3:5). The collective number of warriors and soldiers in both armies was around 3.94 million. Each Akshauhini was under a commander or a general, apart from the Commander-in- chief who was the head of the entire army.

During the Kurukshetra War, the weapons used included the bow and arrows, spear, dragger, sword. The mace was chosen by Bhima and Duryodhana.

Military Formations

During the battle, the commander-in-chief of the army ordered special formations "vyuhas". Each formation had a specific purpose; some were defensive while others were offensive. Each formation had its specific strengths and weaknesses.

Intricate rock carvings showing Abhimanyu entering the Chakra Vyuha

Mahabharata' List of the following Formations:

1. Krauncha vyuha (heron formation)
2. Makara vyuha (crocodile formation)
3. Kurma vyuha (tortoise or turtle formation)
4. Trishula vyuha (the trident formation)
5. Chakra vyuha (wheel or discus formation)
6. Kamala vyuha or Padma vyuha (lotus formation)
7. Garuda vyuha (Eagle formation)
8. Oormi vyuha (Ocean formation)
9. Mandala vyuha (Galactic formation)
10. Vajra vyuha (diamond/thunderbolt formation)
11. Shakata vyuha (Box/Cart formation)
12. Asura vyuha (Demon formation)
13. Deva vyuha (Divine formation)
14. Soochi vyuha (Needle formation)
15. Sringataka vyuha (Horned formation)
16. Chandrakala vyuha (Crescent/Curved Blade formation)
17. Mala vyuha—Garland formation

They may be formations bearing resemblance to animals or they may be names given to strategies and formations.

Rules of War

The two chief commanders met and framed rules of ethical conduct for the war. The rules included:

- Fighting should begin no earlier than sunrise and end exactly at sunset.
- Multiple warriors should not attack a single warrior.
- Two warriors may engage in prolonged personal combat, only if they carry the same weapons and they are on the same mount (no mount, a horse, an elephant, or a chariot).

- No warrior should kill or injure a warrior who has surrendered.
- One who surrenders becomes a prisoner of war and will then be subject to the protections as a prisoner of war.
- No warrior should kill or injure an unarmed warrior.
- No warrior should kill or injure an unconscious warrior.
- No warrior should kill or injure a person or animal not taking part in the war.
- No warrior should kill or injure a warrior whose back is turned away.
- No warrior should attack a woman.
- No warrior should strike an animal not considered a direct threat.
- The rules specific to each weapon must be followed. For example, it is prohibited to strike below the waist in mace warfare.
- Warriors should not engage in any unfair warfare.

Sometimes, most of these laws were broken by both sides.

Course of War

The Kurukshetra War lasted eighteen days. It was fought only during daylight hours. Fighting stopped at sunset. The winner or the defeated was determined not by any territories gained, but by the body counts on each day. This was a war to the death. The winner was the survivor.

Akshauhini

The following are the calculation which is done based on the sub-divisions :

Types of the Division	*Description with Ratio and Numbers*
1-Pati	1-Chariot 1-Elephant 3-Horses with Soldiers 5-Infantry Soldiers
3-Pati	1-Senamukham
3-Senamukham	1-Gulmam
3-Gulmam	1-Ganam
3-Ganam	1-Vahini
3-Vahini	1-Birudanai
3-Birudanai	1-Samu
3-Samu	1-Anihini
10-Anihini	1-Akshauhini
1-Akshauhini	21870-Chariots 21870 – War Elephants 65610-Horses with Soldiers 109350-Infantry Soldiers

Jain Version Mahabharata

Jain version of Mahabharata can be found in the several Jain texts. Harivamsa purana (the story of Harivamsa), Trisasti salakapurusa charitra (Story of the 63 Illustrious Men), Pandava charitra (Story of Pandavas) and Pandava purana (stories of Pandavas) are the Jain versions of Mahabharata.

Professor Padmanabh Jaini comments that unlike in the Hindu Puranas, the names Baladeva and Vasudeva serve as names of two distinct classes of mighty brothers, who appear nine times in each half of time cycles of the Jain cosmology and rule half the earth as half-chakravarties. Jaini traces the origin of these brothers to the Jina charitra by Bhadrabahu (300-400 B.C.).

In Jain version, the main battle is not Mahabharata, but the fight between Krishna and Jarasandha who was killed by Krishna. Ultimately, the Pandavas and Balarama take renunciation as Jain monks and are reborn in heavens, while

Sub-Division

Types of the Division	*Chariot*	*Elephant*	*Horses with Soldiers*	*Infantry Soldiers*	*Head of Division (commander)*
Pathi	1	1	3	5	Pathipal
Senamukha	3	3	9	15	Senamukhi
Gulma	9	9	27	45	Nayak
Gana	27	27	81	135	Gananayak
Vahini	81	81	243	405	Vahinipati
Birudana	243	243	729	1215	Birudanadhipati
Samu/Sena	729	729	2187	3645	Senapati
Anihini	2187	2187	6561	10935	Anikadhipati
Akshauhini	21870	21870	65610	109350	Maha Senapati

The Ratio is 1:1:3:5 through Calculations

Name of the Division	*Chariot*	*Elephant*	*Horses with Soldiers*	*Infantry Soldiers*
1-Akshauhini	21870	21870	65610	109350

Krishna and Jarasandha are reborn in hell. Krishna was reborn in hell because of his exploits while Jarasandha for his evil actions.

Ramayana

The Ramayana is a Sanskrit epic, and it is one of the two great epics of India. It describes the duties of relationships with characters like the ideal father, ideal servant, ideal brother, ideal wife and the ideal king. It explains the doctrines of human existence and the concept of righteousness. Ramayana has greatly influenced on Indian life and culture.

The Ramayana consists of 24,000 verses in seven sections (kândas) and narrates the story of Rama.

Some cultural evidence (the presence of sati[2] in the Mahabharata, but not in the main version of the Ramayana) indicates that the Ramayana predates the Mahabharata. But, the cultural background of the Ramayana reveals the post-urbanisation periods of the eastern part of North India around 400 B.C. while the Mahabharata suggests the Kuru areas of the west from the Rigvedic to the late Vedic period.

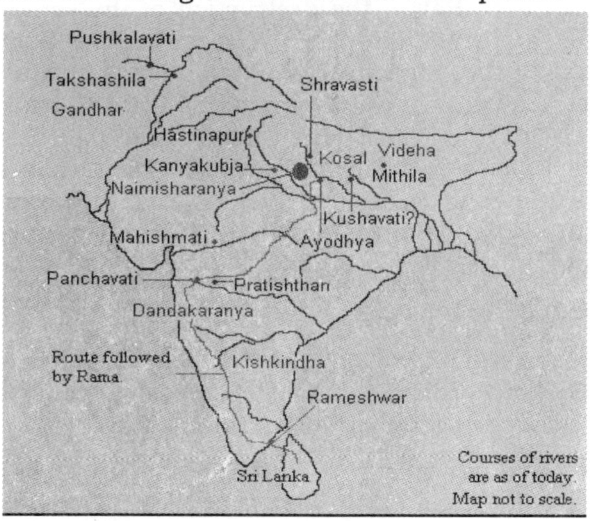

Bharat during Ramayan times.

2. For Example: When Raja Pandu died, Madri entered into sacrificial fire with his body.

The names of the characters Rama, Sita, Dasharatha, Janaka, Vasishta, and Vishwamitra were all known in late Vcdic literature. According to some modern academic view, Vishnu who incarnated as Rama is not Vedic deity, and he came first into prominence with the epics and also during the Puranic period of the later 1st century A.D.

Valmiki's Ramayana is an epic poem of about 50,000 lines. Later Ramayana, like the Mahabharata, is a gradual growth for centuries.

Outline of the Story

The Epic is divided into several major kândas or sections that deals chronologically with the major events in the life of Rama—Bala Kanda, Ayodhya Kanda, Aranya Kanda, Kishkindha Kanda, Sundara Kanda, Yuddha Kanda and Uttara Kanda. The Bala Kanda describes the birth of Rama, his childhood and marriage to Sita. The Ayodhya Kanda describes the preparations for Rama's coronation and his exile into the forest. The Aranya Kanda, describes the forest life of Rama and the kidnapping of Sita by demon king Ravana. The Kishkindha Kanda describes the meeting of Hanuman with Rama, the destruction of the vanara king Vali and the coronation of his younger brother Sugriva to the throne of the kingdom of Kishkinda. The Sundara Kanda narrates the heroism of Hãnuman, his flight to Lanka and meeting with Sita. The Yuddha Kanda describes the battle between Rama's and Ravana's armies. The Uttara Kanda describes the birth of Lava and Kusha to Sita, their coronation to the throne of Ayodhya, and Rama's final departure from the world.

Versions

The original version of Valmiki Ramayana dates back to 1500 B.C. according to some scholars. Recent studies indicate that it is around fourth century B.C.

Famous narrating of Ramayana includes Kamba Ramayana in Tamil (11th-12th centuries A.D.), Sri Rama Panchali or Krittivasi Ramayana by Krittibas Ojha in Bengali (1500 A.D.), and Ramacharithamanas by Tulasidas in Awadhi, which is an eastern form of Hindi (1600 A.D.).

The Ramayana has a profound impact on art and culture in India and Southeast Asia. Ramayana became popular in Southeast Asia during the 8th century A.D. and has influence on literature, temple architecture, dance and theatre.

Multiple versions of the Ramayana are existing today. In particular, the Ramayana in North India differs from South India and the rest of South-East Asia. Father Kamil Bulke, author of Ramakatha, has identified over 300 variations of Ramayana.

Buddhist Version

In the Buddhist version of Ramayana, Dasaratha was the king of Benares and not Ayodhya. According to Romila Thapar, Rama, Sita and Lakshmana were the siblings born to the first wife of Dasaratha. To protect his children from his second wife, the king sent the three in exile to the Himalayas. Twelve years later, all three came back to the kingdom with Rama and Sita as spouses. The abduction of Sita did not occur in this version.

Jain Version

In the Jain epic of Ramayana, it is Lakshmana who ultimately kills Ravana and not Rama as depicted in the Hindu version. In the end, Rama leads an honorable life, renounces his kingdom, becomes a Jain monk and attains moksha. In contrast, Lakshmana and Ravana go to hell. But, it is forecasted that in the end they both will be reborn as honorable persons and attain liberation in their future births. According to Jain texts, Ravana will be the future Thirthankara of Jainism.

BHAGAVAD GITA

Gita is found in the sixth section of Mahabharata, just before the great battle between the Pandavas and the Kauravas. The prominent hero of the Pandavas, Arjuna dragged his chariot in the middle of the battlefield between the two armies. He was accompanied by Krishna, who was his charioteer. Due to despondency, Arjuna throws down his bow and refuses to fight, criticising the immorality of the war.

The situation was extremely grave. Arjuna was the victim of a moral irony. On one side, he was facing persons who deserve his respect and veneration according to dharma (righteousness). On other side, his duty as a warrior demands him to kill them. To Arjuna any kind of victory did not seem to justify such a heinous crime.

When Arjuna refuses to fight, Krishna realises the level of Arjuna's despondency and starts teaching the mysteries of dharmic (right) action in this world. He introduces Arjuna to the structure of the universe, the concepts of prakriti (primordial nature), and the three gunas, the properties that are active in nature. Then he takes Arjuna on a tour of philosophical ideas and ways to greatest happiness. He discusses the nature of theory and action, the importance of righteousness, and the ultimate principle, Brahman. Gita culminates in an overwhelming vision: Krishna allows Arjuna to see his supernatural form, the Vishvarupa, the cosmic form. The rest of the Gita intensifies the ideas and explains the importance of self-control, of equanimity, unselfishness, and devotion. Krishna explains to Arjuna how he can obtain immortality by transcending the properties of primordial matter, but also human character and behavior. Krishna also emphasises the importance of doing one's duty, declaring that it is better to do one's own duty with distinction than to do another's duty well. Finally, Arjuna is convinced and he picks up his bow and prepares himself ready to fight.

The Gita advices humanity to maintain equanimity, and states explicitly that *sthithaprajna* (a person who has stabilised mind) is not disturbed by neither excessive joy nor excessive sorrow. The Gita lays out several paths to greatest happiness: karma yoga for those who are interested in activity or service to humankind; bhakti yoga for those who are interested in devotion. Intellectually interested people can turn towards jnana yoga, the path of knowledge and intellectual discrimination.

It was during the British Raj that the Gita achieved worldwide recognition first time. Many educated Indians were struggling to protect Hinduism against the attack of western culture, and gradually the Gita was considered to embody the essential spirit and deepest truths of Hinduism. The Hindu reformer Rajaram Mohan Roy referred to Gita as "the essence of all shastras", or the essence of all scriptures. By 1912, C.F. Andrews could claim that the Gita had become a common and well-read scripture for the entire educated India. It also appealed to very different group of people, the Theosophists. It was the Theosophists who introduced the Gita to Mohandas K. Gandhi.

Since Gandhi was introduced to the Gita by the Theosophists, he learned to read it in an allegorical way. The mighty battle was really a struggle for Truth—which he saw as another word for God—to be reached through love, and love succeeded violence. He was particularly fascinated by two words: aparigraha (no possession), which suggests the renunciation of money and property to avoid cramping the life of the spirit; and samabhava (equality), which asked him to transcend pain and pleasure, victory and defeat, and to work without the desire of success or fear of failure. The Gita became an inspiration to Gandhi and millions of his followers, a handbook of devotion and action.

The Gita also found a fascinated audience in the West, and a global cross-fertilisation of Gita was followed. It appealed both to the German Romantics, notably Schlege, Humboldt, Goethe, and to the American Transcendentalists, a group in New England also thought that the transcended logic and experience would reveal the deepest truths. The Gita was first translated into English in India in 1785 by Charles Wilkins, a merchant with the East India Company. His translation made a deep impression on the Transcendentalist's leader, Ralph Waldo Emerson. Emerson's poem, "Brahma", elegantly captures some of the essence of the Gita:

If the red slayer thinks he slays,
Or if the slain think he is slain,
They know not well the subtle ways
I keep, and pass, and turn again.

Far or forgot to me is near;
Shadow and sunlight are the same;
The vanished gods to me appear;
And one to me is shame and fame.

They reckon ill who leave me out;
When me they fly, I am the wings;
I am the doubter and the doubt,
And I the hymn the Brahmin sing.

The strong gods pine for my abode,
And pine in vain the sacred Seven;
But thou, meek love of the good!
Find me, and turn thy back on heaven.

The poem is based on verse found in both the Gita and the Katha Upanishad. A century later, another great poet, T.S. Eliot also had a lifelong interest in Indian philosophy and incorporated it into his poetry. Emerson made the Gita required reading for all those who were in rebellion against evangelical Christianity.

Another Transcendentalist, Henry David Thoreau incorporated a version of the Gita's teachings on Karma Yoga into his own lifestyle and philosophy. In 1849, he launched the idea of civil disobedience—an idea that influenced Gandhi's political thinking. Thus, an Indian idea passed through a Western mind and returned transformed to India. And naturally, Gandhi's ideas flowed back westward to inspire two other giants of the twentieth century, Martin Luther King Jr. and Nelson Mandela.

There are hundreds of commentaries on Gita. In the late 19th century, Gita was put to different use: Bal Gangadhar Tilak, in his magisterial interpretation, the Gita-Rahasya, suggested that the Gita urges and promotes action. Tilak argues that it is the devotionalism of Hindus that made them incapable of defending the country against foreign invaders. Krishna's order to Arjuna to take up arms and perform his duty as a warrior was taken literally by the armed revolutionaries who declared Gita to be their indispensable bedside companion. But, Gandhi understood the teachings of the Gita as an allegorical representation of the conflict between knowledge and ignorance within each person and insisted upon the centrality of teachings of Gita that we must perform our duties without expecting the fruits of our labor. Gandhi called the Gita the "Gospel of Selfless Action".

The 18 chapters in Bhagavadgita where each chapter dedicates for certain principles have presented on next page.

From 200 A.D.-Sutra Period

By happy intuition, the seers and thinkers of this era formulated some general principles which appeared to them to explain all aspects of the universe. The volume of philosophical ideas and materials were developed uncontrollably and it was needed to plan an organised system of philosophy. This cutting and summarising work took place in the form of Sutras. Professor Garbe holds that the Samkhya is the oldest school. Next came Yoga, next Mimamsa and then Vedanta, and last of all Vaisesika and Nyaya. The Sutra period and scholastic period cannot be distinguished separately. Both extend to the present day.

300-1200 A.D. Puranas/Mythologies

The Puranas are classic literary texts, written in Sanskrit verses and their composition dates back from the 4th century

Bhagavad Gita Chapters

Chapter	*Name*	*Description*
1.	Vishada Yoga	Yoga of Dejection of Arjuna
2.	Sankhya Yoga	Technique of Theory. Discipline through application of Speculative Doctrines. Samkhya philosophy regards the universe as consisting of two realities: Purusha (consciousness) and Prakriti (matter)
3.	Karma Yoga	Technique of Action: Karma yoga is the science of achieving perfection in action
4.	Jnana Yoga	Technique of Wisdom
5.	Karma Sanyasa Yoga	Technique of Renunciation of Action. (Means performing actions without expecting rewards)
6.	Dhyana Yoga	Technique of Meditation
7.	Jnana Vijnana Yoga	Technique of Wisdom by process of discrimination
8.	Akshara Brahma Yoga	Technique to understand Imperishable, Indestructible Universal Spirit
9.	Rajavidya Rajaguhya Yoga	Technique to recognize Absolute Knowledge and Absolute Secret
10.	Vibhooti Yoga	Technique to understand manifestation of divine attributes. Krishna describes best and outstanding specimen in each class of beings by identifying himself with them
11.	Viswarupa Darshana Yoga	Technique to perceive the Cosmic Form
12.	Bhakti Yoga	Technique of Devotion
13.	Kshetra-Kshtrajna Vibhaga Yoga	Technique of Discrimination between matter and soul
14.	Guna Traya Vibhaga Yoga	Technique of Division of Three Gunas or Qualities (purity, passion and ignorance)
15.	Purushottama Yoga	Technique to understand supreme spirit with its eternal as well as ephemeral aspects
16.	Daivasura Sampad Vibhaga Yoga	Technique of Division between Divine and Demoniacal properties
17.	Shraddhatraya Vibhaga Yoga	Techniques of Three Divisions of Faith (Unselfish, Selfish, and Rude methods)
18.	Moha Sanyasa Yoga	Technique of Renunciation of Delusion

B.C. to about 1,000 A.D. The word "Purana" means "old". Some scholars consider that composing of Puranas started around the time that the composition of the Mahabharata came to end around 300 A.D. Certainly, in its final form the Mahabharata shows puranic features and the Harivamsa also seems as a purana. The special subject of the puranas is the powers and works of the gods. An ancient Sanskrit lexicographer Amarasinha of 5th or 6th century A.D. defined a purana as having five characteristic topics or *panca laksana* (five qualities):

(1) The creation of the universe

(2) Its destruction and renovation;

(3) The genealogy of gods and patriarchs

(4) The reigns of the Manus, forming the periods called Manwantaras;

(5) The history of the Solar and Lunar races of kings.

When the puranas began to be composed first, the belief in particular deities, which is one of the principal marks of the Hindu faith had been established. And to some degree the puranas can be depicted as a form of sectarian literature. Some puranas exhibit devotion to Shiva; in others, the devotion to Vishnu predominates.

There are eighteen major puranas and similar number of minor or subordinate puranas. One method of the classification of puranas organises the traditional three divisions of the gunas or qualities which tend toward purity (*sattva*), passion (*rajas*), and impurity or ignorance (*tamas*),

There are six puranas, where the quality of *sattva* (purity) predominates: Vishnu, Narada, Bhagavata, Garuda, Padma, and Varaha.

The second set of six puranas, where the quality of *rajas* (blind passion) predominates: Brahma, Brahmanda, Brahmavaivarta, Markandeya, Bhavishya, and Vamana.

A third set of six puranas, where the quality of *tamas* (ignorance or impurity) predominates: Matsya, Kurma, Linga, Shiva, Skanda, and Agni.

It is the Puranas that British scholars had in mind when they ridiculed the literature of the Hindus as fanciful and absurd. Genealogies in which certain kings are said to rule for thousands of years, or conceptions of time where tens of thousands of years are said to be a mere instant, were not intended to make the British regard the Puranas as a set of rational religious texts.

However, it requires a very different imagination, as well as interpretive strategy to read the Puranas. The Puranas are works that most beautifully represent the deep mythic structuring of Indian civilisation, expanding, modifying, and transforming the orthodox Brahmanism of the Vedas, importantly by the introduction of the idea of bhakti or devotion.

Puranas assisted in the transition from Brahmanism to Hinduism, particularly a Hinduism that was friendlier to common folks with popular forms of devotion and worship, and arts, crafts, and sciences. The Puranas contain the stories about the gods who had become the objects of devotion as well as the modes of worship of these gods. These gods were no longer Vedic gods, but the gods who form the Hindu trinity. In addition, the Puranas describe about the battle between devas and asuras, and one can undoubtedly understand the struggle within each person between the forces of light and darkness. Though the Puranas are a vast repository of Hindu religious practices—yoga, puja, prayers, sacrifices, customs and traditions—they are not without a sense of humor and irony. They harmonise the metaphysical severity of the Upanishads, the magical and sacrificial knowledge of the Atharva Veda, and the orthodoxy of the Rig Veda.

Puranas consist the narratives of the history of the universe from creation to destruction, genealogies of kings, heroes, sages, demigods, descriptions of Hindu cosmology, philosophy, and geography.

Vyasa, the narrator of the Mahabharata, is traditionally considered the compiler of the Puranas. However, the earliest written versions date from the time of the Gupta Empire (3rd-5th century A.D.) and much material may have been added in the succeeding centuries. They existed in oral form before being written and then incrementally modified later on.

Gavin Flood notes the emergence of the written Purana historically with the rise of devotional cults focusing upon a particular deity in the Gupta period. Common ideas are found throughout the main part of Puranas.

According to American mythologist Joseph Campbell, the mythologies (Puranas) should not be taken as a literal description of historical events happening in our current understanding of time and space, but as a metaphor for the rise of man's cognitive consciousness as it evolved from a prior animal state. In 1924, Joseph Campbell traveled to Europe with his family. On the ship back, he encountered Jiddu Krishnamurti. They discussed Asian philosophy, which sparkled a life-long interest in Hindu and Indian thought in Campbell. Following this trip, Campbell stopped to practice Catholic system.

Function of Myth-Campbell

Campbell often described mythology as having a fourfold function for human society: Metaphysical Function, Cosmological Function, Sociological Function, and Psychological Function.

1. **The Metaphysical Function: Awakening a sense of awe before the mystery of being**

According to Campbell, the absolute mysteries of life cannot be captured directly in words or images. The first function of mythology is to organise waking consciousness to the *mysteries* of this universe *as it is*.

2. **The Cosmological Function: Explaining the shape of the universe**

Myth also functions as a *proto-science*, bringing the observable (physical) world into accord with the metaphysical and psychological meanings rendered by the other functions of mythology. Campbell noticed that the modern dilemma between science and religion on matters of truth is actually between science of the ancient world and that of today.

3. **The Sociological Function: Validate and support the existing social order**

   Ancient societies had to conform to an existing social order if they were to survive at all. This is because they evolved under "pressure" from necessities much more intense than the ones encountered in our modern world. Mythology confirmed that order and enforced it by reflecting it into the stories, often describing how the order arrived from divine intervention.

4. **The Psychological Function: Guide the individual through the stages of life.**

   As a person goes through life, many psychological challenges will be encountered. Myth may serve as a guide for successful passage through the stages of one's life. For example, most ancient cultures used rites of passage as a youth passed to the adult stage. Later on, a living mythology taught the same person to let go of material possessions and earthly plans as they prepared to die.

Evolution of Myth

Campbell's view of mythology was by no means static and he describes how mythologies evolved through time, reflecting the realities in which each society had to adjust. Various stages of cultural development have different, yet identifiable mythological systems. In brief, these are:

The Way of the Animal Powers: *Hunting and gathering societies*

At this stage of evolution religion was animistic, as all of nature was seen as being infused with a spirit or divine presence. At center stage was the main hunting animal of that particular culture and a large part of religion. It focused on dealing with the psychological tension that came from the reality of necessity to kill vs. the divinity of the animal. This was done by presenting the animals as springing from an eternal source and coming to this world as *willing victims*, with the understanding that their lives would be returned to the soil or to the Mother Earth through a ritual of restoration. The act of slaughter then becomes a ritual where both parties, animal and mankind, are equal participants.

The Way of the Seeded Earth: Early agrarian societies

In the beginning, the practice of agriculture spread along with a new way of understanding mankind's relationship to the world. At this time the earth was seen as the Mother, and the myths focused around her life-giving powers. The plant and cultivation cycle was mirrored in religious rituals which often included human sacrifice, symbolic or literal. The main figures of this system were a female Goddess Mother Earth, and her ever-dying and ever-resurrected son/consort, a male God. At this time the focus was to participate in the repetitive rhythm as the world expressed as four seasons, the birth and death of crops and the phases of the moon. At the center of this motion was the Mother Goddess from whom all life springs and to whom all life returns. This often gave her dual functions as both mother and destroyer.

The Way of the Celestial Lights: The first high civilisations

As the first agricultural societies evolved into the high civilisations, the observation of the stars inspired them with the idea that life on earth must also follow a similar mathematically predetermined pattern in which individual beings are but mere participants in an eternal cosmic play. The king was symbolised by the Sun with the golden crown as its main metaphor, while his courts were the orbiting planets. The Mother Goddess remained, but her powers were now fixed within the rigid framework of a clockwork universe. But for the largest part the focus was heavily shifted toward the masculine god Indra or Zeus.

Campbell believed the religions of the world to be the various culturally influenced "masks" of the same fundamental, transcendent truths. All religions can bring one to an elevated awareness above and beyond a dualistic conception of reality, or idea of "pairs of opposites" such as being and non-being, or right and wrong. He quotes from the Rig Veda in the preface to The Hero with a Thousand Faces: "Truth is one; the sages speak of it by many names."

A list of Major Puranas:

Puranas Name	*Number of Verses*	*Comments*
1. Agni	15,400	Deals with ritual worship, cosmology, astrology, history, warfare, sections on grammar and meter, law, medicine, and martial arts. Contains details of Vastu Shasta, the science of construction and Gemology, the science of gems. The text is post-Gupta period and has been dated sometime between the 8th and 11th centuries A.D.
2. Bhagavata	18,000	Narrates Vishnu's ten incarnations and it is a source for bhakthi movement.
3. Bhavishya	14,500	Contains prophecies regarding the future. Parts of the text are drawn from the law book of Manu, including the creation, records of land grants of the 5th century B.C.
4. Brahma	10,000	Describes creation of the cosmos and glorification of Godavari river.
5. Brahmanda	12,000	Describes the cosmos, Brahmanda, literally means Brahma's egg, a term for the universe. It also includes Lalitha Sahasranam according to the Tantric rites.
6. Brahmavaivarta	17,000	Describes the creation and purpose of life and the activities of different gods like Ganesha, Krishna.
7. Garuda	19,000	Describes what happens after a person dies and the kind of treatment he gets for his deeds on earth. It is similar to the concept of Judgment Day in Christianity.
8 Harivamsha	16,000	Describes the creation of the cosmos and the history of the kings of the Solar and Lunar dynasties leading up to the birth of Krishna.

Puranas Name	Number of Verses	Comments
9. Kurma	17,000	Contains information on the incarnation of Lord Vishnu as a tortoise that came to be known as the Kurma avatar.
10. Linga	11,000	Describes the origin of universe, origin of the linga, and emergence of Brahma, Vishnu, and Vedas from the Linga.
11. Markandeya	09,000	Contains the dialogue between two ancient sages, Jaimini and Markandya. The Devi Mahatmya, an important text for the Shaktas is included in this Purana.
12. Matsya	14,000	Describes the first avatar of Lord Vishnu as a fish.
13. Narada	25,000	Describes the greatness of Veda and Vedangas. Narada explains to Sanatkumara the major places of pilgrimages, their location, and their significance.
14. Padma	55,000	In the first part of the text, sage Pulastya explains to Bhishma about religion and the essence of the religion. The second part describes in detail of Prithivi, the earth. Third part describes the cosmos including creation, and description of India, the Bharata Varsha. The fourth part describes the life and deeds of Rama. The fifth part is a dialogue between Shiva and wife Parvathi and the knowledge about religion.
15. Shiva	24,000	Dedicated to Shiva
16. Skanda	81,100	Describes geographical locations of pilgrimage centers in India, with related legends, parables, hymns and stories. The text is devoted to the life and deeds of Kartikeya, a son of Shiva.
17. Vamana	10,000	Describes North India and the areas around Kurukshetra. There are ten

Puranas Name	*Number of Verses*	*Comments*
		characteristics marked in Vamana Purana. They are: 1. Sarga 2. Visarga 3. Sthaana 4. Poshana 5. Uti 6. Vritti 7. Raksha 8. Manvantara 9. Vansha 10. Upaashraya **Sarga** deals with the descriptions of the origin of this universe. **Visarg** describes how a living thing transforms itself from one species to another. **Sthaan, Poshan, Uti and Vritti** deal with the descriptions of various means which are employed by a man for his survival. **Raksha** describes about the various incarnations of Lord Vishnu which he takes for the protection of the humankind. **Manvantara** deals with the complete description of the history of the whole Manvantara (astronomical period of time measurement). **Vansh** describe about the lineage of all kings including Brahma. **Upaashraya** describes the real meaning of Brahma.
18. Varaha	24,000	Describes Varaha (boar) avatar of Lord Vishnu and narrates the rescue of the Earth.
19. Vayu	24,000	The Vayu Purana deals with the following topics: creation and re-creation of the universe; measurement of the time (Kala); origin of fire (Agni), Varuna and a number of gods; origin of animals, birds, trees and creepers; detailed geography of the earth divided into seven dvipas and further sub-divided

Puranas Name	*Number of Verses*	*Comments*
		into the varshas; accounts of inhabitants of different *dvipas*; names and descriptions of the seven *Patalas* (netherworlds); description of the solar system and the movements of the celestial bodies; description of the four yugas and fourteen manvantaras. It also contains chapters on music; duties of the people belong to different castes and funeral rites.
20. Vishnu	23,000	Explains the stories of creation and introduces the concept of four yugas (periods.) The story of Rudra, an intricate story of the Samudra Manthana (churning of the ocean), the famous story of Hiranyakashipu and Prahlada, some topological details of the known world with mentions of lands, tribes, mountains and rivers, concepts of the universe, and the stories of the many births of Jadabharata are discussed. It also discusses the stories of Manvantara (cycles of creation and destruction), the four classes (varnas) and the four stages of life (ashrama) and details of many rituals. The list contains the name of historical kings of Magadha, including kings from the Shishunaga, Nanda, and Maurya dynasties.

From 200 A.D.-Scholastic Period

The Scholastic period also dates from the second century A.D and continues to the present. It is to this period that the great names of Kumarila, Samkara, Sridhara, Ramanuja, Madhva, Vachaspati, Udayana, Bhaskara, Jayanta, Vijnanabhiksu, and Raghunatha belong. Studies indicate that the literature is grossly controversial. Noisy controversialist indulging over subtle theories and twisting arguments, and fighting seriously over the nature of logical universe could be found here. Many Indian scholars' theories more often confuse us. Instead of thought, one can find words. Obscurity of thought, subtlety of logic, and intolerance of disposition mark the dreadful kind of commentators. Nonc would deny their acuteness and enthusiasm. The better side is works are as valuable as the ancient thinkers. Commentators like Sankara and Ramanuja re-state the old doctrine, and their restatement is just as valuable as a spiritual rediscovery.

Indian Music

Highly developed music tradition goes back to early Vedic period (2000 to 500 B.C.) in India. It is possible to distinguish Indian music from its culture and philosophy as it is intertwined in a number of ways. The characteristics of Indian music include accuracy of pitch, clarity of tone, principles of rhythm based on syllable length, and mathematical approach by measures of tala, the beats.

It seems that the Aryans knew a heptatonic scale (a musical scale with seven pitches per octave), and the instructions for chanting the hymns of the Sama Veda, which has been preserved accurately by the Brahmins to the present day. The practice of singing based on notes was popular even from the Vedic times where the hymns in Sama Veda were sung as Sama Gana.

In the later period an anonymous writer composed a textbook on drama, music and dancing, in accordance with the custom of that time attributing it to an ancient sage Bharatha. This Bharatha Natyashastra is the earliest Indian authority on these three arts, out of which India fully developed a system of classical music.

Indians use a system of rhythm called swara: sa, ri, ga, ma, pa, dha, and ni, the seven notes, to scale the degrees. They are used to identify the pitch with the cry of a bird or an animal.

1. The peacock utters, *sa*
2. The chataka-bird, *ri*
3. The goat, *ga*

4. The Kraauncha bird, *ma*
5. The woodpecker with its clear voice, *pa*
6. The frog, excited by love, the note, *dha*
7. The elephant, when hit on the head with the trainer's hook, *ni* (through its nose).

The two main traditions of classical music are Carnatic, found predominantly in the peninsular regions, and Hindustani music, found in the northern and central regions.

Hindustani music

The basic scale of modern Hindusthani music is heptatonic and its seven notes are called sadja, rsabha, gandhara, madhyama, panchama, dhaivata and nishada, abbreviated to sa, ri, ga, ma, pa, dha, and ni. This system also corresponds approximately to European major scale C D E F G A B C. They may be expanded with half-tones of varying intervals classified according to the number of srutis they contain. The sruti[3] is a conceptual interval in which the scale contains 22. The concept of 22 srutis is divided as follows:

Sa	ri	ga	ma	pa	dha	ni
• • • •	• • •	• •	• • • •	• • • •	• • •	• •

A raga is a series of five or more notes, upon which a melody is based. According to orthodox medieval theory there are six basic ragas; the others being raginis, represented as the wives of the masculine ragas. The following is one of the oldest classifications of six original ragas according to modern theory:

1. Bhairava
2. Megha
3. Dipaka
4. Sriraga
5. Kausika
6. Hindola

3. *Sruti* (pitch), *swara* (sound of a single note), *raga* (melody), *tala* (the rhythmic cycles).

The ragas are classified according to the time of day or night for which they are most appropriate. Therefore, Bhairava is suitable to sing at dawn, Megha in the morning, Dipaka and Sriraga in the afternoon, and Kausika and Hindola at night. Bhairava is associated with awe and fear, Kausika with joy and laughter, Hindola, Dipaka and Sriraga with love, and Megha with peace and calm.

Hindustani music is not only influenced by ancient Hindu musical traditions, but also it is enriched by the Persian music. During the Mughal period various types of Gharana became famous.

Carnatic Music

The present form of Carnatic music was developed during fifteenth and sixteenth century A.D. Purandara Dasa is considered as the father of Carnatic music. Later, Thyagaraja of Tanjore and Muthuswamy Dikshitar enriched the style of Carnatic music.

Although there are stylistic differences, the basic elements of sruti, swara, raga and tala build the foundation for both Carnatic and Hindustani music. The Carnatic music is usually sung through compositions, especially the Kritis or Kirtanas, a form developed between the 16th and 20th centuries.

Other Types of Music

Light classical music

Light classical include thumri, dadra, ghazal, chaiti, kajri and tappa.

Bhangra

Bhangra is a lively form of music and dance that originated in the Punjab region to celebrate Vaisakhi, the festival of the Sikhs.

Uttarakhandi Music

Uttarakhandi folk music has its roots in the lap of nature. The pure and blessed music has the feel and the touch of nature and theme related to nature. The folk music is related to the various festivals, religious traditions, folk stories and simple life of the people of Uttarakhand.

Lavani

Lavani comes from the word Lavanya which means beauty. This is one of the most popular forms of dance and music practiced all over Maharashtra. Lavani is a combination of traditional song and dance, which is performed to the beats of "Dholak", a drum like instrument. Dance is performed by women wearing nine-yard saris. Lavani originated in the dry region of Maharashtra and Madhya Pradesh.

Rabindra Sangeet

Rabindranath Tagore was a lofty figure in Bengali music. He composed over 2,000 songs known as Rabindra Sangeet whose form is chiefly influenced by Hindustani classical, Carnatic, Western, Bauls, Bhatiali and different kind of folk songs of India.

Rajasthan Music

Rajasthan has a very diverse cultural collection of musician castes, including Langas, Sapera, Bhopa, Jogi and Manganiyar. The haunting melody of Rajasthan evokes from a variety of delightfully primitive looking instruments. The stringed variety include the Sarangi, Rawanhattha, Kamayacha, Morsing and Ektara. Beating instruments come in all shapes and sizes from the huge Nagaras and Dhols to the small Damrus. Flutes and bagpipers come in local flavors such as Shehnai, Poongi, Algoza, Tarpi, Been and Bankia.

The essence of Rajasthani music is derived from the creative symphony of string instruments, beating instruments and wind instruments accompanied by melodious version of folk singers.

Indians use different kinds of instruments such as Vina, Sitar, Sarod, Sarangi, Flute, and Shahanai.

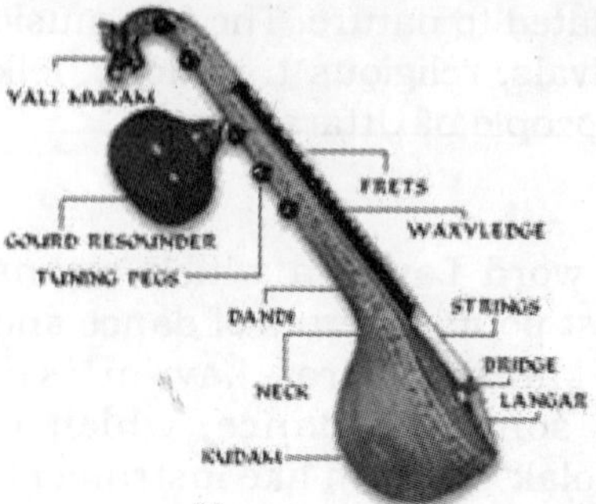

Veena

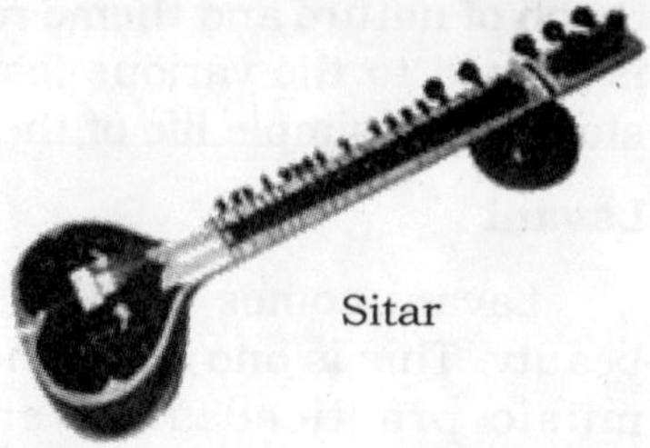

Sitar

Sarod

Sarangi

Flute

Shahanai

Indian Philosophies

Hinduism

Hinduism in its highest manifestation teaches unity in diversity, god is one and the names are many. This characteristic can be seen in all social and religious practices in India. In social order, although people in different parts of the country worship different gods and goddesses, they follow the similar ritualistic procedures throughout India. Although they speak different languages and dress in different styles, there is some kind of unity binding them together.

According to their faith, Hindus are divided into 3 main groups, Vaishnava, Shaiva, and Sakta. Members of these groups live side by side, each believing that the views of others are erroneous. Sometimes some minor clashes may occur, but Hinduism has a very good record of solving its problems in peaceful ways. The basic monotheism of Hinduism has emerged not through the abandonment of all gods, but through the assimilation of many divinities to one great god. This view has made possible many opposing beliefs to live side by side.

The deities in one place include gods and goddesses, the rituals used in worshiping these deities are just as diverse. Although they are different in nature, they adopt Sanskrit incantations and give purely local regional forms.

The Hindu philosophy conceives the Absolute both as personal and impersonal and tries to understand the soul's relationship to this higher Reality.

The six important schools of philosophy emphasized different means of approaches like:

1. Nyaya - Analysis
2. Vaisheshika - The School of Individual Characteristics
3. Sankhya - The Count
4. Yoga - Spiritual Discipline
5. Mimamsa - Enquiry
6. Vedanta - The Essence of Vedas

This last class Vedanta organised the Upanishadic teachings systematically. The important figure in Vedanta philosophy was Shankara of the 9th century. He harmonised many contradictory statements of the Upanishads into a consistent system. According to Sankara, Supreme Self is independent of any need of human offerings or acts of any sort. He argued that on the lower level of truth, the universe was produced by a divine personality by a system of evolution and it passed through many cycles. But in the higher level of truth, this universe is not real. He said, as a rope appears to be a snake in the dark, so, in the ordinary level of this universe, it appears to be true because of illusion. But only the Absolute Brahman, which permeates the whole universe is wholly and truly the real! When this identity is realised, the soul will rise above the mundane illusions and merge with the Truth forever.

Sankara's philosophy also teaches *aham brahmasmi*, "I am the Brahman". Although some argue that Sankara's philosophy is vanishing, it is indeed very strong in learned and intellectual people in India.

Theistic philosopher Ramanuja of eleventh and 12th century A.D. initiated Sri Vaishnava movement and advocated *Jnanayoga,* the way of knowledge. He promoted devotion to god. According to Ramanuja, salvation could be gained by unconditional surrender to god and humbly waiting for his grace. Ramanuja's god was personal. In Ramanuja's theory, although an individual is a fragment of god, he is never completely identical with god. In the highest level, the soul is personally joined with him, but not one with him, and retains some degree of self-consciousness. Thus, the liberated soul is one with God but yet separate! Hence, Ramanuja's philosophy is known as qualified monism, Vishishtadvaita.

Madhwacharya of 13th century promoted a doctrine of devotion (Dwaita philosophy). According to Madhwa, God, souls, and matter are eternally distinct. He did not teach salvation as union with God, but salvation is dwelling near god forever. According to him, god saves his devotees by his grace; without his grace, intense devotion and strict morality are of no use. But God's grace is showered without fail on those who lead righteous path. Evil souls are expelled to eternal damnation. This concept contradicts to popular belief that all souls have a chance to rise again. A. L. Basham says Madhwa philosophy is influenced by Christianity.

Theism has great inspiration on Hindu reformers. The teachings of the Vedas, Upanishads and works of great masters were in Sanskrit. Only educated Brahmins could be able to study and understand them. It was the hymnodists who composed devotional songs in local languages and carried the message of devotion to the people. A common man understands the doctrine of *moksha*, liberation though the stories and songs written in regional languages. Thus, hymnodists changed the way of Hinduism.

Among these religious poets, Kabir was an important reformer. At his time, India was dominated by Muslims and they opposed image worship. His goal was to unite both the Hindu and the Muslim and convince them that they were the children of the same Father. He touched the most controversial practices like caste, idol worship, pilgrimage, and reverence for sacred places and tried to bring them into a common community by saying,

> If God be within the mosque, then to whom does
> this world belong?
> If Ram be within the image which you find upon
> your pilgrimage, then who is there to know
> what happens without?
> Hari is in the East; Allah is in the West;
> Look within your heart, for there you will find
> both Ram and Karim.
> All the men and women of the world are his living forms.
>
> There is nothing but water at the holy bathing Places;
> and I know that they are useless,
> for I have bathed in them.
> The images are all lifeless, they cannot speak;
> I know, for I have cried aloud to them,
> The Purana and the Koran are mere words;
> lifting up the curtain, I have seen.

Kabir gives utterance to the words of experience;
and he knows very well that all other things are untrue.

(Kabir's Poem - Translated by Rabindranath Tagore)

His hymns were welcomed by both theist and non-theist because they had universal appeal.

There were many hymn singers throughout India. All hymnodists are fundamentally theist and teach devotion is the surest way of salvation. Many hymnodists discouraged the rigidity of caste.

Vallabhacharya (1479–1531) taught that salvation could be achieved by simple worship of Krishna without renouncing the worldly pleasures. He organised a *Mutt*, a church in Mathura. The head of the Mutt, called as Maharaja, was treated with all respect thinking that he was the incarnation of Vishnu upon earth. The ignorant and foolish laymen used to give the Maharaja the full use of their possessions including their wives. A number of scandals led to reform the Vallabha cult, and they stopped this practice of immorality. It seems Hinduism has tried all kinds of paths to reach God or gain salvation on a trial and error basis!

Aurobindo tried the modern evolution method. He proclaimed the ancient idea that there is an eternal self and consciousness. All beings are united in that one eternal self but are separated by ignorance. To prove this, he used the evolutionary theory. "Evolution is the process by which it liberates itself. Consciousness appears in matter, and once having appeared, it grows higher and higher towards greater perfection. Life is the first step of this release of consciousness; mind is the second. But, the evolution does not end with mind; it awaits release into something greater, a consciousness which is spiritual and supramental." He argued that by following certain disciplines one can reach this state.

900 B.C. & 600 B.C.—Jainism

According to scholars, Parshvanatha was an historical person who lived in the 9th century B.C. In the 6th century

B.C., Vardhamana Mahavira became one of the most prominent Jainism teachers. He organized a large group of disciples and taught them an ascetic doctrine in order to achieve enlightenment. The disciples referred to him as Jina, which means "the conqueror".

Jainism prevailed even before Parshvanatha or Vardhamana. It is said that the Yajurveda mentions the names of three Tirthankaras-Rsabha, Ajitanatha and Aristaneme. The Bhagavata endorses the view that Rsabha was the founder of Jainism.

Deciphering of the Brahmi script by James Prinsep in 1788 enabled the reading of ancient inscriptions in India and established the antiquity of Jainism. The discovery of Jain manuscripts has added significantly to revise Jain history. Archaeologists have encountered Jain remains and artifacts at Maurya, Sunga, Kushan, Gupta, Kalachuries, Rashtrakuta, Chalukya, Chandel and Rajput sites. Several western and Indian scholars have contributed to the reconstruction of Jain history.

Jainism started spreading in South India from the 3rd century B.C. when Badrabahu, a preacher of Jainism, came to Karnataka from Bihar. Shravanabelagola has the world famous monolithic statue of Lord Bahubali. Similar Monolithic statues of Lord Bahubali are in Dharmasthala, Venur and Mysore. In all of these temples, the holy festival of Mahamastakabhisheka will be held once in every 12 years.

Jains have successfully sustained this longstanding religion to the present day and have significantly influenced and contributed to ethical, political, and economic sectors in India. Jains have the highest degree of literacy for a religious community in India. Jain libraries are the oldest in the country.

Structure of Jain Universe and Time Cycles

According to Jain thinking, the universe was never created, nor will it ever stop to exist. Therefore, it is *eternal*. It has no beginning or end. Within the universe there will be regular changes, movements and modifications in accordance with the macro phases of the time cycles. The universe consists of infinite amount of *Jiva* (life force or souls), and infinite amount of Ajiva (lifeless objects).

Jainism believes that not only gods, human beings, demons, animals and insects are inhabited by souls, but also plants of all types of species, earth and stones, everything originated from the earth like rivers, ponds, seas, and raindrops, flames and all fires, and gases and winds of every kind are inhabited by souls. Thus the whole universe is full of life. In every breath of wind, in every handful of earth, souls are imprisoned. When a match is struck to that soul-being, the soul of that being may one day become a man and born, only to die again when the match is blown out. In every stone on the road a soul is locked in a prison of silent suffering, unable to escape the careless foot kicks it or to cry out at its pain. The more tightly it is bound by matter, greater the pains are.

Karma Theory in Jainism

According to Jains, karma is of material nature. They perceive that thoughts and ideas affect our character and create or modify the tendencies of our souls. Karma is a material force, matter in a subtle form. It is a kind of matter, which is in the subtle form of particles to manifest karma, fills all cosmic space. It has the peculiar property of developing the effects of merit and demerit. The soul by its interaction with the outer world becomes literally penetrated with the particles of subtle matter. These become karma and build up a special body called karma sharira, which does not leave the soul till its final emancipation. The karmic matter retards the radiance of the soul. Karma works in such a way that every change which takes place leaves a mark which is retained and built into the organism to serve as the foundation for future action. It is actually present and acting in the nature of the human souls. To obtain liberation from karma, Jainism emphasizes that one has to try to transgress this karma cycle.

Customs and Practices

Jains are strict vegetarians. They prevent eating root

vegetables in general, because cutting root from a plant kills other parts of the plant. In addition, according to Jain texts, root vegetables contain huge amount of microorganism called nigodas. They eat before the night falls. They filter water so as to remove any small insects that may be present and boil the water before the drinking.

Jain monks and nuns practice strict ascetism and attempt to make their present birth is their last one to escape from the cycle of transmigration. Jain monks and nuns walk barefoot and sweep the ground in front of them to avoid killing insects or other tiny beings.

Major Sects

Jainism is mainly divided into two major sects: Shvetambar and Digambar. Jainism has a distinct thought on the principal of Tirthankar worship. The physical form is not worshipped, but their characteristics, virtues, and qualities are glorified and imitated. Tirthankaras strictly reject idol worship. However, Mur Tippujak and Digamabar branch allow praying before idol in order to help them in motivating and focusing thoughts.

Digambar

In Digambar tradition, idols of Thirthankars are worshipped. However they are not decorated with ornaments. The Digambar monks who have reached the highest stages of spiritual state do not wear any clothes. They carry in their hands a special kind of pot and a broom made of fallen peacock's feathers. They eat food once a day with both their palms folded in the shape of a bowl without using a plate.

Jain contributions to Indian culture

Jains have contributed to the culture and language in the Indian states Gujarat, Rajasthan, Tamil Nadu, and Karnataka. Ancient Tamil books titled Manimegalai, Naaladiyar, Silapathigaram, Seevaka Sinthamani, etc. were written by Jain scholars. Between 9th and 13th century, Kannada writers were predominantly of the Jain and Veerashaiva faiths. Jains were the earliest known promoters of Kannada literature. Pampa, 900 A.D. known as Adikavi

Pampa, is one of the greatest Kannada poets of all time. He was a court poet of Chalukya King Arikesari. The Jain writers Adikavi Pampa, Ponna and Ranna heralded the age of

General view of inside main hall of Luna Vasahi Jain Temple at Mt. Abu in Rajasthan

Palitana Temple

Highly decorated ceiling of Vimal Vasahi Jain temple at Mt. Abu in Rajasthan

classical Kannada in the 10th century. The earliest known Gujarati text, Bharat-Bahubali Ras was written by a Jain monk. Some important people in Gujarat's Jain history were Acharya Hemachandra Suri and his disciple, and the Chalukya ruler Kumarapala.

Jains literature exists mainly in Prakrit, Sanskrit, Gujarati, Rajasthani, Marathi, Kannada, Tamil, Malayalam, and Tulu.

600 B.C.-Buddhism

Vardhamana of Jainism and Gautama Buddha of Buddhism were contemporaries. Guerinot has highlighted the date and the birth of Vardhamana and Gautama Buddha. Vardhamana was born at Vaisali about 599 B.C. while Gautama Buddha was born at Kapilavastu about 567 B.C. Vardhamana died at Pawa in 527 B.C. while Gautama died at Kusinagar about 483 B.C.

Two major branches of Buddhism are recognised: Theravada, "The School of the Elders" and Mahayana, "The Great Vehicle".

Buddhism was born in India twenty five hundred years ago, inspired by Siddhartha Gauthama Buddha's life and his teachings. Buddha's teachings are the revelations to the people who are suffering from the pain of birth and death cycle. He spread this knowledge for the sake of humanity. Three things are necessary to take refuge in Buddhism. They are the Buddha, the Dharma, and the Sangha.

As a prince, Gauthama was never exposed to pain, suffering, old age, or any illness. Since an oracle told that Gauthama would become a sanyansi (saint) if he saw a sick person, old men or any kind of suffering, his father arranged a strict atmosphere so that Gauthama could never come into contact with any suffering. At the age of twenty one, accidentally he encountered a dead body, an old man, and a beggar on his way back from a retreat. Then, Siddhartha Gauthama determined to find the way out from suffering, renounced the family, all worldly pleasures, and entered the forest in search of salvation. There, he observed rigorous penance. After six years of strict mental and physical discipline, he attained Enlightenment under the Bodhi-tree. He realized the cause of pain and suffering. Gauthama Buddha's teachings are the four Noble Truths:

1. Life is full of suffering
2. The cause of suffering is human desire
3. Cessation of suffering (*nirvana*) is attainable
4. The discipline of morality, meditation, and wisdom is the path to attain *nirvana*

Gautama's doctrine contained no theology, no metaphysics: it was essentially logic, psychology and practical ethics. What is important is not the knowledge of structure of the universe but one's relations to the universe. His teaching was essentially psychological, dedicated to the liberation of the individual human being alone.

According to Buddha, the cause of human-suffering is not from outside, but humans themselves. A person commits *karma*, the cause of suffering, by thoughts, words, and deeds through his body, mind and intellect. People are self-creating themselves by desire for life, for pleasure, for power, for possession since whatever a person thinks that he becomes. The deeds performed through thinking good, speaking good, and doing good produce good *karma*, that is *punya*; and deeds performed through bad intentions produce bad *karma* that is papa. Both kinds of people have to experience their *karma* according to their deeds. Good merits produce happiness, such as good health, high status, long life, wealth, power, pleasure, taking birth in heaven, and bad merits produce unhappiness such as poverty, poor health, untimely death, and taking birth as subhuman beings. A person is born as a human being due to his past *karma* and accumulates merits for his future births. According to Buddha's worldview, there are several levels of life, like god, animal, ghostly and human forms. Below the earth is the hell and above is heaven.

Buddha said, through meditation, the meditator attains selfless state and understands the real nature self and the world. This is Enlightenment. Buddha called it *nirvana*. The ultimate goal of Buddhism is *nirvana*, freedom from suffering.

This moral perfection and *nirvana* cannot be attained in one life, and it may take many lives. Buddhism offered a panacea, a progression from offering (*dana* or donation) to morality to meditation. Respect and service to holy monks develop morality. Eventually, morality leads a person to be able to live the monastic life which is full of moral purity and meditation. In one's life, a person may not attain *nirvana*, but he will be born again to perpetuate his unfinished journey, ultimately reaches *nirvana*.

Buddha travelled throughout the northeastern part of India to spread his message and died in 483 B.C. at the age of 80 in Kushinagar.

Hinayana (Theravada)

In Buddhism, there are two major traditions, Hinayana (Theravada) and Mahayana. It was the ancient custom in India to rely on human memory for the preservation and passing on the knowledge from generation to generation. For about four hundred years, Buddha's teachings, utterances and discourses were carried on in the memories of his disciples. There was a possible threat that with the lapse of time many sects may form and interpret divergence of opinions on Buddha's teachings. To save the true Dharma, five hundred fully trained *arhants* gathered together at Rajagraha to hold the Theravada First Council with an object to recite loudly Buddha's Dharma and Vinaya to preserve, learn, master, and to follow. The assembled *Arhants* composed many great works based on Buddha's teachings. Among them *Vinaya-pitaka, Sutta-pitaka, Abhidhamma-pitaka, the Tipitaka* are in Pali language. These are the most authoritative source of orthodox Buddhism. They are called Theravada.

After a century, a group of monks desired to reform certain disciplines in Buddhism. They gathered in a Second Council at Varsali, but the rebellious minority group did not oblige to accept the orthodox as majority, split off from the main body, and called themselves *Mahasanghikas*. Their chief work was *Mahavastu* which emphasizes a different interpretation on *Sutta* and *Vinaya* and rejects some practices written in original Pali canon. Theravada held the notion that everything, past, present, and future exists but denied any permanent substance in an individual being including transcendental nature of the Buddha. Theravadins believed that Buddha was a man, neither God nor creator, or a myth or legend. Several Theravada Councils have been held in order to purify the records, at first spoken and later written down the great works.

Mahayana

Mahayana is the second phase of Buddhism. The meaning of Mahayana is "Great Vehicle". Buddhist Doctrine Dhamma is conceived as a ferry-boat which carries laymen across the ocean of this world of suffering to the salvation, *nirvana.*

Hinayana emphasised the role of Arhant, a person who has been liberated from the cycle of birth and death. Four centuries later, the notion of *arhant* ideal faded because fewer and fewer monks reached the goal and it was replaced by Bodhisattva ideal. The promoters of Mahayana gave much importance to laymen because they considered people are as important as "dharma". They attacked selfish monks who favored their own welfare, and demanded that saints should accept a common fate with their fellowmen. They induced monks to become more useful to the people. Eventually, monks acting as astrologers, weather makers, physicians, etc. mingled themselves into the flow of the society.

Mahayana's most instructive work is "the Perfection of Wisdom". The Mahayana is a way of life with a specific idea of spiritual perfection and the path which leads to *nirvana.* It puts forth many ideals from mythological concept to magical forces. The Bodhisattva ideal says how the Bodhisattvas take birth again and again to serve the suffering people. In mythological doctrine, the celestial Bodhisattvas become objects of a religious sect. *Avalokiteshwara* helps all beings with compassion by a capacity of transforming himself into any shape he desired; *Manjusri* disperses wisdom; *Maitreya,* the coming Buddha, holds an elixir pot and leads many to Enlightenment; *Kshitigarba* looks after the welfare of the dead; *Samanthabhadra* dispels all dangers; *Sakyamuni* is original Buddha and he is described as eternal savior; *Amitabha* presides over a Pure Land named Sukhavati; *Bhaisajyaguru* Buddha is Master of Healing.

Thus, Buddha's teachings have been developed from Hinayana to Mahayana undergoing many purifications and modifications from time to time.

The *Dharmachakra* represents the Noble Eightfold Path

The Mahayana dominated Nepal, Tibet, China, Korea and Japan. The Hinayana dominated Ceylon (Sri Lanka), Burma (Myanmar) and Siam (Thailand).

The Noble Eightfold Path

Buddha's "The Noble Eightfold Path" describes the way to the end of suffering:

1. Right View—*Prajñâ*: Prajna is the wisdom that purifies the mind.
2. Right Intention—*Shila*: Shila is the ethics or morality, or abstention from unwholesome deeds.
3. Right Speech—*Vaac*: Speaking in a truthful and non-hurtful way.
4. Right Action—*Karma*: Acting in a non-harmful way.
5. Right Livelihood—*Aajivana*: A non-harmful livelihood.
6. Right Effort—*Vyayama*: Making an effort to improve.
7. Right Mindfulness—*Smriti*: Awareness to see things with clear consciousness.
8. Right Concentration—*Samaadhi*: Correct meditation or concentration, as explained by the first four jhanas.

Magadha Empire

684 B.C. - 550 A.D.-Magadha Empire

Among the sixteen Mahajanapadas, the kingdom of Magadha became an important Empire under a number of dynasties. During Ashoka Maurya's leadership, the kingdom of Magadha had emerged as a major power and possessed an unparalleled military.

The kingdom of the Magadha approximately represents the modern districts of Bihar, Nalanda, Aurangabad, Patna, Gaya, and parts of Bengal in the east. On the north it was surrounded by the river Ganges, on the east by the river Champa, on the south by the Vindhya Mountains and on the west by the river Sone.

Magadha Empire ascended to world dominion during 7th and 6th century B.C. A few centuries later Magadha became a classical world as equal to Rome. The founder of Magadhan Dynasty was Bimbasara, a contemporary of Gautama Buddha. Magadhan state was situated across two of the greatest international trade routes of the Indian world: navigation through river streams on the Ganges and the land route through important meeting place of Gaya. An enthusiastic military man, Bimbasara, was the first ruler to discover the fighting potential of the armored war-elephants, the heavy tanks of those days.

The two great epics Ramayana and Mahabharata mention the name of Magadha Empire. Magadha Empire was a part of the 16 Mahajanapadas. It was mostly republican in nature and the administration was divided into judicial, executive and military functions.

Ajatshatru even built a huge fort around his capital Pataliputra. With an unmatched military force and advanced forms of weaponry, the Magadha Empire conquered neighborhood places and extended its territories.

After the death of King Udayan, the Magadha Empire started to decline very rapidly. Internal disturbances and corruption within the kingdom led to its decline. Finally,

Magadha Empire was taken over by the powerful Nanda Dynasty who ruled the kingdom until Mauryas replaced their Empire.

Although the Magadhan nation was as old as the later Vedas, it remained a small state for many centuries far away in the east, remote from the great centers of Kurus and Panchalas where Indian Culture was in full development. It was considered as a barbarian country because its population was mixed, partly Aryanised and incompletely Brahmanised. However, economic efficiency seems to have been the defining factor of Magadhan life: roads and pathways, irrigation canals and dams, granaries, everything was built faster and on a larger scale than other states. Because of their cultural inferiority consciousness, many young men from Magadha were sent to Takshashila faraway in the northwestern state of Gandhara to acquire education.

Magadha Dynasties

684-320 B.C.

Brihadratha Dynasty, Pradyota Dynasty, Harayanka Dynasty, Shisunaga Dynasty ruled Magadha. Afterwards the Nanda Dynasty, Maurya Dynasty, Sunga Dynasty, Kanva Dynasty, Gupta Dynasty expanded beyond Magadha.

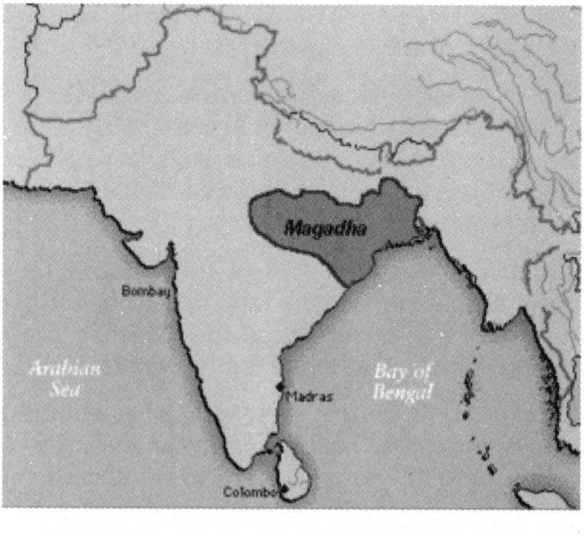

1700-799 BC - Brihadratha Dynasty

According to the Puranas, the Magadha Empire was established by the Brihadratha Dynasty. The first prominent Emperor of the Magadhan branch of Bharathas was Emperor Brihadratha. His son Jarasandha appears in popular legend Mahabharata and slained by Bhima.

799-684 B.C.—Pradyota Dynasty

The Brihadratha Dynasty was succeeded by the Pradyota Dynasty, which ruled for 138 years. One of the Pradyota traditions was that the prince should kill his father to become king. During this time, it is said that there were high crimes in Magadha. The people revolted against the dynasty and elected Haryanka to become the new king, which ended the power of the Pradyotas and established the Haryanka Dynasty.

684-413 B.C.—Haryanka Dynasty

The Haryanka Dynasty established the Magadha Empire in 545 B.C., whose center was Rajagriha. Later it became Pataliputra, near the modern day Patna. King Bimbisara expanded the boundaries of his kingdom through matrimonial partnerships and conquest. Bimbisara was imprisoned and killed by his son Ajatashatru. Under Ajatashatru's rule the dynasty reached highest level. His son Udayabhadra succeeded his father. Under his administration, Pataliputra became the largest city in the world. This dynasty survived until 413 B.C. and was defeated by the Shishunaga Dynasty.

413–345 B.C.—Shishunaga Dynasty

Shishunaga Dynasty defeated Haryanka Dynasty and ruled Magadha until 345 B.C. Shishunaga was the founder of a dynasty of ten kings, assumably his ten sons, called Shishunaga Dynasty. The Shishunaga Dynasty was one of the largest Empires of the Indian subcontinent at that time.

The kingdom had a series of bloody succession. King Anuruddha succeeded Udaybhadra through assassination, and his son Munda succeeded him in the same manner,

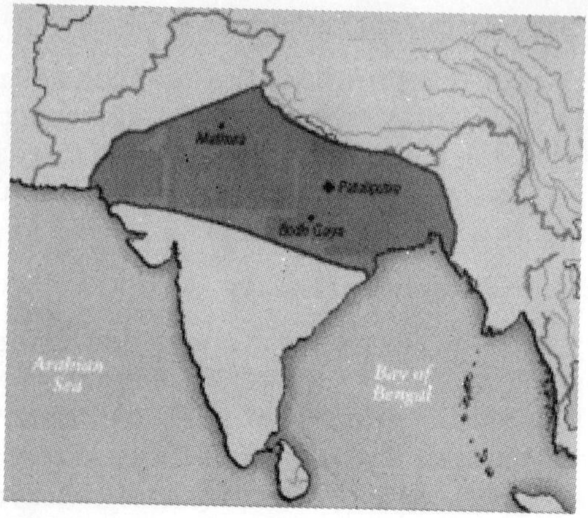

and his son Nagadasaka followed the same path. Due to this bloody rule, a civil revolt directed the development of the Nanda Dynasty.

345 -321 B.C.-Nanda Dynasty

There is some confusion about Nanda's origin. According to some studies, the Nanda Dynasty was founded by an illegitimate son of king Mahanandin of the previous Shishunaga Dynasty. Another record states that the Nandas who grabbed the throne of the Shishunaga Dynasty were of low origin. Mahapadma Nanda was known as destroyer of all the Kshatriyas. Dhana Nanda extended the empire to a greatest degree. He was defeated by Chandragupta Maurya and lost his empire.

The Nandas were followed by the Maurya Dynasty.

324-184 BC—Maurya Dynasty

Chandragupta Maurya: In 321 B.C., Chandragupta Maurya established the Maurya Dynasty after defeating the Nanda king Dhana Nanda.

In 326 B.C., Magadha was the most powerful state in India. Chanakya Kautilya met a young man of great energy and ability, Chandragupta Maurya, while they both were hiding in the vindhya forests. Forming forces, fusing penetrating thought and forceful action, they raised an army of outlaws, fanned the anti-foreign feeling of the Indians in western India. They went to war against the small Macedonian fortified military regions left behind by Alexander, and soon became masters of the lower Indus Valley. In a short period of time, the Mauryas conquered the whole of western India and then turning east, defeated the Magadhan army led by the Bhadrasila. Thus, he became the emperor not only of Magadha, but also for almost united India for the first time in history. At first time as an Emperor, he concluded a treaty with Alexander's successor, Seleukos, according to which he received the entire territory of modern Afghanistan and Baluchisthan.

Using Gandhara as his base, Chandragupta led a rebellion against the Magadha Empire and ascended the throne at Pataliputra in 321 BC. There are no Indian records of Chandragupta Maurya and almost all that is known is based on the diaries of Megasthenes, the ambassador of Seleucus at Pataliputra, as recorded by Arrian in his Indika.

Chandragupta's son Bindusara expanded the kingdom Turkestan down to modern Mysore and comprised most of the northern India and the Deccan. Only Kalinga remained independent.

During the reign of Chandragupta Maurya, Chinese travellers came to India on pilgrimages. It is known from Fa Hien, who visited Pataliputra in the fifth century A.D. He describes that the magnificent palaces built seven hundred years before by Ashoka still existed. The Greeks in the third century B.C. had judged them to be the finest in the world, and the Chinese who visited them in Gupta times felt nothing but awe and admiration. A comparison between the Greek and Chinese descriptions about the life in India seven hundred years apart reveals great admiration about the remarkable civilisation displayed during their visit. It can be noticed by their documentation that severe system of government of Mauryas with its countless spies and secret service seems to have softened somewhat by the time of the Guptas.

One of the remarkable characteristics of that period was the frequent contacts between India and China – India sending missionaries, China sending back pilgrims.

Arthashastra

Kautilya is a great Indian philosopher-statesman and contemporary of Aristotle. It is believed that his most famous book "Arthashashtra" was misplaced for more than 1400 years. It was lost at the end of the Gupta Dynasty in India, around 500 A.D. and was not rediscovered until early in the 20th century. It was considered as a classical economic thought, which covered the areas of international trade, taxation, labor system, government, administration, metallurgy, and every part of early life in India. This aspect of Kautilya's philosophy of government and economic has been overlooked by historians for a long time.

Unfortunately, translation of Arthashastra from Sanskrit to English and other languages did not occur until 1920's and 1930's. The goal of Kautilya was to increase the monarch's wealth. Economists such as Adam Smith and David Hume did not have the opportunity to study the Kautilya's thoughts on the best policies and practices for creating and enhancing nations's wealth.

Adam Smith published his book "The Wealth of Nations" in 1776 enumerating the labour theory of value and its benefits to enhance the wealth of the nation. This book is a *magnum opus* of the Economist in the western world. But, two thousand before Adam Smith, Kautilya apprehended that fair wages to be paid to workers based on the amount of time spent on the job, the amount of output created, and the skills necessary to peroform the required tasks in his book "Arthashastra". He promotes a wage system, which remunerates workers for the wealth they have created and encourages them to work efficiently.

Kautilya clearly recognised that international trade in goods and services is a major means for increasing the national wealth as well as its citizens. He recommends the king that the wealth and well being of the kingdom can be improved by fair and efficient tax system, which will create revenue for economic growth. Kautilya imposed a heavy taxation on imported foreign goods of luxury. On common things, light duties were imposed.

Kautilya endorses the use of tariffs on both import and export as revenue-raising strategy for the king.

Following are the excerpts from Arthashastra as described by Kautilya two thousand years ago in India.

On Administration

It is the duty of *Gopa*, village accountant, to attend to the accounts of five or ten villages as ordered by the Collector-General.

By setting up boundaries to villages, by numbering plots of grounds as cultivated, uncultivated, plains, wet lands, gardens, vegetable gardens, fences (*váta*), forests, altars, temples of gods, irrigation works, cremation grounds, feeding houses (*sattra*), places where water is freely supplied to travellers (*prapá*), places of pilgrimage, pasture grounds and roads, and thereby fixing the boundaries of various villages, of fields, of forests, and of roads, he shall register gifts, sales, charities, and remission of taxes regarding fields.

Also having numbered the houses as taxpaying or non-taxpaying, he shall not only register the total number of the inhabitants of all the four castes in each village, but also keep an account of the exact number of cultivators, cow-herds, merchants, artisans, laborers, slaves, and biped and quadruped animals, fixing at the same time the amount of gold, free labor, toll, and fines that can be collected from it (each house). He shall also keep an account of the number of young and old men that reside in each house, their history (*charitra*), occupation (*ájíva*), income (*áya*), and expenditure (*vyaya*).

Kautilya has provided an exhaustive and illustrative description of the duties, responsibilities and role of the king, prince(s), ministers, and other state officials.

The Arthashastra classifies legal matters into civil and criminal and it specifies elaborate guidelines for administering justice in terms of evidence, procedures and witnesses. Furthermore, Kautilya strongly believed in Dandniti (punishment), though he maintained that penalties must be fair and just, and proportionate to the offence committed. He recommends cruel punishments for criminal activities, which many people condemn those policies.

Because of its harsh political pragmatism, the *Arthashastra* has often been compared to Machiavelli's The Prince[4].

Kautilya distinguished six different kinds of interests: compound interest, periodical interest, stipulated interest, daily interest, and the use of a pledged article. Indeed the idea of expressing interest as a percent originated in India.

Kautilya identified several areas of State intervention to facilitate the economic life of the country. They are as follows:

1. The superintendent of slaughterhouse
2. The superintendent of prostitutes
3. The superintendent of ships

4. Niccolo Machiavelli was an Italian author, who wrote "Prince" around 1500 A.D. It is about political science describing how a Prince should rule the country. He Explains different kinds of states, republics and principalities, discusses what qualities a prince should apply so that he can best control his kingdom. He discusses military knowledge, liberality and parsimony, to be loved or to be feared, trustworthiness, good and bad reputations. Machiavelli also deals with how to handle money, princes do not need to think that people should be trustworthy. He mentions which class of people is best to be kind to and to listen to the needs and wants of like the peasants, the aristocracy, or the soldiers. He states that it is best to listen to people because they will offer you the best protection in times of war and will best keep you in power if you do what they need and want.

4. The superintendent of passports (authorization)
5. The office of the city superintendent.

Kautilya's idea of the Passport corresponds to the modern version of the document that helps movement of people. This is perhaps the first instance of an institutionalised concept of passports that regulate the flow of people across national and international borders. Kautilya said that "whoever is provided with a pass shall be at liberty to enter or to go out of the country".

Kautilya realised that the role of the State was to ensure that commercial activities do not violate laws or are harmful for the consumer and if the State did not establish and enforce codes of conduct, it would raise transaction costs.

Kautilya states that "Adulteration of grains, oils, alkalis, salts, scents, and medicinal articles with similar articles of poor quality shall be punished with a fine".

According to Kautilya, agriculture was the most important economic activity. In his view the cultivatable land is better than mines because mines fill only the treasury while agricultural production fills both treasury and store houses.

Kautilya considered trade as the pillar of economic activity and in consonance with this, the Arthashaṣtra details every aspect of trade.

It is amazing to note the wide range of subjects and area of specialties in which education was imparted during Kautilya's time. Medicine, mathematics, military education, commercial education, statecraft, the arts, architecture are some of the areas in which extensive training was provided. Some of the eminent institutions of learning that flourished during the time included Nalanda and Takshila.

The Duties of Government Superintendents

"Whoever imposes punishment as deserved becomes respectable. For punishment (*danda*) when awarded with due consideration, makes the people devoted to righteousness and to works productive of wealth and enjoyment; while punishment, when ill-awarded under the influence of greed and anger or owing to ignorance, excites fury even among hermits and ascetics dwelling in forests, not to speak of householders.

"Native, born of high family, influential, well trained in arts, possessed of foresight, wise, of strong memory, bold, eloquent, skillful, intelligent, possessed of enthusiasm, dignity, and endurance, pure in character, affable, firm in loyal devotion, endowed with excellent conduct, strength, health and bravery, free from procrastination and fickle mindedness, affectionate, and free from such qualities as excite hatred and enmity—these are the qualifications of a ministerial officer (*amâtyasampat*)

"When in the court, he shall never cause his petitioners to wait at the door, for when a king makes himself inaccessible to his people and entrusts his work to his immediate officers, he may be sure to engender confusion in business, and to cause thereby public disaffection, and himself a prey to his enemies. He shall, therefore, personally attend to the business of gods, of heretics, of *Brahmans* learned in the Vedas, of cattle, of sacred places, of minors, the aged, the afflicted, and the helpless, and of women;—all this in order (of enumeration) or according to the urgency or pressure of those works. All urgent calls he shall hear at once, but never put off; for when postponed, they will prove too hard or impossible to accomplish. Having seated himself in the room where the sacred fire has been kept, he shall attend to the business of physicians and ascetics practising austerities; and that in company with his high priest and teacher and after preliminary salutation (to the petitioners). Accompanied by persons proficient in the three sciences (*trividya*) but not alone lest the petitioners be offended, he shall look to the business of those who are practicing austerities, as well as of those who are experts in witchcraft and *Yóga*.

"In the happiness of his subjects lies his happiness; in their welfare his welfare; whatever pleases himself he shall not consider as good, but whatever pleases his subjects he shall consider as good. Hence the king shall ever be active and discharge his duties; the root of wealth is activity, and of evil its reverse. In the absence of activity acquisitions present and to come will perish; by activity he can achieve both his desired ends and abundance of wealth.

"If she is desirous of a second marriage (*kutumbakama*), she shall be given on the occasion of her remarriage (*nivesakále*) whatever either her father-in-law or her husband or both had given to her. The time at which women can remarry shall be explained in connection with the subject of long sojourn of husbands.

"If a widow marries any man other than of her father-in-law's selection (*svasurapratilo-myenanivishta*), she shall forfeit whatever had been given to her by her father-in-law and her husband.

"A woman, hating her husband, cannot dissolve her marriage with him against his will. Nor can a man dissolve his marriage with his wife against her will. But from mutual enmity, divorce may be obtained (*parasparam dveshanmokshah*). If a man, apprehending danger from his wife desires divorce (*mokshamichhet*), he shall return to her whatever she was given (on the occasion of her marriage). If a woman, under the apprehension of danger from her husband, desires divorce, she shall forfeit her claim to her property; marriages contracted in accordance with the customs of the first four kinds of marriages cannot be dissolved.

Rules Regarding Laborers and Co-operative Undertaking

"A servant neglecting or unreasonably putting off work for which he has received wages shall be fined 12 *panas* and be caught-hold of till the work is done. He who is incapable to turn out work, or is engaged to do a mean job, or is suffering from disease, or is involved in calamities shall be shown some concession or allowed to get the work done by a substitute. The loss incurred by his master or employer owing to such delay shall be made good by extra work. An employer may be at liberty to get the work done by (another) provided there is no such adverse condition that the former shall not employ another servant to execute the work, nor shall the latter go elsewhere for work.

Protection of Artisans

"Those who can be expected to relieve misery, who can give instructions to artisans, who can be trusted with deposits, who can plan artistic work after their own design, and who can be relied upon by guilds of artisans, may receive the deposits of the guilds. The guilds (*sreni*) shall receive their deposits back in time of distress.

"Artisans shall, in accordance with their agreement as to time, place, and form of work, fulfill their engagements. Those who postpone their engagements under the excuse that no agreement as to time, place and form of work has been entered into shall, except in troubles and calamities, not only forfeit ¼th of their wages, but also be punished with a fine equal to twice the amount of their wages. They shall also make good whatever is thus lost or damaged. Those who carry on their work contrary to orders shall not only forfeit their wages, but also pay a fine equal to twice the amount of their wages.

"*Scavengers.* Of whatever precious things sweepers come across while sweeping, one-third shall be taken by them and two-thirds by the king. But precious stones shall be wholly surrendered to the king. Seizure of precious stones shall be punished with the highest amercement. A discoverer of mines, precious stones, or treasure troves shall, on supplying the information to the king, receive 1/6th of it as his share; but if the discoverer happens to be a peon (*bhritaka*), his share shall be only 1/12th of it. Treasure troves valued beyond 100,000 shall wholly be taken by the king. But if they are of less value, the discoverer shall receive 1/6th of it as his share.

Medical Practice

"Physicians undertaking medical treatment without intimating (to the government) the dangerous nature of the disease shall, if the patient dies, be punished with the first amercement. If the death of a patient under treatment is due to carelessness in the treatment, the physician shall be punished with the middle-most amercement. Growth of disease due to negligence or indifference (*karmavadha*) of a physician shall be regarded as assault or violence.

The Elements of Sovereignty

The king, the minister, the country, the fort, the treasury, the army and the friend are the elements of sovereignty. Of these, the best qualities of the king are:

Born of a high family, godly, possessed of valour, seeing through the medium of aged persons, virtuous, truthful, not of a contradictory nature, grateful, having large aims, highly enthusiastic, not addicted to procrastination, powerful to control his neighbouring kings, of resolute mind, having an assembly of ministers of no mean quality, and possessed of a taste for discipline;—these are the qualities of an inviting nature. Inquiry, hearing, perception, retention in memory, reflection, deliberation, inference and steadfast adherence to conclusions are the qualities of the intellect.

Valor, determination of purpose, quickness, and probity are the aspects of enthusiasm. Possessed of a sharp intellect, strong memory, and keen mind, energetic, powerful, trained in all kinds of arts, free from vice, capable of paying in the same coin by way of awarding punishments or rewards, possessed of dignity, capable of taking remedial measures against dangers, possessed of foresight, ready to avail himself of opportunities when afforded in respect of place, time, and manly efforts, clever enough to discern the causes necessitating the cessation of treaty or war with an enemy, or to lie in wait keeping treaties, obligations and pledges, or to avail himself of his enemy's weak points, making jokes with no loss of dignity or secrecy, never brow-beating and casting haughty and stern looks, free from passion, anger, greed, obstinacy, fickleness, haste and back-biting habits, talking to others with a smiling face, and observing customs as taught by aged persons;—such is the nature of self-possession. The qualifications of a minister have been described in the beginning, middle, and at the close of the work. Possessed of capital cities both in the centre and the extremities of the kingdom, productive of subsistence not only to its own people, but also to outsiders on occasions of calamities, repulsive to enemies, powerful enough to put down neighboring kings, free from miry, rocky, uneven, and desert tracts as well as from conspirators, tigers, wild beasts, and large tracts of wilderness, beautiful to look at, containing fertile lands, mines, timber and elephant forests, and pasture grounds, artistic, containing hidden passages, full of cattle, not depending upon rain for water, possessed of land and waterways, rich in various kinds of commercial articles, capable of bearing the burden of a vast army and heavy taxation, inhabited by agriculturists of good and active character, full of intelligent masters and servants, and with a population noted for its loyalty and good character;—these are the qualities of a good country.

- A wise king can make even the poor and miserable elements of his sovereignty happy and prosperous; but a wicked king will surely destroy the most prosperous and loyal elements of his kingdom.
- Hence a king of unrighteous character and of vicious habits will, though he is an emperor, fall a prey either to the fury of his own subjects or to that of his enemies.
- But a wise king, trained in politics, will, though he possesses a small territory, conquer the whole earth with the help of the best-fitted elements of his sovereignty, and will never be defeated.

Chanukya writes extensively about king's duties on war and peace, army, traitors, enemies, external and internal dangers, spies, etc.

Megasthenese's Indica

Megasthenes was a Greek historian and an ethnographer in the Hellenistic period. He was born in modern day Turkey and came with Alexander the Great as an ambassador of Seleucus. He was an author of the book "Indica" in which he wrote his exeperiences about India, its geography, its people, its culture and manners.

It is said that the original book "Indica" of Megasthenese was lost. But, parts of his writings were recovered and have been preserved by various ancient authors both in Greek and Roman. Those fragments were collected by Dr. Schwanbeck and translated by J.W. McCrindle and presented in "Ancient India" as described by Megasthaenese and Arrian. It gives a picture of India in 300 B.C. during Maurya's period.

The following excerpts are gathered from "Ancient India" and from "The Cambridge History of India, Vol. I" and produced here to get a glance of India as Megasthanese and Arrian saw it in 300 B.C:

"India has many huge mountains which abound in fruit-trees of every kind, and many vast plains of great fertility, but all interconnected by a multitude of rivers. The greater part of the soil is under irrigation, and consequently bears two crops in the course of the year. At the same time, it is abundant with animals of all sorts—beasts of the field and fowls of the air—of all different degrees of strength and size. As its soil supplies food in generous surplus, India is abundant with elephants, which are of monstrous bulk making these animals exceed in strength those that are bred in Libya. Since they are caught in great numbers by the Indians and trained for war, they turn the extent of victory most of the times.

"The inhabitants, having abundant means of subsistence, exceed in consequence the ordinary stature, and are distinguished by their proud bearing. They are also found to be well skilled in the arts, as might be expected of men who inhale a pure air and drink the very finest water. And while the soil bears on its surface all kinds of fruits, which are known for cultivation, it also has numerous underground veins of all sorts of metals, like gold and silver, copper and iron in no small quantity, and even tin and other metals, which are used in making articles and ornament, as well as the implements and accessories of war.

On Caste System

"The whole population of India is divided into seven castes, of which the first is formed by the collective body of the Philosophers. In number they are lesser to the other classes, but in point of dignity they are greatest over all. For the philosophers, being exempted from all public duties, are neither the masters nor the servants of others. However, they are engaged by private persons to offer the sacrifices due in lifetime, and to celebrate the funeral rites of the dead for they are believed to be most dear to the gods and to be the most conversant with matters pertaining to Hades (lord of the dead). In return to such services they receive valuable gifts and privileges. To the people of India at large they also render great benefits. At the beginning of the year, they forewarn multitudes about droughts and wet weather, and also about propitious winds, and diseases, and other topics capable of profiting the hearers. Thus the people and the sovereign, learning beforehand what is to happen, always make adequate provision against a coming deficiency, and never fail to prepare beforehand what will help in a time of need. The philosopher who makes mistake in his predictions suffers humiliation and then he observes silence for the rest of his life.

"The second caste consists of the Farmer, who appears to be far more numerous than the others. Being exempted from fighting and other public services, they devote the whole of their time to tillage. No enemy would do any harm to a farmer at work on his land because these men of this class are regarded as public benefactors and are protected from all injury. The land, thus remaining unravaged, and producing heavy crops, supplies the inhabitant with all that is requisite to make life very enjoyable. The farmers themselves, with their wives and children, live in the village, and entirely avoid going into town. They pay a land-tribute to the king, because all India is the property of the crown, and no private person is permitted to own land. Besides the land-tribute, they pay into the royal treasury a fourth part of the produce of the soil.

"The third caste consists of the Herdmen and Shepherds, and in general of all herdsmen who neither settle in towns nor in villages, but live in tents. By hunting and trapping they clear the country of noxious birds and wild beasts. As they apply themselves eagerly and assiduously to this pursuit, they free India from the pests with which it abounds,—all sorts of wild beasts, and birds which consume the seeds sown by the farmers.

"The fourth caste consists of the Artisans. Of these some are armorers, while others make the implements which farmers and others find useful in their different occupation. This class is not only exempted from paying taxes, but even receives maintenance from the royal exchequer.

"The fifth caste is the Military. It is well organised and equipped for war, holds the second place in numbers, and gives itself up to idleness and amusement in the times of peace. The entire force—men-at-arms, war-horses, war-elephants, and all—are maintained at the king's expense.

"The sixth caste consists of the Overseers. It is their province to inquire into and superintend all that goes on in India, and make report to the king, or, where there is not a king, to the magistrates.

"The seventh caste consists of the Councillors and Assessors,—those who deliberate on public affairs. It is the smallest class, looking at number, but the most respected on account of the high character and wisdom of its members. From their ranks the advisers of the king are taken, and the treasurers of the state, and the arbiters who settle disputes. The generals of the army also, and the chief magistrates, usually belong to this class.

"Such are the parts into which the body of politic in India is divided. No one is allowed to marry out of his own caste, or to exercise any work or art except his own: for instance, a soldier cannot become a farmer or an artisan, a philosopher.

("It appears strange that Megasthenese has divided the people of India into seven Castes. Herodotus, however had divided the people of Egypt into seven castes, namely priests, soldiers, herdsmen, swineherds, tradesmen, interpreters, and steersmen; and Megasthenes may therefore have taken it for granted that there were seven castes in India. It is a curious fact that, from the time of Alexander's expedition to a comparatively recent date, geographers and others have continually drawn analogies between Egypt and India.")

On Administration

"Indian officers are appointed even for foreigners, whose duty is to see that no foreigner is wronged. If any one of them loses health, they send physicians to attend him, and take care of him. If he dies, they bury him and deliver such property to his relatives. The judges also decide cases in which foreigners are concerned, with the greatest care, and come down sharply on those who take unfair advantage.

On Manners of the Indians

"The Indians live sparingly, especially when in camps. They dislike a great undisciplined multitude, and consequently they observe good order. Theft is of very rare occurrence. Megasthenese says that those who were in the camp of Sandrakottos (Chandragupta[5]) with 4,00,000 men, found that the thefts reported on any one day did not exceed the value of two hundred drachmae (currency used in Greece), and this was among the people who had no written laws, and are ignorant of writing. Nevertheless, they live happily enough remaining simple in their manners with meager resources. They never drink wine except at sacrifices. Their beverage is liquor composed from rice instead of barley, and their food is principally rice. The simplicity of their laws and their contracts is proved by the fact that they seldom go to law. They have no suits about pledges or deposits, nor do they require either seals or witnesses, but make their deposits and faithful to each other. They generally leave their houses and property unguarded.

"These things indicate that they possess good, calm sense; but other things they do which one cannot approve: for instance, that they eat always alone and they have no fixed hours when meals are to be taken with all in common, but each one eats when he feels inclined. The contrary custom would be better for social and civil life.

5. The name of Chandragupta is written by the Greeks Sandrokottos, Sandrakottas, Sandrakottos, Androkottos, and Sandrokuptos.

"Their favourite mode of exercising the body is by friction, applied in various ways, but especially by passing smooth ebony rollers over the skin. Their tombs are plain and the mounds rose over the dead lowly. In contrast to the general simplicity of their style, they love fine clothes and ornament. Their robes are worked in gold and ornamented with precious stones, and they wear flowered garments made of the finest muslin. Attendants walking behind hold up umbrellas over them: for they have a high regard for beauty, and use every device to improve their looks. Truth and virtue they hold alike in esteem. Hence, they accord no special privileges to the old unless they possess superior wisdom. They marry many wives, whom they buy from their parents, giving in exchange a yoke of oxen. Some marry hoping to find in them willing helpmates; and others for pleasure and to fill their houses with children. The wives prostitute themselves unless they are compelled to be chaste. No one wears a crown at a sacrifice or libation, and they do not stab the victim, but strangle it so that nothing mutilated, so that it could be presented to the deity with full form.

On Punishment

"A person convicted of bearing false witness suffers mutilation of his extremities. He who mutilates any one not only suffers the loss of the same limb in return, hut his hand also is cut off. If he causes an artisan to lose his hand or his eye, he is put to death.

On King

"The care of the king's person is entrusted to women, who also are bought from their parents. The guards and the rest of the soldiery attend outside the gates. A woman who kills the king when drunk becomes the wife of his successor. The sons succeed the father. The king may not sleep during the daytime, and by night he is obliged to change his couch from time to time, with a view to defeat plots against his life.

"The king leaves his palace not only in time of war, but also for the purpose of judging cases. He remains in court for the whole day, without allowing the business to be interrupted, even though the hour of rubbing with cylinder of wood arrives. He continues hearing cases while the friction, which is performed by four attendants, is still proceeding. Another purpose for which he leaves his palace is to offer sacrifice; a third purpose is to go to the hunting, for which he departs in Bacchanalian fashion. Crowds of women surround him, and outside of this circle spearmen are ranged. The road is marked off with ropes; passing within the ropes is a death, for man and woman alike. Men with drums and gongs lead the procession. The king hunts in the fields and shoots arrows from a platform. At his side stand two or three armed women. If he hunts in the open grounds he shoots from the back of an elephant. In case of women, some are in chariots, some on horses, and some even on elephants, and they are equipped with weapons of every kind, as if they were going on a campaign.

On Elephants

"India possesses a vast number of huge elephants, which far surpass those found elsewhere both in strength and size. The period of gestation is at shortest sixteen months, and at furthest eighteen months. Like mares, they generally bring forth one young at a time, and gives milk for the young for six years. Most elephants live to be as old as an extremely old man, but the most aged live two hundred years.

"A private person is not allowed to keep either a horse or an elephant. These animals are considered to be the special property of the king and persons are appointed to take care of them.

"The manner of hunting the elephant is like this. Round a bare patch of ground is dug a deep ditch about five or six stadia in extent, and over this is thrown a very narrow bridge which gives access to the enclosure. Into this enclosure are introduced three or four of the best-trained female elephants. The men themselves lie in ambush in concealed huts. The wild elephants do not approach this trap in the daytime, but they enter it at night, going in one by one. When all have passed the entrance, the men secretly close it up. Then, introducing the strongest of the tame fighting elephants, they fight it out with the wild ones, whom at the same time they weaken with hunger. When the latter are now overcome with fatigue, the boldest of the drivers dismount unobserved, and each man creeps under his own elephant, and from this position creeps under the belly of the wild elephant and ties his feet together. When this is done, they provoke the tame ones to beat those whose feet are tied until they fall to the ground. Then, they bind the wild ones and the tame ones together neck to neck with thongs of raw ox-hide. To prevent them shaking themselves in order to throw off those who attempt to mount on them, they make cuts all round their neck and then put thongs of leather into the incisions, so that the pain obliges them to submit to their fetters and to remain quiet. They reject the elephants, which are too old or too young to be serviceable, and the rest were taken away to the stables. Here they tie their feet one to another, and fasten their necks to a firmly fixed pillar and tame them by hunger. Afterwards, they restore their strength with green reeds and grass. They next teach them to be obedient, by soothing them, some by coaxing words, and others by songs and the music of the drum.

"Some of them take up their drivers when fallen in battle, and carry them off to a safety place from the battle field. Others, when their masters have sought refuge between their forelegs, have fought in their defense and saved their lives. If in a fit of anger they kill either the man who feeds or the man who trains them, they pine so much for their loss that they refuse to take food, and sometimes die of hunger.

"Most of them live as long as men who attain extreme longevity and some live over two hundred years. They are liable to many infectious viral diseases and are not easily cured. The remedy for diseases of the eye is to wash it with cows' milk. For most of their other diseases black wine are administered to them. For the cure of their wounds they are made to swallow butter, for this draws out iron.

On Kalanos and Mandanis

"Megasthenese says that self-destruction is not a doctrine of the philosophers, but committing that kind of acts are regarded as foolish of those who with severe temper stabbing themselves, or throwing themselves down from a peak, or those reluctant to pain drowning themselves, or those capable of enduring pain strangling themselves, or those of obsessive temperaments throwing themselves into the fire.

"Kalanos was a man of this brand. He was ruled by his passions and became a slave to Alexander. On this account, he was condemned by his countrymen. But, Mandanis was applauded because when messengers from Alexander invited him to go to the son of Zeus (Alexander), with the promise of gifts if he complied, and threats of punishment if he refused, he did not go. Alexander, he said, was not the son of Zeus, for he was not a master of the larger half of the world. For himself, he wanted none of the gifts of a man whose desires nothing could satiate; and as for his threats he did not have any fear. He knew that if he lived, India would supply him with enough food and if he died, he would be delivered from the body of flesh now afflicted with age, and would be translated to a better and a purer life. Alexander expressed admiration of the man, and let him have his own way.

"Kalanos followed the Makedonian army from Taxila. According to Plutarch, his real name was Sphines, and he received the name Kalanos among the Greeks because when saluting persons, he used the Sanskrit word καλε (kalyan or good) instead of the Greek χαιρε (hail or jai).

"Beyond Palibotra[6] is Mount Maleus on which shadows in winter fall towards the north, in summer towards the south, for six months alternately. In that region the Bears are seen but once a year, and not for more than fifteen days. Those living near the river Indus in the regions that flows southward are scorched more than others by the heat, and the complexion of the people is visibly affected by the great power of the sun. The mountains are inhabited by the Pygmies.

"But those who live near the sea have no kings. The

6. Pataliputra (Patna)

Pandaean nation is governed by females, and their first queen is said to have been the daughter of Hercules.

"Heracles begat a daughter in India whom he called Pandaia. To her he assigned that portion of India which lies to southward and extends to the sea. He distributed the people subject to her rule into 365 villages, giving orders that one village should bring to the treasury the royal tribute each day.

On Brahmins

"The Brahmins have the greatest prestige, since they have a more consistent rigid system. As soon as they are conceived in the womb, men of learning take charge of them. These go to the mother and ostensibly sing a charm tending to make the birth happy for mother and child, but in reality convey certain virtues, counsels aid suggestions; the women who listen most willingly are held to be the most fortunate in childbearing. After the birth, the boys pass on from one set of teachers to another in succession, the standard of teachers rising with the age of the boy. The philosophers spend their days in a grove near the city, under the cover of an enclosure of right size, on beds of leaves and skins, living sparely, practicing celibacy and abstinence from flesh· food, listening to grave discourse, and admitting such others to the discussion as may wish to take part. He who listens is forbidden to speak, or even to clear his throat or spit, on pain of being ejected from the company that very day as incontinent. When each Brahman has lived in this fashion for thirty-seven years, he departs to his own property, and lives now in greater freedom and luxury, wearing muslin robes and some decent ornaments of gold on his hands and ears, eating flesh, so long as it is not the flesh of domestic animals, but abstaining from pungent and highly-seasoned food. They marry as many wives as possible to secure good progeny; for the larger number of wives, the larger the number of good children is likely to be. Since they have no slaves, they depend all the more upon the administrations of their children as the nearest substitute. The Brahmins do not admit their wives to their philosophy.

"The chief subject on which the Brahmins talk is death; for this present life, they hold, is like the season passed in the womb, and death for those who have cultivated philosophy is the birth into the real, the happy, life. For this reason they follow an extensive discipline to make them ready for death.

"They say none of the accidents, which befall on men, are good or evil. If they were, one would not see the same things causing grief to some and joy to others - men's notions being indeed like dreams - and the same men grieved by something which at another moment they will turn and welcome. Their teaching about nature is in parts naive for they are more admirable in what they do than in what they say, and the theoretic proofs on which they base their teaching are mostly fable.

"In many points however their teaching agrees with that of the Greeks-for instance, that the world has a beginning and an end in time, and that its shape is spherical; that the Deity, who is its Governor and Maker, interpenetrates the whole; that the first principles of the universe are different, but that water is the principle from which the order of the world has come to be; that, beside the four elements, there is a fifth substance, of which the heavens and the stars are made[7]; that the earth is established at the centre of the universe. About generation and the soul their teaching shows parallels to the Greek doctrines, and on many other matters. Like Plato too, they interweave fables about the immortality of the soul and the judgments inflicted in the other world and so on.

Writing: Language

That writing was common not only for literary purposes, but also in public business as per existing edicts of Ashoka. Writing correspondence letters was perfectly usual and written documents were employed in the courts of law. Moreover, the administration was versed in bookkeeping and registration on a large scale and systematically arranged.

7. This is the akasha, or all-pervading element, of ancient Indian philosophy. It may be compared with the ether of modern physical science.

Concerning the condition and organisation of the vast Maurya Empire, the Greeks have provided us with a considerable body of valuable information. Arthashastra also furnishes the means of describing the complete polity existing at the time, its land system, its fiscal system, its administrative system, its law, its social system, its literature and religion, we get an opportunity to read and understand rare Indian history during Maurya rule. Until Akbar comes to picture, we do not have much information about India. India was struggling for its existence fighting with invaders, one after another, losing its identity.

On Palace

"The palace is a walled building, with women's apartments, gardens, and tanks in the rear. In front of these is the innermost court, where the king on awakening is saluted by the various domestic officials and, according to Aelian[8] also by an elephant. The next is the station of a sham body-guard of dwarfs, hunchbacks, wild men, etc.; the outermost of all, communicating with the exterior, is occupied by armed attendants, by ministers and associates.

"Everything bespeaks precaution. The structure of the palace itself includes mazes, secret and underground passages, hollow pillars, hidden staircases, collapsible floors against fire, poisonous animals and other poisons creatures. There are diverse specifications, including trees, which snakes avoid; parrots and sarika birds, which cry out on seeing a serpent; other birds which are affected by the sight of poison. Everyone has his own apartments, and none of the interior officials are allowed to communicate with the outside. The women are carefully watched by attendants, male and female; not even their relatives are admitted to them, except in time of childbirth or illness. All employees coming from outside, such as nautch women (dancers) need to undergo bath and massage and change their dress before admission. Material objects, as they pass in and out, are placed on record and under seal. The king changes his apartment every night.

8. Greek military writer of the 2nd century, who lived in Rome.

"The kitchen is in a secret place, and there is a multitude of tasters. The signs of poison in the delicious food and in the demeanor of the persons are carefully noted. Medicaments must pass similar test. The instruments of the shampooer and others must be handled by the body-guard, and the persons themselves to be bathed. Articles of ornament and apparel are inspected by female slaves. Cosmetics are first tried on those who apply them. If actors are admitted, the orchestra and other accessories separate them from the spectator.

"The king rides or drives in the company of high officials. When he embarks upon a ship, the same is the ease; no other vessel must be near, and troops are stationed on the shore. Similar precautions apply in the hunt also.

On Administration

"Foreign emissaries are received in durbar. The king inspects his armed troops, mounted on elephant or horse. As he progresses, the roads are lined on both sides by police who keep away all armed persons. Whenever ascetics and cripples enter a procession, banquet, festival, or wedding, attendants should take them away apart.

On Other Things

"Their customs are very strange when compared with our own, but the following are still more strange; for Megasthenese states that the tribes inhabiting the Kaukasos[9] have intercourse with women in public, and eat the bodies of their relatives, and that there are monkeys which roll down stones. Herodotus has noted the existence of both practices among certain Indian tribes.

"The Indians neither put out money at usury, the lending of money, at exorbitant interest rates, nor know how to borrow. To perform a wrong doing is contrary to established usage for an Indian; therefore, they neither make contracts nor require securities.

---

9. The mountain range which runs from northwest to southeast between the (Black Sea) and the Caspian Sea.

Megasthenese, in the second book of his Indica says that when the Indians are at supper, a table like a tripod is placed before each person. Upon it a golden bowl is placed, into which they first put boiled rice and then they add many delicates prepared according to Indian recipes.

304–232 B.C. Ashoka the Great

The Maurya Empire was inherited by Bindusara's son Ashoka the Great, grandson of Chandragupta Maurya. Emperor Ashoka's remarkable achievements are known mainly through numerous inscriptions carved on rock and stone. He extended the Empire up to Tamil Land and proved that he was one of the great emperors of all times.

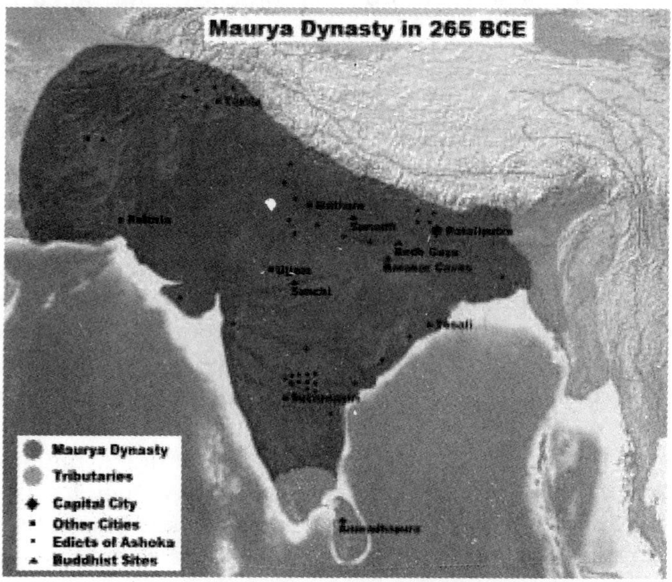

After noticing the massacre in Kalinga war, he renounced bloodshed and converted to Buddhism following the policy of non-violence or ahimsa. Ashoka spread the Buddhism across the entire East Asia and South-East Asia. Ashoka was exceedingly tolerant in matters of religion and fallowed absolute faithfulness to the Eightfold Path prescribed in Buddhism. He started the social welfare duties like digging of wells and irrigation canals; construction of roads, hospitals and public gardens all over the Empire. Widows, orphans and the disabled were looked after and supported financially by the administration. State warehouses at the countryside, filled with provisions for the relief of unexpected famines. He created a special department for the benevolent administration of aboriginal tribes, endowed many schools and universities, improved the taxation system, included the income of his own private estates in the state budget and spread economical justice all over India.

In Ashoka's time, the old Indian art reached the climax of its perfection. Because they worked in perishable material (mostly wood), the earlier works of the culture era have been destroyed. A great archaeologist, Sir John Marshall commented, "The extraordinary precision and accuracy which characterizes all Maurya work, and which has never, we venture to say, been surpassed even the finest workmanship of Athenian buildings".

Amaury de Reincourt writes, "Gradually artistic inspiration had been overcome by engineering skill in Maurya India. Technological progress from the seventh century B.C. onward must have been remarkable and suggests the possibility of a real industrial revolution. Complex irrigation works had multiplied – a vast network of canals with sluices spread all over northern India, varied water rates being levied on the customers. Roads and large highways, in no way inferior to those of the Roman Empire, connected all important cities. One great highway ran from Taksasila in the northwest to distant Pataliputra. Pillars marking distances, caravansaries and rest houses, store houses, lined all the main highways. Life was full of bustle and activity, trade flourished, education was widespread and it is highly probable that there was a higher percentage of literacy among the population than that existing at present. The immense bureaucracy worked with precision and efficiency, taxing, regulating, inspecting—all under the personal supervision of the emperor."

The dependable source of events and occurrences in Ashoka's life known from his own inscriptions are as follows:

(1) In the 9th year after his coronation, he began the conquest of the Kalinga country, *i.e.,* Orissa. The slaughter and suffering caused by the conquest produced a lasting impression and it was the turning-point in his mind and career. Thereafter, he joined the Buddhist order as a lay disciple.

(2) His devotion to Buddhism faith began two and a half years later, about the end of the eleventh year from his coronation. When he became a member of the Sangha, or order of monks, he travelled from place to place like the wandering Buddhist and Jain brothers displaying energy, as he phrases it. This energy took the form of visits and gifts to Brahmins, ascetics, and old people, instructions and discussions relating to the Buddhist Dharma or religious rules and principles.

(3) At the end of this tour, he issued the first of his religious proclamations, a slogan to his officials to adopt the principles of energetic action and he also ordered that this message should be engraved everywhere, upon rocks and on stone pillars. The practice of carving Buddhist sentiments in this manner on noticeable objects became wide practice. It is still visible in Tibet, Central Asia, China, and throughout the Buddhist world.

(4) 'During the 13th and 14th year, Ashoka's activities must have been at its height. He issued nearly sixteen memorandums of which fourteen are found engraved throughout his empire. In these records, which engraved in his fourteenth year, Ashoka gives an account of the administrative and other measures which he had adopted. He instructed to dig wells by the roads, to provide medical aid for men and animals, to open animal hospitals, to propagate medical or useful plants not only in his own territories, but in neighbouring territories also like independent and quasi-independent states of South India and the north-west frontier, even as far as the Greek kingdom

of Antiochus and beyond. Then he had made regulations restricting the slaughter of animals for food and especially on occasions of festivals and public shows. He had issued persuasive appeals for kindness and consideration in family relationships, in dealings with Brahmins and teachers, in the mutual attitudes of different sects. He had condemned what he regarded as excess of profitless (i.e. Brahman) ceremonies in public and private life, which had instilled economic burden.

(5) In his 13th year, he instituted quinquennial (every five years) circuits of the leading officials for the purpose of proclaiming the moral law as well as for the discharge of their normal functions.

(6) In the 14th year, he appointed high officials, entitle *dharma mahamatras* with the duty of instilling piety, rectifying misfortune or wrong, organising charitable endowments and gifts. Some of these officers stood in special relation to the establishments and benevolences of his various endowments, and the operations of others extended even to the foreign countries.

At the same time he gave instruction for the periodical public recitation of these admonitions, and repeats his intention of instituting quinquennial circuits for the benefit of the Kalinga officials. His sons, the Viceroys in Taxila and Ujjain, followed a similar practice at intervals of three years.

(7) In his 13th and again in his 20th year, he dedicated cave-dwellings in the Barabar hills for the use of monks of the Ajivika sect.

(8) In his 15th year, he enlarged the stupa of the Buddha Kanakamuni, and during the 21st year, he personally visited this site and that of Buddha's own birth-place.

As regards to the aged and the poor, they are placed under the care of religious officials. Here we see the greatness of Ashoka who implemented a system to take care of aged and poor when there was no "poor law" existed anywhere in the world.

185-73 B.C.-Shunga Dynasty

After fifty years of Ashoka's death, his grandson Brihadratha was assassinated by the then commander-in-chief Pusyamitra Sunga; he founded Sunga Dynasty in 185 B.C. When Brihadratha was taking the Guard of Honour, armed forces of Pushyamitra Sunga assassinated Brihadrata and Pushyamitra ascended the throne.

73-43 B.C.-Kanva Dynasty

A Brahmin of Kanva gotra, Vasudeva, established the Kanva Dynasty in Magadha and ruled the eastern part of India. After the collapse of the Kanva Dynasty, the Satavahana Dynasty of Andhra kingdom replaced the Magadha kingdom as the most powerful Indian state.

240-550 A.D. - Gupta Dynasty

A minor line of the Gupta clan continued to rule Magadha after the disintegration of the Empire.

240-280 A.D. - Srigupta and Ghatotkacha

It is estimated that time for the reign of Sri Gupta is probably 240–280 A.D. Modern historians think that Sri Gupta and his son were Kushans. His son and successor Ghatotkacha ruled from 280–319 A.D.

280-319 A.D. - Chandragupta I

Ghatotkacha (280–319 A.D.) had a son named Chandragupta (not Chandragupta Maurya) In a deal, Chandragupta married Lichhavi princes of Magadha, Kumaradevi. Chandragupta expanded his power, conquering a great part of Magadha, Prayag, and Saketa. He established a kingdom -Gupta- stretching from the Ganges River to Prayag. It came to be known as "Gupta Dynasty".

335-380 A.D. – Samudragupta

Samudragupta succeeded his father in 335 A.D. and

ruled for about 45 years, until his death in 380 A.D. In his rule, he incorporated nearly twenty kingdoms into his Empire. The title of Samudragupta was give to him as he acquired many kingdoms by his conquests (*Samudra* referring to the "oceans"). He was a talented military leader and supporter of art and literature. He was a poet and musician by himself. He was a firm believer in Hinduism and worshipped Lord Vishnu.

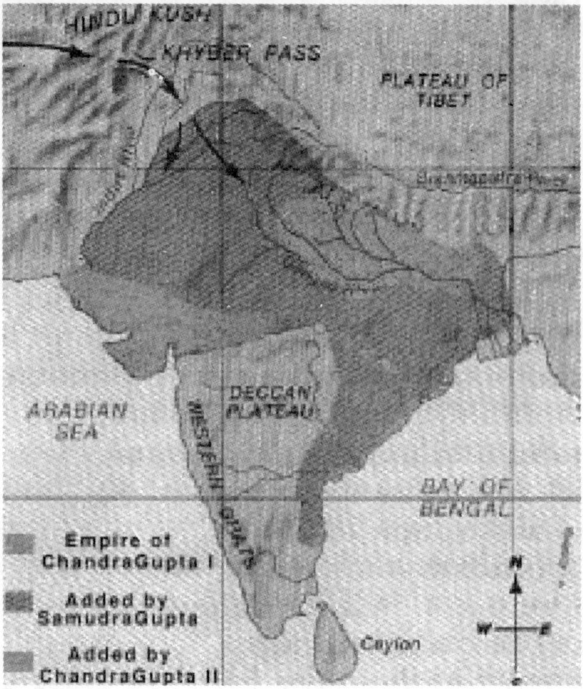

Ramagupta

According to some historians, Samudragupta's eldest son Ramagupta, who succeeded him, was a weak leader.

380-413 A.D.-Chandragupta II

Chandragupta II, also called Vikramaditya, was the son of Samudragupta, who ruled the Empire from 380 to 413 A.D. Chandragupta II married princess of Kadamba of

Kuntala region, a princess of Naga lineage. Making wedding alliances through by himself and his children, he expanded his Empire drastically. This act extended his control from coast-to-coast, eventually establishing a second capital at Ujjain.

415-455 A.D.-Kumaragupta I

Chandragupta II was succeeded by his second son Kumaragupta I. He ruled the Empire until 455 A.D.

455-467 A.D.-Skandagupta

Skandagupta, son and successor of Kumaragupta I is generally considered to be the last of the great Gupta rulers. He fought against the invading Hunas from the northwest. But the expenditure of the wars exhausted the Empire's resources and ended in decline.

Later kings are known as Puru gupta, Narasimhagupta Baladitya, Kumaragupta II, Budhagupta, and Kumaragupta III. They ruled Gupta Empire until 550 A.D.

Gupta Administration

Reports of the inscriptional records of the Gupta Empire illustrates that there was a hierarchy of administrative divisions from top to bottom. The territories were called by diverse names such as Rajya, Rashtra, Desha, Mandala, Prithvi and Avani. It was divided in to 26 regions, which were designed as Bhukti, Pradesha and Bhoga. Regions were also divided into Vishayas and placed under the control of the Vishayapatis. A Vishayapati managed the Vishaya with the help of the Adhikarana, which consisted of four representatives: Nagara sresthi, Sarthavaha, Prathamakulika and Prathama Kayastha. A wing of the Vishaya was called Vithi.

The Gupta Dynasty was one of the largest political and military Empires in ancient India. This period has been called the "Golden Age of India" because of its accomplishments in science, mathematics, astronomy, engineering, religion, philosophy, art, literature, dialectic, literature, logic, trade, technology that developed the essentials known as Hindu culture. The decimal system, including the concept of zero was invented in India during this period. The peace and prosperity created under the leadership of Guptas enabled to pursue scientific and artistic endeavours in India.

The cultural creativity of magnificent architecture, sculpture, and painting was accomplished in this period. The Gupta period presented great scholars such as Kalidasa, Aryabhata, Varahamitra, and Vatsyayana who made great advancements in many academic fields.

Chess is said to have originated in this period. Early form of Chess in 6th century was known as Chaturanga, which means four divisions of the military. Infantry, cavalry, elephants, and chariots in the game represent the modern pawn, knight, bishop, and rook, respectively.

The ancient text Kama Sutra in Sanskrit literature was written by the Indian scholar Vatsayana. Aryabhata, a noted mathematician-astronomer lived in Gupta period and contributed significantly towards astronomy and mathematics.

The Earliest Buildings

Buildings of primitive India, as among the poorer classes of to-day, the materials most commonly used were mud or mud bricks, bamboo canes, and other kinds of wood. The simplest kinds of dwellings were constructed of screens of bamboo in woven with palm branches or the like, the roofs being flat or arched. The bamboos were lashed together at the apex and tied in near the lower end, thus forming a singularly strong framework of curvilinear form, while the walls were strengthened to resist the outward thrust. In other cases, the walls were constructed from unbaked brick or mud, and the subsequent material was also used as a covering for the flat roofs or for plastering the screens of the walls on the wattle and daub principle. At a later date cut timbers came to be used in the more flashy dwellings, and provided opportunities for the development of that exuberant surface decoration in which the genius of India has always excelled.

These materials left their character deeply and permanently impressed on Indian architecture. From the use of the bamboo came the curvilinear type of roof which later was reproduced in cut timber and subsequently in stone, and from which the familiar chaitya arches used over doorways and windows were evolved. Log capitals[10] were imitated in stone, and the more finished timbering of walls, roofs, and gateways in stone including every detail down to the nail-beads were copied with care and accuracy by the masons of later days.

As a precaution to protect against destructive insects, wooden poles were set in jars of earthenware as a pot and foliage base (probably insect repellent herbal plants), so beautifully developed in the Gupta age. An outstanding illustration of the influence used by wood in contrast with brick construction is to be found in the pillars of the cave temples. In the earliest examples, the stone pillars are noticeably copied from wooden prototypes and are relatively slender, though sufficiently thick enough for their purpose. In the later examples, the pillars are heavy and cumbersome, not because extra strength was required, but because they were copied from the brick-in-mud pillars of famous viharas, which required much thicker in proportion to their height than columns of stone.

Huns invasion and the decline of Gupta Empire

Skandagupta was followed by weak rulers Purugupta, Kumaragupta, Budhagupta, Narasimhagupta, Kumaragupta III, Vishnugupta, Vainyagupta and Bhanugupta until 480 A.D. By 500 A.D., much of the Empire in northwest was conquered and occupied by Hunas.

10. Upper most of a column, a horizontal part in classical architecture that rest on the columns.

Middle Kingdoms of India

230 B.C. - 1279 A.D.-Middle kingdoms

Middle kingdoms of India refer to the political entities in India from 2nd century B.C. after the decline of the Maurya Empire and the parallel rise of the Satavahana Dynasty. This was a classical period of India. India had the largest economy in the world. Middle Kingdoms survived for 1,500 years and ended in the 13th century A.D.

The Northwest

Following the breakdown of the Mauryan Empire, the Indus Valley and Gangetic plains of the north-west attracted a chain of invaders between 200 B.C. and 300 A.D.

Eventually the invaders became Indianized as they were influenced by society and philosophy across the Gangetic plains. This period has featured by both intellectual and artistic achievements inspired by cultural diffusion of the new kingdoms across the Silk route.

600 B.C.-Gandhara

Gandhara is the name of an ancient kingdom located in modern day northern Pakistan and eastern Afghanistan. Its main cities were Purushapura (modern Peshavar) literally meaning City of Man, and Takshashila, modern Taxila.

The Gandhara people were settled on the banks of Kabul River down to its confluence with the Indu since the Vedic times. Later Gandhara included parts of northwest Punjab. Gandhara was located on the northern trunk road and was a centre of international commercial activities. It was an important channel of communication with ancient Iran, India and Central Asia. The kingdom was ruled from capitals at Taxila, Purushapura (Peshawar) on the Indus Valley. According to the Puranas, they were named after Taksha and Pushkara.

The region shows southern Central Asian culture in the Bronze Age and the Gandhara grave culture, likely corresponding to immigration of Indo-Aryan speakers and the center of Vedic civilisation. Gandhara had played an important role in the epic of Ramayana and Mahabharata. Great scholars such as Panini and Kautilya lived in this cosmopolitan environment.

600-500 B.C.—Persian and Greek Conquests

Much of the northwestern subcontinent, present-day eastern Afghanistan and Pakistan, came under the rule of the Persian Achaemenid Empire in 520 B.C.

In 326 B.C. Alexander the Great conquered Asia Minor and the Achaemenid Empire, reaching the northwest frontiers of the Indian subcontinent. There he defeated King Porus and conquered much of the Punjab. Alexander's march towards east placed him in confrontation with the Nanda Empire of Magadha. His army exhausted and frightened by the possibility of facing larger Indian armies at the Ganges River refused to march further. Plutarch writes the concerns of Alexander's army:

> "As for the Macedonians, however, their struggle with Porus blunted their courage and stayed their further advance into India. For having done all they could do to repulse an enemy who mustered only twenty thousand infantry and two thousand horse, they violently opposed Alexander when he insisted on crossing the river Ganges also, the width of which, as they learned, was thirty-two furlongs, its depth a hundred fathoms, while its banks on the further side were covered with multitudes of men-at-arms and horsemen and elephants. For they were told that the kings of the Ganderites and Praesii were awaiting them with eighty thousand horsemen, two hundred thousand footmen, eight thousand chariots, and six thousand fighting elephants."

Alexander was convinced and returned back.

The Persian and Greek invasions had important repercussions on Indian civilisation. The political systems of the Persians influenced future forms of governance on the subcontinent, including the administration of the Mauryan Dynasty. In addition, the region of Gandhara, or present-day eastern Afghanistan and northwest Pakistan, became a melting pot of Indian, Persian, Central Asian, and Greek cultures. It also gave birth to a hybrid culture, Greco-Buddhism, which lasted until the 5th century A.D. and influenced the artistic development of Mahayana Buddhism.

The Indo-Greeks ruled various parts of northwestern India until the end of the 1st century B.C. and then they were conquered by the Scythians and Kushans.

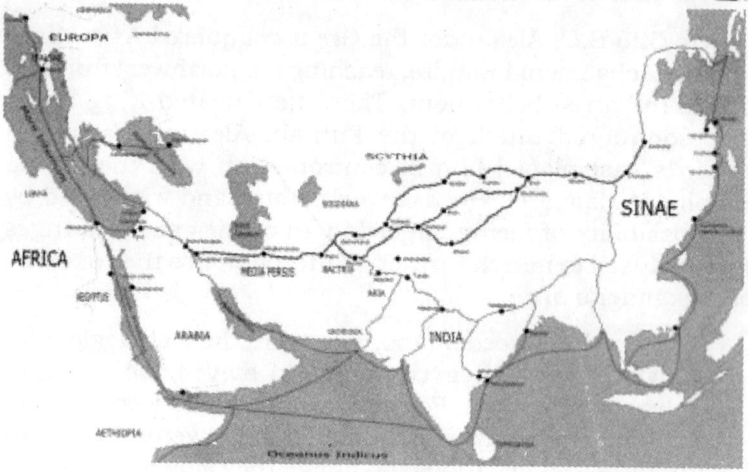

Silk Route

200 B.C.-10 A.D.—The Indo-Greeks

The Indo-Greek Kingdom was founded when the Greeco-Bactrian king Demetrius invaded India early in the 2nd century B.C. through Hindu Kush.

During the two centuries of their rule, the Indo-Greek kings combined the Greek and Indian languages and symbols and mingled ancient Greek, Hindu and Buddhist religious customs culminating into a rich combination of Indian and Hellenistic influences. Finally, the Indo-Greeks disappeared from politics around 10 A.D. after the invasions of the Indo-Scythians.

200 B.C.-400 A.D.—The Indo-Scythians Sakas

The Indo-Scythians are the offshoot of Sakas (Scythians),

who migrated from the middle of the 2nd century B.C. crossing southern Siberia into Bactria, Sogdiana, Arachosia, Gandhara, Kashmir, Punjab, and into some parts of Western and Central India, Gujarat, Maharashtra and Rajasthan. The first Saka king in India was Moga who founded Saka rule in Gandhara and gradually extended dominance over north-western India. Their rule in India ended in 395 A.D.

The Scythian (Sakas) and Parthian (Pahlava) invaders of India are often mentioned in Sanskrit literature, and always in association with each other and with the Yavanas. But, as this literature is not historical, scholars have referred to Greek and Chinese historians, to the inscriptions of Persia and India, and to coins for information about their origin and their rule in India.

Therefore, it is possible that Sakas reached India indirectly, and like Pahlavas, they came through Ariana (W. and S. Afghanistan and Baluchistan) by the great highway, associated in modern times with the Bolan Pass.

100 B.C – 400 A.D.-The Yavanas

The Yavanas were living beyond Gandhara. Yavanas, Sakas, Pahlavas, and Hunas were all considered as Mlechhas. This name was used to refer their cultural differences with the Vedic culture that prevailed in the Kuru Panchala kingdoms. The Mahabharata compliments the all-knowing Yavanas as the architects of vimanas (aerial vehicles). It is said that in the ports of southern India, the early Tamil poems speak about the settlement of the Yavanas.

Old Persian inscriptions of Darius show that the Yavanas and Persians applied to all Greeks without distinction and they are the name of the Ionians of Asia Minor who were conquered by Cyrus in 545 B.C. Therefore, Greeks were known in India at a time when a large portion of the northwest was still under the Persian rule. The occurrence of the word Yavana in a grammatical rule of Panini (IV, 1.49) is a clear indication that it had been adopted into Sanskrit before the middle of the 4th century B.C. Its Prakrit equivalent, Yona, is used in the inscriptions of Ashoka to describe the Hellenic sovereigns of Egypt, Cyrene, Macedonia, Epirus, and Syria. There is no doubt that in all Indian documents earlier than the 3rd century A.D., the term Yavana denotes a person of Greek descent. In spite of the fact, like other foreign settlers in India, many of the Yavanas had become Hinduised and had adopted Indian names. At a later date, foreigners generally are classified as Yavanas.

12 BC–100 A.D.—The Indo-Parthians (Pahlavas)

Parthians[11] conquered the Indo-Scythians. The Indo-Parthian Kingdom was founded by Gondophares around 20 B.C. The kingdom existed briefly until it was captured by the Kushans in the late 100 A.D.

The Pahlavas

Pahlava Kingdom is recognised as a kingdom of an Iranian tribe. They are the same as the Parasikas. Some texts describe as the Pahlavas are identical to Pallavas, a dynasty of Southern India. Pahlavas might have migrated to south India over a period of time through navigation for trading purpose. It is also mentioned in the epic Mahabharata and it does not distinguish between the Pahlavas and Pallavas.

35-405 A.D.—The Western Satraps

The Western Satraps or Western Kshatrapas 35-405 A.D. were Saka monarchs of the western and central part of India: Saurashtra, Malva, Gujarat, Maharashtra, Rajasthan and Madhya Pradesh states. The word Kshatrapa stands for satrap (governor) and its equivalent in Persian Ksatrapavan, which means viceroy or governor of a province. In total, there were 27 independent Western Satrap monarchs during a period of 350 years.

100-300 A.D.—The Kushans

The Kushan Empire was established in Bactria, which is now the northern Afghanistan, Tajikistan and Uzbekistan. They extended their regions to incorporate the Punjab and most of the Ganges basin conquering a number of kingdoms

11. Parthia is a region of north-eastern Iran.

across the northern part of India. The Kushans occupied the central part of the main Silk Route and had control over land route enabling them to conduct trade between India, Persia, China, and Roman Empire.

240–410 A.D.—The Indo-Sassanid Kushanshahs

A new Persian Dynasty, the Sassanid Kushanshahs conquered territories and eventually Kushans were replaced by Hephthalite Hunas in 410 A.D.

500–600 A.D.—The Hephthalite Huns

The Hephthalite Huns were another Central Asian nomadic people to invade. Their exact origins and background remains unknown. Some argue that they were initially a group of people living near the Great Wall of China and some argue they were Turkic people.

489-632 A.D.—The Rais

The Rai Dynasty ruled Sindh from 489-632 A.D. They were followers of Buddhism.

300–900 A.D.—The Shahis

The Shahi Dynasties ruled parts of the Kabul Valley in eastern Afghanistan and old territories of Gandhara. They were split into Buddhist Shahis and Hindu Shahis.

Gangetic Plains and Deccan

The Gangetic Plains and Deccan

Following the decline of the Mauryan Empire, the Gangetic area broke up into several states. In the Deccan, the Chalukyas began developing a strong nation and spreading the cultural and military power that was in the hold of Indo-Gangetic Plain.

230 B.C.—220 A.D.—The Satavahanas

The Satavahana Empire started as feudatories to the Mauryan Empire. They became independent and declared independence some time after the death of Ashoka. The Satavahanas originally ruled in the areas of current

Telangana and other coastal Andhra areas as well as Pune. They fought against Sungas, Kanvas and protected their territory from Sakas, Yavanas and Parthivas. Four or five Kings of Satavahana Dynasty ruled the Empire until 220 AD., and it declined following the rise of its feudatories.

The Satavahanas ruled a large and powerful Empire that endured the attacks from Central Asia. Apart from their military power, their business and naval activities enabled them to establish Indian colonies in South-East Asia.

They created a cultural bridge between Indo-Gangetic Plain and southern part of India, and played an important role in trade and transfer of ideas and culture.

The Satavahanas influenced South-East Asia by spreading Hindu culture, language and religion. They contributed a great deal towards the development of art. They spoke Telugu and Maharashtra Prakrit.

Their coins had images of ships.

193 B.C.—170 A.D.—The Kharavela

Kharavela was the king of Kalinga. He restored the power of Kalinga after it had been destroyed by Ashoka. He was the third king of the Chedi Dynasty. Not much information is available about this king. Some information could be found from his well-known inscription Hathigumpha.

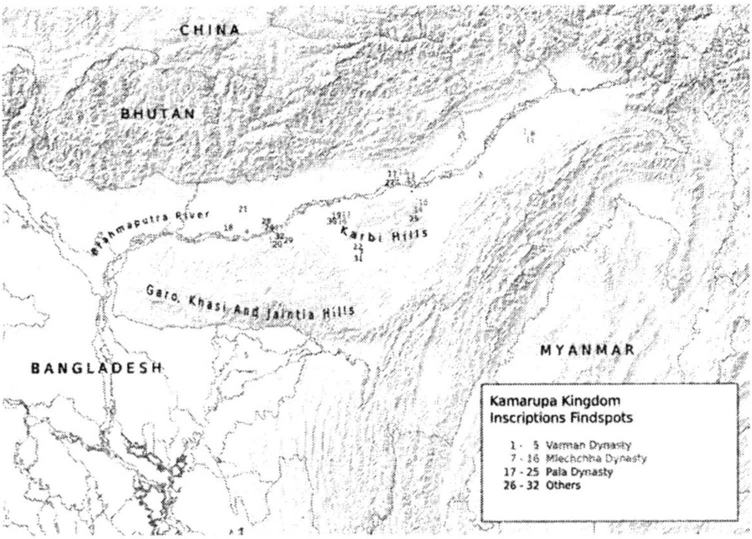

Northeast India

350–650 A.D.—The Varman Dynasty

The Varman Dynasty ruled Kamarupa (Assam), founded by Pushya Varman in the 4th century A.D. The kingdom under the Varman rulers extended up to the Korotoa River in the west and Sadia River in the east and included the Sylhet division of present-day Bangladesh. The Varman Dynasty ruled until 650 AD. Not much information is available about this dynasty. This dynasty included the rulers: Pushyavarman, Samudravarman, Balavarman, Kalyanavarman, Ganapativarman, Mahendravarman, Narayanavarman, Bhutivarman, Chandramukhavarman, Sthithavarman, Susthitavarman, Supratishitavarman, and Bhaskaravarman.

650- 900 A.D.—Mlechchha Dynasty

The Mlechchha dynasty ruled Kamarupa (Assam) from their capital at Hadapeshvar in the modern day Tejpur after the decline of Varman Dynasty. The rulers were aboriginals. According to some historical records, there were twenty one rulers in this dynasty. The Mlechchha dynasty in Kamarupa was followed by the Pala Dynasty. Some of the rulers of Mleccha Dynasty: Salasthamba, Vigrahastambha, Harshadeva, Balavarman II, Pralambha alias Salambha, Harjjaravarman,Vanamalavarmadeva, Jayamala alias Virabahu, Balavarman III, and Tyagasimha.

900–1100 A.D.—The Pala Dynasty of Kamarupa

The Pala Dynasty of Kamarupa (Assam) succeeded the Mlechchha Dynasty and ruled until the end of the 12th century A.D. The Palas of Kamarupa were Vaishnavas. This dynasty obtained their lineage from the Varman Dynasty. This dynasty included the rulers: Brahmapala, Ratnapala, Indrapala, Gopala, Harshapala, Dharmapala, and Jayapala.

250–500 A.D.—The Vakatakas

The Vakataka Empire was the contemporaries of the Gupta Empire and the descendants of Satavahanas. Vindhyashakthi was the founder of the Vakata Empire. They ruled over modern day states of Madhya Pradesh and Maharashtra during the 3rd and 5th century A.D.

Vakatakas were famous for encouraging arts, architecture and literature. The stone built Buddhist viharas and chaityas of Ajanta Caves were built under the sponsorship of the Vakataka rulers. Ultimately, they were defeated by the Chalukyas.

Vakataka rulers: Vindhyashakti, Pravarasena, Rudrasena, Prithvisena, Rudrasena II, Divakarasena, Prabhavatigupta (female), Damodarasena, Narendrasena, Prithvisena II, Sarvasena, Vindhyasena, Pravarasena II, Devasena, and Harisena.

606–647 A.D.—Harshavardhana

After the collapse of the Gupta Empire, the Gangetic plains were divided into several small states. Harshavardhana of Kannauj was able to unite them together under his rulership briefly. This unity did not last long beyond his reign and his Empire was divided again soon after his death in 647 AD.

Harshavardhana was a Mahayana Buddhist. He was a tolerant ruler and supported all faiths: Vedas, Buddhism, and Jainism. The great Indian mathematician Brahmagupta lived in the Empire of Harshavardhana.

According to the Chinese Pilgrim Xuanzang, who visited Harsha's kingdom in 636 A.D., Harsha built several stupas in the name of Buddha. Harshavardhana was also a supporter of art and literature. He contributed numerous endowments to the University of Nalanda.

Harshavardhana himself was a famous author. He composed three Sanskrit plays—Nagananda, Ratnavali, and Priyadarsika. Bana, in his first historical poetic work in Sanskrit language, composed Harsha Charitha, which describes India's natural environment and vitality of life at that time.

550-1018 A.D—Gurjaras

The Gurjaras played a great role in history of Northern India nearly 500 years. Modern day Rajasthan was under the rule of Gurjars with capital at Bhimal, located approximately 50 miles northwest of Mount Abu. Gurjars origin is unknown.

420–624 A.D.—The Vishnukundinas

The Vishnukundina Empire was one of the Middle Kingdoms of India and was an Indian Dynasty that ruled over the Deccan, Orissa, and parts of South India during the 5th and 6th century A.D.

For administrative purpose, the Empire was divided into a number of Rashtras and Vishyas. The king was the highest authority in the administration of justice. The Vishnukundin rulers instituted various kinds of punishments for variety of crimes. They were known for their impartial judgment and high sense of justice.

The Vishnukundins were also great supporters of learning. They founded colleges for learning Vedas. Indra Bhattaraka established many schools for imparting education on Vedic literature.

Many of the Vishnukundin kings were recognized with authorship of numerous books. Vikramendra Varma I was described as a Mahakavi. In addition, an incomplete work on Sanskrit called "Janasraya Chando Vichiti" was written by Madhava Varma IV, who was called "Janasraya". Sanskrit language enjoyed the royal support.

The Vishnukundins were responsible for construction of a numerous cave temples dedicated to Shiva. The cave structures at Bezwada (Vijayawada), Mogalrajapuram, Undavalli caves, and Bhairavakonda were dated to this period.

The Vishnukundin reign ended with the conquest of the eastern Deccan by the Chalukya, Pulakesin II.

475–767 A.D.—The Maitrakas

The Maitraka Empire ruled Gujarat in western India. Senapati Bhatarka, the founder of the dynasty, was a military governor under Gupta Empire. Vallabhi was their capital.

The background of Maitrakas is unknown. The name Maitraka may have been derived from Mithra, the Sun God. Later they became Buddhist. Gunamati and Sthiramati were two famous Buddhist scholars of Vallabhi. Vallabhi was famous for its all-embracing nature and the students from all over the country including the Brahmana boys visited it to have higher education in material and religious subjects.

600-1036 A.D.—The Gurjara Pratiharas

The Gurjara Pratihara Dynasty ruled much of Northern India.

It was the last great Empire in Northern India before the Muslim conquest. Its main reputation belongs to its successful resistance to the foreign invasions from the west. This was recognized by the Arab writers themselves.

Historians of India are surprised to know the slow progress of Muslim invaders in India compared to their fast spread in other parts of the world. It was the power of the Gurjara Pratihara army that effectively controlled the progress of the Muslims beyond the limits of Sindh. It was regarded that the control of the Indian border in the west was the chief contribution of the Gurjara Pratiharas to the history of India.

600–1950 A.D.—The Rajputs

The Rajputs were of Hindu origin who ruled the region stretching from the Gangaetic plains to the Afghan mountains. Their dynasties made the transition from Buddhist ruling dynasties to Hindu ruling dynasties.

After the collapse of Gupta Empire, the first Rajput kingdoms rose to power in 5th and 6th century A.D. They ruled the Indian subcontinent from 6th century to 20th century A.D., and Southeast Asia from 9th to 15th centuries. Nepal was the last Empire of Rajputs which ended in 1950. At the time of India's independence in 1947, Rajputs ruled in the princely states of Rajasthan and Saurashtra.

Rajput kingdoms competed against Arabs, Moguls, Mongols, Afghans and Turkic people. They gained their reputation by fighting these battles with rules of polite conduct rooted in their staunch adherence to tradition and Hindu dharma. The Rajput Kings protected their kingdom against Arabs and other Central Asian Empires for several centuries. A few Rajput Kings did convert to Islam and eventually an alliance was formed with the Mughals.

Eventually they had to face Muslim invasion. During the British Raj, after the third Anglo-Maratha War in 1817-1818, Rajputs entered into subsidiary alliance with the East India Company and became princely states under the British Raj.

Rajputs were also the former royal family of Mysore making marriage alliances with the Rajput royalty of Gujarat and Madhya Pradesh in the 20th century. It is said that the Mysore royal family Arasu caste belongs to Rajput ancestry. The founder of the dynasty, Yaduraya was a Rajput from Kathiawar.

Pratapkumari Devi, the spouse of Maharaja Krishnaraja Wadiyar IV was a Rajput princess from Bansda in Gujarat.

The marriage which took place in 1900 was arranged by the Maharani Regent at that time, Vanivilas Sannidhi. Pratapkumari Devi died at the Bangalore Palace in 1953.

Sathyapremakumari, the first wife of Maharaja Jayachamaraja Wadiyar, was a Rajput princess from Charkhari State in Madhya Pradesh. Krishnaraja Wadiyar had arranged the marriage which took place in 1938.

All the three daughters of Kanteerava Narasimharaja Wadiyar and sisters of Jayachamaraja Wadiyar had been married outside the Mysore State. Princess Sujayadevi and Princess Vijayadevi had been married to the royal houses in Gujarat. The third sister, Jayachamundeshwari had married the Maharaja of Bharatpur in Rajasthan.

One of the sons-in-law of Jayachamaraja Wadiyar is from the former Rajput royal family of Wadhwan in Gujarat.

942 –1244 A.D.—The Solankis

The Solankis were Hindu Gurjar Rajput tribes, also known as Agnivanshi Rajput Dynasty who ruled parts of western and central India between the 10th and 13th century A.D. Solankis have also been called Chalukyas. According to the inscription found in the Veera Narayana temple in Gadag in Dharwar, their ancestor was a Chandravanshi who ruled from 1029 to 1063 A.D. According to some historians, Solankis descended from 6th-century Badami Chalukya. The name Solanki comes from Chalukya, an ancient Indian Dynasty.

The Solankis were patrons of the great seaside temple of Shiva, Somnath temple, in Kathiawar.

800-1327 A.D.—The Paramaras

Adjoining to the kingdom of Chalukyas was the Paramaras in Malwa with minor branches in the territories to the north. The Paramaras emerged as feudatories of the Rashtrakutas and rose to prominence during the reign of Bhoja. An attack by the Chalukyas weakened the Paramaras in 1143.

King Bhoj was a ruler of Malwa from 1010 to 1060 A.D. He was a genius in several subjects as well as a philosopher in medieval India. His extensive writings cover philosophy, poetry, medicine, veterinary science, phonetics, yoga and archery. Under his rule, Malwa became an intellectual centre of India. Bhoj also founded the city of Bhopal to secure the eastern part of his kingdom.

800–1200 A.D.—The Tanwars (Tomara)

The Tanwar Dynasty ruled Indraprastha, the modern day Delhi. This dynasty is considered as the genealogical descendants of Chandra Vanshi Pandavas and ruled small states and villages. They ruled from modern day Kannauj and Delhi and later defeated by Ghadavalas of Kannauj and later by Chauhans of Ajmer. A total of 19 Tomar rulers ruled Thansar, modern day Haryana and Delhi. Jaipal Tuar was ruling at the time of Gaznavid invasion in 10th century A.D.

800–1200 A.D.—The Chauhans

The Chauhan Dynasty was one of the four main Rajput dynasties of that time. Chauhan dynasties spread in several places in northern India and in the state of Gujarat in the west. Inscriptions associate them with Sambhar, the salt lake area in the Amber, the modern day Jaipur. Chauhans developed political policies that lead them to fight against the Chalukyas and the invading Muslims. In the 11th century, they founded the city of Ajayameru (Ajmer) in the southern part of their kingdom, and in the 12th century captured Dhilika (the old name of Delhi) from the Tomaras and captured some of their provinces along the Yamuna River.

Under the King Prithiviraj III, the Chauhan Kingdom became an important state in the north. He became famous in folk tales and historical literature because he resisted and prevented the invasion by Mohammed of Ghor in the battle. The Chauhan kingdom became destroyed after Prithviraj and his armies fled the battlefield against Mohammed of Ghor in 1192 A.D. at the second battle at Tarain.

750–1174 A.D.—The Palas

Pala Empire was a Buddhist Dynasty that ruled north-eastern region of India. The Palas were followers of the Mahayana and Tantric systems of Buddhism. The first ruler Gopala, a son of a warrior, came to power in 750 A.D. in Gaur by a democratic election according to Tibetan scholar Taranatha. This event is recognised as one of the first democratic elections in South Asia since the time of Mahajanapadas. Gopala unified Bengal territories and brought peace and prosperity in the region. The period of anarchy ended with his election. Palas constructed many temples and works of art, and supported Universities of Nalanda and Vikramashila. Somapura Mahavihara built by Dharmapala is the famous Buddhist Vihar in India.

The Pala kings devoted themselves in public welfare and social reform. The Palas adopted the policy of religious tolerance and co-existence of Buddhists and Hindus. Pala kings won the heart of the people by welfare activities like constructing lakes and establishing towns.

The earlier version of Bangla language was born at the time of Palas. The Buddhist works of Charyapada, mystical poems are the earliest forms of Bangla language. This Proto-Bangla language was used as the official language in Tibet, Myanmar, Java and Sumatra. Texts on every type of knowledge were compiled during the Pala Rule.

- **On philosophy**: Agama Shastra by Gaudapada, Nyaya Kundali by Sridhar Bhatta, Karmanushthan Paddhati by Bhatta Bhavadeva.
- **On Medicine**: Chikitsa Samgraha, Ayurvedidvipika, Bhanumati, Shabdachandrika, Dravya Gunasangraha by Chakrapani Datta.
- Shabda-Pradipa, Vrikkhayurveda, Lohpaddhati by Sureshwara.
- Chikitsa Sarsamgraha by Vangasena.
- Sushrata[12] by Gadadhara Vaidya.

12. Sushrata was an ancient Indian surgeon and the author of the book Sushruta Samhita, in which he explains over 300 surgical procedures, 120 surgical instruments, and classifies human surgery in 8 categories.

- Dayabhaga, Vyavohara Matrika and Kalaviveka by Jimutavahana, and so on.
- Atisha compiled more than 200 texts.
- The great epic "Ramacharitam" written by Sandhyakar Nandi, the court poet of Madanapala was another masterpiece of the Pala literature. The Pala copperplate inscriptions were of excellent literary value. These distinctive inscriptions are in Gaudiya Style.

Palas created excellent art and sculpture monuments, a distinctive form of Buddhist art known as the Pala School of Sculptural Art.

The Sailendra Empire of Java, Sumatra and Malaya were a colony of Palas. Tibet's culture and religion are greatly influenced by Palas. Palas spread Buddhism to Tibet and around the world through Buddhist missionaries.

The Pala dynasty rulers include: Brahmapala, Ratnapala, Indrapala, Gopala, Harshapala, Dharmapala, Jayapala, Timgyadeva, and Vaidyadeva.

1070–1230 A.D.—The Senas

The Pala Dynasty was followed by the Sena Dynasty who took Bengal under their control during the 12th century. The founder of Sena Dynasty was Hemanta Sen who was a member of the Pala Dynasty. The second ruler of this dynasty, Vijay Sen, defeated the last Pala king Madanpala and established his sovereignty. Finally, they were defeated by the Muslims.

The Sena Dynasty revived Hinduism and promoted Sanskrit literature. It is believed that Jayadeva was a poet of the court of King Lakshman Sen in 12th century A.D. Jayadeva was a famous Sanskrit poet and author of Gita Govinda.

The Sena rulers include: Hemanta Sena, Vijay Sena, Ballal Sena, Lakshman Sena, Vishwarup Sena, and Keshab Sena.

900-1050 A.D.—Candras

The Candra Dynasty who ruled eastern Bengal was contemporaries of the Palas.

1028–1434 A.D.—The Eastern Gangas

Eastern Ganga and Western Ganga dynasties were distinct from each, but remotely related to Indian dynasties. The Western Gangas ruled in Mysore state Gangavadi from 250-1004 A.D. The Eastern Gangas ruled Kalinga, modern day Orissa, from 1028 to 1434 A.D.

The Eastern Ganga Dynasty ruled Kalinga, which consisted parts of Orissa, West Bengal, Jharkhand, Chattisgarh, and Andhra Pradesh. They protected their kingdom from the constant attacks of Muslim rulers. This kingdom flourished through trade and commerce, and the wealth was generally used for the construction of temples.

Eastern Ganga Dynasty was established by King Anantavarma Chodaganga Deva (1070–1150) and ruled by illustrious rulers in this dynasty. He was a very devoted person and a supporter of art and literature. He was renowned for having built the famous Jagannatha Temple of Puri in Orissa. King Narasimhadeva I (1238-1264) was famous for building Konark Sun Temple, a World Heritage site at Konark in Orissa.

During the reign of Eastern Ganga period, a new style of temple architecture came into existence, known as Indo-Aryan style architecture. This dynasty came to an end under the leadership of King Bhanudeva IV in the early 15th century.

The Eastern Ganga Dynasty rulers include Ananta-Varma Chodaganga, Ananga Bhima Deva II, Anangabhima Deva III, Narasimha Deva, Bhanu Deva I, Narasimha Deva II, Bhanu Deva II, Narasimha Deva III, Bhanu Deva III, Narasimha Deva IV, and Bhanu Deva IV.

Southern India

The South

In the early period of history, the Southern India saw various small kingdoms rise and fall, and the spread of the Buddhism and Jainism up to the southern end of India. After the fall of the Gupta Empire, there was a gradual shift of balance of power from the northern states to the southern states, both in military and in culture.

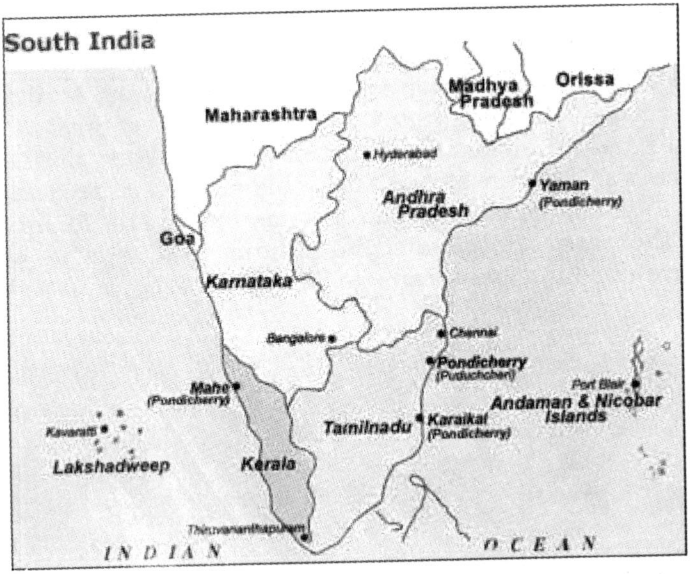

Southern India in those days had a high regard in the world for its booming Civilisations. The southern areas had a great geopolitical advantage over the northern regions. Northern regions were repeatedly devastated and weakened by the foreign invasions, while south was safe from outside invaders. Therefore, they were more prosperous and freer to devote themselves to cultural pursuits and remained distinct from the rest of the subcontinent.

The Deccan known as South Land (dakshinapatha), stretching down to south of the Vindhya mountain ranges to the Tungabhadra River, was covered with dense jungles and populated by aboriginal tribes akin to the old Dasyus (the known enemies of the Vedic Aryans). Penetration across the thickly forested Vindhya mountains was extremely difficult and hazardous, but the powerful Aryans overran the Deccan in increasing number from 7th century B.C. They civilized the aborigine tribes; they gave their languages and literatures, their artistic styles and technology, their social structure and political ideas. But, Fa Hien, a Chinese pilgrim who travelled India in 399 B.C. wrote the Deccan was still sparsely populated and dangerous, swarming with leopards, tigers, snakes and monkeys.

The history of Deccan comes to light after the collapse of Maurya Empire, when the Dravidian-speaking Andhras, founded an enduring state that included most of the Deccan and survived almost five hundred years. When northern India was overrun by the Yueh-chis and Huns devastated northern India, the Deccan became an asylum for many northerners. Buddhists and Hindus lived side by side peacefully until Islam came to dominate India.

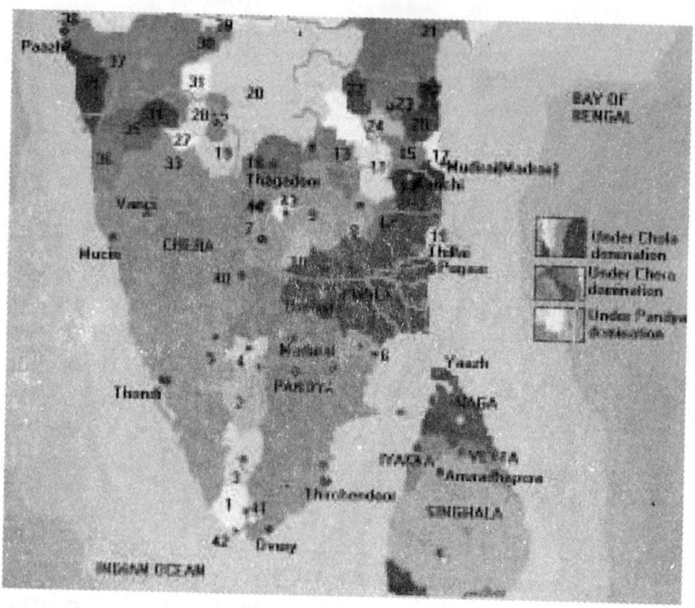

Political South India, 210 B.C.

Brahmins and Buddhists penetrated the formidable Venkata Hills and entered Tamil Land where they met strong powerful kingdoms that would not submit to the northern rule. In the Tamil Land, large states existed even before Ashoka's reign and had great wealth and prosperity due to amazing growth of foreign trade that was taking place at the time. Approximately at the same time, the great cultures in China, India and Greeco-Roman world were passing into Civilisation. Foreign trade was becoming an economic factor of paramount importance. Megasthanese[13] has mentioned the power of the Pandya state (modern Madhurai) in his Indica. A generous nature provided these southern states with many riches for which the rest of the world thirsted such as pearls, corals, rice, pepper, ginger, sandalwood, cinnamon, and ivory. As early as 450 B.C., rice and peacocks had been sent to Greece from south. The fabulous wealth of Tamil Land became an epitome all over the known world; gold poured into South India in exchange for spices. Vast numbers of Roman coins have been found at Madurai, and Roman colonies and mercenaries were numerous all over south.

When northern India descended into cultural sterility, South India provided Indian Civilisation with a remarkable cultural rebirth. One after another, great dynasties arose in South India. All noteworthy Indian thinkers between the seventh and thirteenth century came from the south: Shankara from Malbar (Kerala), Ramanuja from Kanchi, Madhva from South Canara, and Nimbarka and Vallabha from Andhra Pradesh.

From the middle of the 7th and 13th century, regionalism was the central theme of political or dynastic history of South Asia. Three features commonly characterised the sociopolitical realities of this period.

---

13. Megasthenes (350-290 B.C.) was a Greek ethnographer in the Hellenistic period and author of the book Indica. He was born in Asia Minor (Modern day Turkey) and became an ambassador of Seleucus I of Syria to the court of Sandrocottus (Chandragupta Maurya) in Pataliputra, India.

- First, the spread of Brahmanical religions through Sanskritisation of local cults and organisation of Brahmanical social order.
- Second, the ascendancy of the Brahman priestlyhood and landowning groups who later governed regional institutions and political developments.
- Third, because of numerous fluctuating dynasties which faced perennial military attacks, regional kingdoms faced frequent defeats but never extinguished.

Tamil Nadu's history dates back to pre-historic times and archaeological evidence indicate that this area was one of the longest steady habitations in India. In Adichanallur, 24 km from Tirunelveli, archaeologists from the Archaeological Survey of India excavated 169 clay urns including human skulls, skeletons and bones, in addition to husks, grains of rice, charred rice, and Neolithic celts, providing evidence to confirm that they belonged to the Neolithic period, 3,800 years ago. The archaeologists have suggested that the script used at the site is very rudimentary form of Tamil Brahmi.

Most of the pre-Dravidian tribes in the country's south of the Vindhya Mountains adopted the speech of the proto-Dravidians, notably in the centre and south of the peninsula, the Tamil, Kannada, and Telugu regions.

In Gujarat, the waves of Aryan immigration gradually submerged Dravidian blood and speech. In Maharashtra, the same influences eliminated the language and the same has happened in Kalinga (now Orissa), where a Dravidian language, the Telugu, survives only in the southern districts.

Long before the beginning of the Christian era, the Dravidian South had developed a considerable culture of its own, and its inhabitants had possessed powerful kingdoms, some of which carried a thriving trade with Western Asia, Egypt, and later with the Greek and Roman empires.

300 B.C.-200 A.D.—The Sangam Era Kingdoms

There were three ancient Tamil states in South India: Chera on the west, Chola on the east, and Pandya on the south. They were fighting each other in quest of regional supremacy. They are mentioned in Greek and Ashoka sources as important Indian kingdoms beyond the Mauryan Empire. A collection of ancient Tamil literature, known as Sangam Academy provides useful information about life in these kingdoms during 300 B.C. to 200 A.D. There are several facts of imposition of Aryan traditions from the north into a predominantly native Dravidian culture.

Dravidian social order was based on different ecological regions rather than on the Aryan varna pattern. Tribal rulers emerged as kings as people moved from pastrolism toward agriculture supported by irrigation based on rivers and wells and maritime trade with Rome and Southeast Asia.

Discoveries of Roman gold coins in various sites confirm an extensive South Indian connection with the outside world. The city of Madurai, the capital of the Pandyan Kingdom, in present day Tamil Nadu, was the center of intellectual and literary activity. Poets and lyricists composed anthologies of poems and description on Tamil grammar. By the end of the 1st century B.C., South Asians moved back and forth by overland trade routes, which enabled Buddhist and Jain missionaries and other travelers to fusion, many cultures.

Sangam literature

Sangam literature interacts with emotional and material topics like love, war, governance, trade and bereavement.

The Indologist Kamil Zvelebil mentions A.K. Ramanujan's quotes: "In their antiquity and in their contemporaneity, there is not much else in any Indian literature equal to these quite and dramatic Tamil poems. In their values and stances, they represent a mature classical poetry: passion is balanced by courtesy, transparency by ironies, and nuances of design, impersonality by vivid detail and austerity of line by richness of implication. These poems are the earliest evidence of the Tamil genius who were part of proto-Dravidian Jain culture."

500 B.C.—1345 A.D.—The Pandyan Dynasty

Pandya kingdom seems to have been founded in the 5th century B.C. by Pandya, a person of the agricultural class. The word Pandya is derived from the Tamil word "Pandi" meaning bull. Bull is a sign of masculinity and valour. Pandya became the nickname of the first Pandyan king of Madurai, Kulasekharan Pandya because he was built like a bull and was used as a personification of masculinity.

The Pandyas and their capital city Madurai were well known to the ancient Greeks and Romans. Megasthenes, a Greek ambassador of Seleukos at the court of Chandragupta Maurya mentions about the Pandyan kingdom around 300 BC. and gives an elaborate report of the Pandyan kingdom, which according to him was govern by women. He mentions that Heracles was the ruler of a southern country and Pandyan queen at the time, *Pandaia* was a daughter of Heracles. He says, "Heracles begat a daughter in India whom he called Pandaia. To her he assigned that portion of India which lies to southward and extends to the sea while he distributed the people subject to her rule into 365 villages, each of which was expected to meet the needs of the royal household for one day in the year." Since a story Silappadikaram refers to an example of a cowherdess who says that it was her turn of the day to supply ghee to the royal household of Madurai, Dr. Devakunjari maintains that this statement was probably a kind of payment to the queen.

Emperor Augustus of Rome at Antioch was aware of the Pandyan and met a Pandyan ambassador with letters and gifts from this ancient Tamil Kingdom. Strabo, a Greek historian, geographer and philosopher, wrote that an ambassador from a South Indian King known as Pandyan visited Emperor Augustus Caesar. Records indicate that the Pandya kingdom was described as *Pandyan Mediterranea* by *Periplus* and *Modura Regia Pandyan* by Ptolemy.

Ptolemy shows great knowledge of the interior of the Tamil country and mentions a number of inland cities of the Pandoonoi, namely, Tainour (Thenur), Peringkarei (Perunkarai), Korindiour, Tangala or Taga and Akour.

Madurai, the capital of Pandyans was in the south far away from the coast. They also had extensive trade links with the Southeast Asian countries.

There were constant wars and conflicts between Cholas, Pandyas and Pallavas. The kingdoms were conquered and replaced by each other several times.

In the 8th century A.D. Pallavas were replaced by the Pandyas. During the 13th century Marco Polo mentioned Pandyan Kingdom as the richest Empire in existence at that time. Meenakshi Temple at Madurai is the best examples of Pandyan Temple architecture. The Pandyas excelled in both trade as well as literature and they managed the pearl fisheries along the South Indian coast, between Sri Lanka and India, which produced some of the finest pearls known in ancient world.

Again the Pandyan kingdom was replaced by the Cholas who assumed the title as Chola Pandyas in the 11th century. After being overshadowed by the Pallavas and Cholas for centuries, Pandyan glory was briefly revived by Maravaramban Sundara Pandyan and by Jatavarman Sundara Pandyan in 1251.

300 BC - 600 A.D.—The Cheras

The early Cheras ruled parts of Kerala (Malabar) state, Kongu Nadu, Salem, and Dharmapuri from time immemorial. Cherans, who spoke Tamil language ruled from the capital of Karur in the west and traded significantly with West Asian kingdoms.

Their kingdom extended over the Malabar Coast, Karur, Coimbatore and Salem Districts in South India, which now is a part of present day Kerala and Tamil Nadu. The Chera kings were constantly engaged in conflicts with their neighboring kingdoms. To establish political associations,

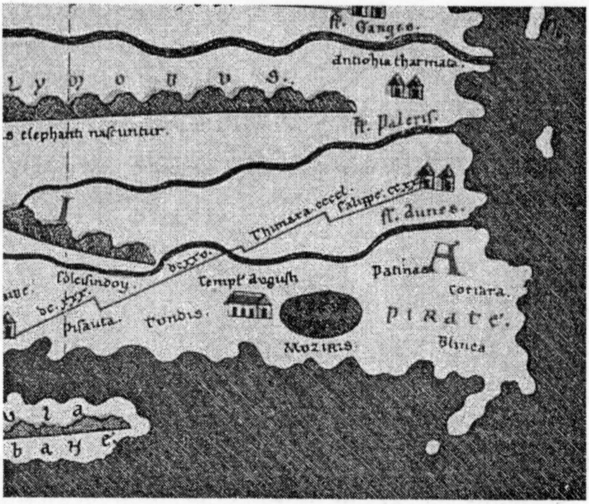

Muziris in the Pandyan Kingdom of Southern India as shown in the Tabula Peutingeriana[14] (A map of Roman settlements and road map) with depiction of a Temple of Augusti, a demonstration of Indo-Roman relations during Pandya period.

they sometimes inter-married with the families of the adversary kings.

Cheras were Shaivite Hindus. Cheras had their own mother goddess Kottravai who was eventually incorporated into the present day form of Devi. Other religious traditions like Jainism and Buddhism came to this area during the period of the Chera Kings.

In Sanskrit, "Kera" means "coconut" and Kerala (Kera Alam) means Kera kingdom. Pliny, the Roman historian of

---

14. The Tabula Peutingeriana is a map of the Romans and it was the state-run courier and transportation service of the Roman Empire. It was made by a monk in Colmar in the 13th century. It is a Parchment scroll assembled from eleven sections, a medieval reproduction of the original scroll. It is a very schematic map: the land masses are distorted, especially in the east-west direction. The map shows many Roman settlements, the roads connecting them, rivers, mountains, forests and seas. The distances between the settlements was also given. Besides the totality of the Empire, the map shows the Near East, India and the Ganges, Sri Lanka, and even an indication of China. It shows a "Temple to Augustus" at Muziris, one of the main port cities in the 1st century B.C. for trading purpose with the Roman Empire on the southwest coast of India.

the first century, who most likely visited Kerala, called the area *Caelobothras* in his Natural History. The Peiplus of the Erythraen Sea states that Chera as *Cerobothra* whose capital was Karur.

300 B.C—1300 A.D.—The Chola Dynasty

The Chola Dynasty was a Tamil Dynasty. The earliest records of this Hindu Dynasty could be found from the inscriptions from the 3rd century B.C. of Ashoka. Pillars of Ashoka inscriptions mention Cholas among other kingdoms existed on friendly terms with him although independent of Ashoka. Cholas continued to rule various territories until the 13th century A.D. The origin of the Chola Dynasty can be found in ancient Tamil literature, inscriptions and Sangam period literature.

There are also brief notices on the Chola country and its towns, ports and commerce furnished by the Periplus of the Erythrean Sea[15] (*Periplus Maris Erythraei*). Greek Geographer and Astronomer Ptolemy has described that the Chola town of Kaveri Poompattinam, also known as Poompuhar as an important sea port that had trade connection with the Roman Empire and China. Roman coins from the early centuries have been found near the Kaveri delta.

The history of the Cholasoccurs in periods: early Cholas 235 B.C.—161 B.C., Interregnum (200–848 A.D.), Medieval Cholas (848-1070 A.D.), and Later Cholas (1070-1279 A.D.)

By the 9th century under Rajaraja Chola and his son Rajendra Chola, the Cholas emerged again as a prominent power in south Asia. Their Empire extended as far as Bengal. Rajaraja Chola conquered most of South India and parts of Sri Lanka. Rajendra Chola's navies moved forward and occupied the coasts from Burma to Vietnam, the Andman and Nicobar Island, Lakshadweep, Sumatra, Java, Malaya,

15. The Periplus of the Erythraean Sea is a Greek periplus, which, describs navigation and trading routes from Roman-Egyptian ports through the coasts of Arabian Gulf, Indian Ocean, Northeast Africa, and India. Periplus means "Sailing around".

and Pegu islands. He conquered Mahipala, the king of the Bengal, and celebrated victory building a new capital Gangaikonda Cholapuram (City of Gangas purchased by Chola).

Under Cholas, the Tamil excelled in art, religion, and literature. Monumental architecture in the form of majestic temples and sculptures in stone and bronze reached an elegance and refinement.

The age of the Medieval Cholas (850–1200) was the golden age of Tamil culture and literature. Jain and Buddhist authors flourished as well. Jivaka Chintamani by Tirutakkatevar and Sulamani by Tolamoli are notable works. Kamban's Ramavatharam, also known Kamba Ramayanam is a great epic in Tamil literature produced in this period.

Cholas were the staunch followers of Hinduism. Throughout their history, they were never persuaded by Buddhism or Jainism influence.

250–600 A.D.—The Kalabhras

An unidentified dynasty called Kalabhras defeated all three Tamil kingdoms between the 4th and the 7th century A.D. Little of their identification or the time is known except that they ruled over the entire southern end of India during the 3rd to the 6th century, conquering the Sangam kingdom. They supported Jainism and Buddhism. They were contemporaries of the Kadambas and the Western Ganga Dynasty.

Ultimately, they were overthrown by the Pallavas and Pandyas.

345–525 A.D.—The Kadambas

The Kadamba Dynasty was an ancient royal family of Karnataka that ruled from Banavasi, Uttara Kannada district. At the peak of their power under King Kakushtavarma, they ruled large parts of Karnataka. The Kadambas were the first indigenous dynasty to use Kannada, the language of the natives at an administrative level. In the history of Karnataka, this period is a starting point in the study of the development of region as an enduring geo-political entity and Kannada as an important regional language.

The dynasty was established by Mayurasharma in 345 AD. The Kadambas were contemporaries of the Western Ganga Dynasty of Talkad.

350–1000 A.D.—The Western Gangas

The Western Ganga Dynasty was an eminent ruling dynasty of ancient Karnataka in India. They initially ruled from Kolar and later moved their capital to Talkad.

Even though it is a small kingdom, the Western Ganga's contribution to organised political order in the government, culture and literature are considered very important. The Western Ganga kings demonstrated benevolent tolerance to all faiths but they were well-known for their patronage towards Jainism. They built world famous Jain monuments like Shravanabelagola and Kambadahalli. The kings of this dynasty promoted fine arts, literature in Kannada and Sanskrit. An important work in Kannada prose is Chavundaraya's Chavundaraya Purana. Several classics were written on numerous subjects varying from religion to elephant management.

600–1200 A.D.—Badami Chalukyas

The Chalukya Empire, natives of the Aihole and Badami territory in Karnataka were landlords under the Kadambas at first. They ruled large parts of southern and central India between the 6th and the 12th century. They encouraged the use of Kannada in addition to the Sanskrit language in their administration. Pulakesi I selected the hill fortress in Badami as his centre of power. The Aihole inscription of Pulakesi II, written in classical Sanskrit language and old Kannada script dated 634 A.D. states his triumph against the Kingdoms of Kadambas, Western Gangas, Mauryas of Puri, Kingdoms of Kosala, Malva, Lata and Gujaraths of southern Rajasthan.

There are other theories about the origin of Chalukyas like they were successors of the Seleukia Empire[16] of Iraq

16. Seleukia was the capital of the Seleucid Empire in ancient Mesopotamia on the Tigris River.

because of the similarity in the name of Chalukya. They argue that Seleukias continued their enmity as far as the territories of India with the Pallavas, who thought to be descendents of Pahlavas or the ancient Parthians of Iran.

The Kappe Arabhatta record in tripadi meter is known as the earliest available record in Kannada poetics. Chalukya Dynasty has left a legacy of a particular kind of architecture. They built more than one hundred and fifty monuments, which are in Malaprabha basin in Karnataka. The temples at Pattadakal, Mahakuta, Aihole, the cave temples of Badami are their most renowned monuments. A painting in Ajanta cave shows Pulakesin II receiving the Ambassador of Iran.

400–800 A.D.—The Pallavas

The Pallavas were the emperors of the Dravidian country and rapidly adopted Tamil ways. Originally, Pallavas were executive officers under the Satavahana Empire. After the fall of the Satavahanas, they started to control some parts of Andhra and Tamil territories.

Around 580 A.D. Pallavas emerged into prominence and dominated the south India for 150 years. They ruled a large segment of Tamil Nadu with Kanchipuram as their capital. They conquered the Cholas and ruled as far as south of the Kaveri River. Pallavas were great temple builders and Dravidian architecture reached its peak during the Pallava rule.

The Pallavas supported Buddhism, Jainism, and the Brahminical faith and were supporters of music, painting, and literature. Their greatest architectural monuments are in Mahabalipuram, which include Shore Temple and the various other temples carved from granite monoliths, and the Varaha cave temple at Mahabalipuram. Once it was a prosperous port.

700–1100 A.D.—The Eastern Chalukyas

Eastern Chalukyas were of South Indian dynasty, closely related to the Chalukyas of Vatapi Badami and their kingdom was located in the modern day Andhra Pradesh. Pulakesin

II, the famous Kannada king of Chalukya of Badami, defeated the eastern Deccan and appointed his brother Kubja Vishnu Vardhana as Viceroy. After the death of Pulakesin II, it became an independent kingdom. Initially their capital was Vengi and later they shifted it to Rajamundry (Rajamahendravaram).

Eastern Chalukyas promoted the development of Telugu culture, literature, poetry and art. It is said that it was golden period in Andhra's history.

600–1000 A.D.—The Rashtrakutas

The Rashtrakuta Empire was a noble dynasty ruling major parts of southern, central and northern India between 6th and 10th century A.D.

The Rashtrakutas rapidly became the most powerful Deccan Empire. The rule of Govinda III implies a new era with Rashtrakuta victories against the Pala Dynasty in Bengal, Gurjara Pratihar in northwest, ultimately capturing Kannauj.

The centre of the Rashtrakutas Empire included almost all of Karnataka, Maharashtra, and some parts of Andhra Pradesh.

The Rashtrakuta Empire at its peak spread from Kanyakumari in the south to Kannauj, UP in the north and from Banaras in the east to Bharuch Gujarat in the west.

Rashtrakutas built many fine monuments in the Deccan and the most extensive and extravagant works are the monolithic temple at Ellora and Pattadakal.

Inscriptions and other literary reports illustrate that the Rashtrakutas selected the crown prince based on hereditary. The crown did not pass on to the eldest son always. Skills and abilities were considered more important than hereditary.

The Rashtrakutas kings supported the popular religions of the day to maintain the peace, law and order in the spirit of religious tolerance.

Records mention that there were more castes prevalent

than the four commonly known castes in the Hindu social system. Some records mention that there were sixteen castes including the four basic castes of Brahmins, Kshatriya, Vaishya and Shudras. Brahmins enjoyed a superior rank in Rashtrakuta society and Jains enjoyed a special position. The Zakaya or Lahud caste specialised in dance and acrobatics. People who engaged in the professions like sailing, hunting, weaving, cobblery, basket making and fishing belonged to specific castes or subcastes. The Antyajas caste did menial services to the wealthy.

Capital punishment was not given to Kshatriya sub-castes or Brahmins. As an alternate punishment to impose the law, a Brahmin's right hand and left foot was severed, leaving that person disabled in case of severe crimes.

The professions of Brahmins were related to education, judiciary, astrology, mathematics, poetry, philosophy or administrative jobs. Children of Kshatriyas were admitted to Vedic schools together with Brahmins, but the children of Vaishya and Shudra were not allowed.

During the 8th through the 10th century they stressed the importance of Kannada language correlating Sanskrit in their administration. Rashtrakuta inscriptions are in both Kannada and Sanskrit. They encouraged literature in both languages, and literature prospered under their rule.

King Amoghavarsha I composed Kavirajamarga in Kannada. It is a guide to poets (Kavishiksha) to standardise the various styles, which are in Kavirajamarga.

One of the famous writer Pampa composed Adipurana, written in champu style (mixed prose-verse style). His other popular work is VikramarjunaVijaya, also known as Pampa Bharatha is a classic work. In a Kannada version of Mahabharata Pampa chooses Arjuna as a hero.

Another great Jain writer in Kannada was Ponna. He received the title Ubhaya Kavichakravathi (King of poet in two languages) for his domination over Kannada and Sanskrit. Ponna was famous for his works in Kannada:

ShanTippurana, Bhuvanaika-Raramabhyudaya, Jinaksara-male and Gatapratiagata.

The Rashtrakutas contributed extensively to the architectural legacy in the Deccan. Initially, the Ellora was a part of Buddhist caves created approximately in the 6th century A.D. Later the area was occupied by Jains monks whose structural details illustrate Pandyan influence. The Rashtrakutas renovated these Buddhist caves and the rock-cut shrines.

1000–1200 A.D.—The Western Chalukyas

In the late 10th century, the Western Chalukyas, also known as the Kalyani Chalukyas, rose to power by defeating Rashtrakutas under whom they were serving as feudatories. Kannada continued as their language of administration, and the Kannada and Sanskrit literature was abundant in their time

In 1076, the rise of the most famous king of Chalukya family, Vikramaditya VI and his fifty year sovereignty was an important period in Karnataka's history. His victories over the Cholas in the late 11th and early 12th century ended the Chola influence in the Vengi territory.

Bijjala II, the powerful ruler of this dynasty, was a commander during the rule of Chalukya Vikramaditya VI. Grabbing the opportunity of fading power of Chalukhyas, Bijjala II declared independence in 1157 and occupied their capital Kalyani. His rule was interrupted by his murder in 1167 as the last Chalukya regained control over Kalyani. Eventually, Chalukyas were defeated by the Seuna Yadavas.

Important architectural works were built by these Chalukyas, particularly in the Tungabhadra river valley.

850–1334 A.D.—Yadavas

The Seuna or Yadava Dynasty was an Indian Dynasty which ruled a kingdom covering from Tungabhadra to Narmada Rivers, including Maharashtra, North Karnataka and some parts of Madhya Pradesh. Their capital was at Devagiri, modern day Daulatabad in Maharashtra.

Originally, Yadavas were feudatories of the Western Chalukhyas. Around the middle of the 12th century, they defeated Western Chalukhyas and established their rule. Their leadership peaked under Singhana II.

The basics of Marathi culture was designed by the Yadavas and the traditional values of Maharashtra's social life developed during their rule. Yadavas are called as Jadhavas also.

Ancient Indian literature describes about the Yadavas as they were descended from a mythical king Yadu. Yadava clans include Chedis, Vidarbhas, Satvatas, Andhakas, Kukuras, Bhojas, Vrishnis and Shainyas and are descended from Kroshta, the younger son of Yadu.

Modern historian, Romila Thapar argues that since Yadavas are identified as Chalcolithic Black and Red ware time people, they were not Indo-European speakers. She writes about the Yadavas kinghip system. Yadavas kinship system shows that they had cross-cousin marriage practice, which is strongly prohibited in the Indo-Aryan system. In Bhagavata as well as in Vishnu Purana, there is a mention that Krishna married Rukmini, a Vidarbha princess. His son Pradyumna married Kakudvati, daughter of Rukmi, brother of Rukmini. Pradyumna's son Aniruddha married Subhadra, granddaughter of Rukmi.

1083-1323 A.D.—The Kakatiyas

The previous history of the Kakatiyas is not available. Based on some inscriptions, historians regard that Kakatiyas were from Andhra Pradesh. After the decline of Chalukya dynasty, they became independent. According to some historians Kakatiyas was a South Indian Dynasty that ruled parts of Andhra Pradesh from 1083 to 1323. They were one of the great Telugu kingdoms that survived for centuries. Prolaraja was the first king of Kakatiyas followed by Rudra, Mahadeva, Ganapati, Rudramba, and Pratapa Rudradeva II.

The Kakatiya Dynasty was considered as one of the golden ages in Telugu history. The territory was governed by

Telugu speaking rulers who promoted literature, art and architecture. The Thousand-pillar Temple in Hanumakonda was built during this period.

The famous Kohinoor diamond was unearthed in Golconda at the Kollur mine and was specifically mined from the Rayalaseema (Land of Stones) diamond mine during the rule of the Kakatiya Dynasty.

Muslim invasion caused the decline of the Kakatiya Dynasty. Rudradeva was defeated by Khilji dynasty and looted the Kohinoor diamond. Later Bahamani Sultan Ahmad Shah occupied the kingdom of the Kakatiyas.

1000–1200 A.D.—The Kalachuris

Two Kalachuri families are known to history: the Kalachuris of Sarayupara[17] and the Kalachuris of Ratanpur. The Sarayupara family ruled a territory in the Central India (west Madhya Pradesh and Rajasthan) along the banks of the Sarayu, modern day Ghaghara River in the Bahraich and Gonda regions of Uttar Pradesh. The Kalachuri kings were known as the Kalachuris of Chedi or Haihaya. Kokalla I was the founder of the dynasty. They founded their kingdom in Madhya Pradesh with their capital at Tripuri near Jabalpur. The family originated in the late 8th century and lasted until the end of 11th century. Its kingdom extended from the Ghaghara River to the Gandak River and included the cities of Bahraich, Gonda, Basti, and Gorakhpur.

1130–1184 A.D.—Southern Kalachuris

Other southern Kalachuri ruled over parts of Karnataka overthrowing Chalukyas of Kalyana in the early part of the 12th century A.D.

They ruled parts of the Deccan expanding over areas of modern day North Karnataka and parts of Maharashtra. Kalachuris rose to power between 1156 and 1181 A.D. This period produced two striking personalities: Bijjala, who destroyed Chalukyas rule and achieved the Kalachuri independence. Another personality was eminent

17. Sarayu river is modern day Ghaghara river.

Basaveshwara, who undertook revolutionary movement of religious and social reform called Virasaiva movement.

It is said that Bijjala, a viceroy of this dynasty established the dominance over Karnataka. Their rule was a brief and chaotic, but very important from the socio-religious perspective. A new cult called the Lingayat or Virashaiva cult originated during these times. A distinct and purely indigenous form of Kannada literature called Vachanas was developed during this time. Notable works like Virupaksha Pandita's Chennabasavapurana, Dharani Pandita's Bijjalarayacharite and Chandrasagara Varni's Bijjalarayapurana were also written during this period.

1026–1343 A.D.—The Hoysalas

The Hoysala Empire was a renowned Kannada Empire in South India that ruled modern day state of Karnataka between the 10th and the 14th century. Due to vanishing Western Chalukya power, the Hoysalas declared their independence. Based on the numerous inscriptions, historians refer that the founders of Hoysala Dynasty were natives of Malnad of Karnataka. Hoysala rulers were mountain people of Malnad in Karnataka, situated on elevated region of Western Ghats range. Originally, the capital of the Hoysalas was situated at Belur. Later in the early 12th century, they successfully conquered the Cholas in the south in the battle of Talakad and shifted their capital to Halebidu.

Veera Ballala II, the Hoysala ruler defeated Pandyas when they invaded the Chola kingdom extending their grip over Tamil province in 1225 A.D. According to some folklore, Veera Ballala founded the city of Bangalore[18].

18.1. Folklores, guesses, historical evidences, and inscriptions provide different theories of the source of the name "Bangalore". Around 5th Century, Ganga rulers constructed a township near Kengeri for their security guards—recognised as Bengavalu in Kannada. Obviously it was known as Bengavaluru, which later on changed to Bengaluru.

2. There is another story relating to 12th century when Hoysala king, Veera Ballala II, came on a hunting tour and lost his way. The hungry king was treated by an old woman with *benda kalu* (boiled beans)

In the early 13th century Muslim invasion began in South India. After waging war against Muslim rulers, Veera Ballala III died in the battle at Madurai in 1343. Consequently, Hoysala Empire and the territories administered by Harihara I, founder of Vijayanagara Empire, merged together. This new kingdom flourished for another two centuries with Vijayanagara as its capital.

During the period of Hoysalas, unique type of Kannada literary meters such as *Ragale, Sangatya* (to be sung with the accompaniment of a musical instrument), *Shatpadi* (six line) became popular.

Hoysalas were tolerant of all religions. During the rule of the Hoysalas, three important religious developments took place in Karnataka inspired by three philosophers, Basaveshwara, Madhvacharya, and Ramanujacharya.

Although Sanskrit literature remained popular during the Hoysala rule, royal patronage for local Kannada scholars increased.

The Hoysalas supported scholars such as Janna, Rudrabhatta, Harihara and Raghavanka, whose works are everlasting masterpieces in Kannada literature. In 1209, the Jain scholar Janna wrote Yashodharacharite, story of a king who planned to perform a ritual sacrifice of two young boys to a local deity Mariamma. Feeling shame on his decision, the king liberated them and renounced the practice of human

---

and water. The grateful king remembered this place as "Bendakaluru" which eventually became Bengaluru.

3. Another story tells that because many Venkataramana Swamy temples were built by Kempe Gowda . Venkataru became Benkaturu and finally Bengaluru.
4. Another story tells that Benacha kalluru (Benachu is quartz stone found in plenty in this area) became Bengaluru.
5. Another theory traces the name to Benge trees found in "Bengeuru" which became Bengaluru.
6. Bangalore also had other names such as Devarayapattana (16th century) and Kalyanapura. It is interesting to note that Bengaluru near Kodigehalli was the parental house of Kempe Gowda's mother and of his wife. This must have encouraged him to name the city as Bengaluru.

sacrifice. King Veera Ballala I honored Janna for this work and gave him the title Kavichakravarthi (Emperor of Poets).

Based on Vishnu Purana, Rudrabhatta wrote Jagannatha Vijaya relating the life of Lord Krishna in Champu style.

Harihara wrote the *Girijakalyana.* Raghavanka introduced the Shatpadi meter into Kannada literature in his Harishchandra kavya.

Philosopher Madhvacharya wrote Bhashya on Brahmasutras and several polemical works.

Another famous writing was Rudraprshnabhashya by Vidyatirtha.

The Hoysala architecture style is described as Karnataka Dravida style differentiated from the conventional Dravida style, and is considered as an independent architectural practice with many unique features. The Hoysalas extended the Vesara style architecture beginning from Chalukyas, ending with Hoysala architectural style as illustrated in the construction of the temples at Belur and Halebidu.

1336–1646 A.D.—Vijayanagara Empire

The Vijayanagara Empire, referred as the Kingdom of Bisnaga by the Portuguese, was a South Indian Empire located in the Deccan Plateau of modern day Karnataka. The Empire was established by Harihara I and his brother Bukka Raya I in 1336 A.D. The Empire, named after its capital city of Vijayanagara (City of Victory), is now a World Heritage Site in Karnataka state. The writings of European travelers such as Domingo Paes, Fernao Nune, Robert Sewell and Niccolo Da Conti and the literature in local languages provide important information about its history. Archaeological excavations at Vijayanagara have discovered the Empire's power and wealth.

The founders of Vijayanagar Empire Harihara I and Bukka Raya I were originated from Kuruba community and were related to Kakatiya kingdom. They were controlling northern parts of the Hoysala Empire at the end of their

rule. They were supported and inspired by Vidyaranya, a sage at the Sringeri monastery and his brother Sayana to fight Muslim invasion in South India.

Vijaynagar Empire consolidated under Harihara I and began to expand and prosper under Bukka Raya. Vijayanagar was more defensible and secure for its location between 14th and 16th century. They designated varaha (boar) as their emblem. Before the rise of the Vijayanagara Empire in early 14th century, the Hindu kingdoms of the Deccan were repeatedly invaded by Muslims from north. The Hoysala Empire was the only remaining Hindu kingdom preventing Muslim invasion. After the death of Hoysala King Veera Ballalla III during a battle against the Sultan of Madurai in 1343, the Hoysala Empire merged with the emerging Vijayanagara Empire.

Ultimately, the Empire came under the rule of Krishnadevaraya, the son of Narasa Nayaka of Tuluva community.

Vijayanagara Empire dominated Southern India and defended their kingdom from Deccan Sultanates. The Empire reached its peak during the rule of Krishnadevaraya. It captured the areas, which were under the Sultanates in the northern Deccan and the territories in the eastern Deccan, including Kalinga.

After Krishnadevaraya, the Empire gradually declined and feudatories of the Vijayanagar Empire—Mysore, Keladi Nayakas, Nayaks of Madurai, Nayaks of Tanjore, and Nayakas of Chitradurga—declared independence.

Writings by foreign travellers and recent excavations in the Vijayanagara have unearthed information about the Vijayanagar Empire's history, fortresses, scientific developments and architectural innovations.

The kings of the Vijayanagara Empire followed the methods to govern their provinces developed by their predecessors, the Hoysala, Kakatiya and Pandya kingdoms and maintained the well-functioning administrative schemes.

The kingdom's economy mainly depended on agriculture. Its capital city was a thriving business centre that included a flourishing market in large quantities of precious gems and gold. Lavish temple-building provided employment to thousands of masons, sculptors, and other skilled artists.

Merchants from many nations including Arabs, Persians, Northwestern Iran, and Afghanistan were settled in Calicut, attracted by the booming business. Ship building prospered and ships sailed to the Red Sea ports of Aden and Mecca with Vijayanagara goods and sold as far away as Venice. Cotton yarn was exported to Burma and indigo to Persia. Chief imports from Palestine were copper, quicksilver (mercury), vermilion, coral, saffron, colored velvets, rose water, knives, colored camlets[19], gold and silver. Persian horses were imported and silk arrived from China. Spice trade was very popular in India, especially Pepper. Pepper was so highly valued. Therefore, the workers on shipping vessels were prevented from having pockets on their dresses presuming that they may steal this black gold! A mineral rich region, Machilipatnam was the main source for high quality iron and steel exports. The Kollur region dealt in diamond mining business.

19. Fabric made of camel hair.

Most of the information on the social life in Vijayanagara Empire is known from the writings of foreign visitors and from research in the Vijayanagara area. The Hindu caste system was prevalent and untouchability was part of the caste system. The Muslim communities were represented by their own group in coastal Karnataka. But the caste system did not stop distinguished persons from being promoted to high ranking posts in the army and administration. In civil life, Brahmins enjoyed a high level of respect. Most Brahmins concentrated on religious and literary matters. Free from material wealth and power made them ideal arbiters in local judicial matters.

Although it was voluntary, the practice of Sati was common in Vijayanagar and commonly observed among the upper classes.

Women were actively involved in matters such as administration, business and trade, and involvement in the fine arts. Until then it was considered as the monopoly of men. Tirumalamba Devi wrote Varadambika Parinayam, and Gangadevi wrote Madhuravijayam and they were notable women poets of that period.

Portuguese visitor Domingo Paes was at Vijayanagara during the reign of Krishnadevaraya. He gives invaluable information on the walls, gates, streets and markets of the city, major temples of the city, including the Virupaksha at Hampi, and its row of pillars bazaar. Paes describes the Mahanavami festival beginning with the preparations within the king's palace where ceremonies were held at the House of Victory, all decorated with precious cloths. According to Paes, the festival included numerous processions of animals, warriors and courtly women, as well as wrestling matches, fireworks and other entertainments.

Rich men wore the Peethambara Kulavi, a tall Turban made of silk and decorated with gold. Jewellery was used by men and women and records tell the use of anklets, bracelets, finger-rings, necklaces and ear rings of various types. During celebrations, men and women adorned themselves with flower garlands and used perfumes. In contrast to the commoners whose lives also were modest, the lives of the kings and queens were full of ceremonial pomp in the court. Queens and princesses had numerous attendants who also lavishly dressed and adorned with fine jewellery.

Domingo writes:

"The city of Bidjanagar is such that the pupil of the eye has never seen a place like it, and the ear of intelligence has never been informed that there existed anything to equal it in the world.

Roy gave orders for the entertainment of mussulmauns in his service; allotted those jaghires, erected a mosque for their use in the city of Beejanuggur, and commanded that no one should molest them in the exercise of their religion. He also ordered a Koran to be placed before his throne, on a rich desk, that the mussulmauns might perform the ceremony of obeisance in his presence, without sinning against their laws. Physical exercises were popular with men and wrestling was an important male preoccupation for sport and entertainment. Gymnasiums have been discovered inside royal quarters and records write about regular physical training for commanders and their armies during peace time."

The Vijayanagara kings were tolerant of all religions and sects as understood by writings by foreign visitors.

During the rule of the Vijayanagar Empire, poets, scholars and philosophers wrote in Sanskrit and in the regional languages, Kannada, Telugu and Tamil. Their literature consisted subjects like religion, biography, fiction, music, grammar, poetry and medicine. The Telugu language became a popular literary medium, reaching its peak under the rule of Krishnadevaraya

Many kings of Vijayanagar Empire were themselves litterateurs and authored classics such as King Krishnadevaraya's Jambavati Kalyana, a poetic and dramatically skillful work.

Vijayanagara architecture is a brilliant combination of the Chalukya, Hoysala, Pandya, and Chola styles. The previous temple building traditions in South India came in the Vijayanagara Architecture style. The combination of all faiths and vernaculars inspired architectural innovation of Hindu temple construction using the local granite. The Empire's support enabled fine arts and literature to reach new heights in the languages of Kannada, Telugu, Tamil and Sanskrit. Karnatic music also prospered.

A feature of Vijayanagara architecture shows the multi-ethnic trend of the great city is the presence of many secular structures bearing Islamic features. While political history describes the ongoing encounters between the Vijayanagara Empire and the Deccan Sultanates, the architectural record shows a more creative interaction. Vijayanagar kings had employed many Muslims in their army and court, some may be Muslim architects. This harmonious exchange of architectural ideas must have happened during the periods of peace between the Hindu and Muslim kingdoms. The "Great Platform" popularly known as Mahanavami Dibba has carvings that illustrate a broad range of royal figures receiving guests, enjoying entertainments, and hunting expeditions.

Kannada, Telugu and Tamil languages were used in the Empire. The Empire minted coins at Hampi, Penugonda and Tirupati with Sanskrit, Kannada and Telugu legends usually carrying the name of the ruler. Gold, silver and copper were used to issue coins called Gadyana, Varaha, Pon, Pagoda, Pratapa, Pana, Kasu and Jital. The coins contained the images of various Gods including Balakrishna, Venkateshwara, Goddesses such as Bhudevi and Sridevi, divine couples, animals such as bulls and elephants and birds. The earliest coins featured Hanuman and Garuda.

Indian Philosophers

788-820 A.D.—Adi Shankaracharya

By the fifth century, the South Indian religious outlook was different because of several religions existing together with Vedic sacrifice and non-Vedic traditions like Buddhism and Jainism. There existed Hindu schools of Philosophy, Sankhya, Vaisheshika, Buddhism, Carvaka and Jainism. A sentiment of Buddhism or Jainism domination provoked Hindus and a large Hindu revival movement reached its peak in the seventh century.

Adi Shankaracharya was an Advaita philosopher who had a tremendous influence on the growth of Hinduism through his non-dualistic (monism) philosophy. He promoted the greatness and importance of the Hindu scriptures, the Vedas, Upanishads and gave new life to Hinduism at a time when Buddhism and Jainism were achieving popularity.

Shankara was a brilliant dialectician and his teaching soon became the standard philosophy of intellectual Hinduism.

Shankaracharya's Advaitha Philosophy (Monism)

His teachings are based on the unity of the Atman and Brahman.

Advaita Vedanta declares that the one unchanging entity, Brahman, alone exists, and that changing entities do not have absolute existence.

Advita argued that the Brahman presented in the Upanishads is the static and is undistinguished absolute reality. Therefore, false perception of difference is due to avidya or ignorance.

For Shankara devotion

and piety were merely the first steps of the spiritual ladder. Full salvation could only be achieved by the knowledge born of meditation. Other philosophers, however, strongly disagreed with him.

Adi Shankara emphasized the importance of the Vedas. His efforts helped Hinduism to recapture its old strength and popularity. He travelled on foot to various parts of India to propagate the study of the Vedas through discourses and debates with other thinkers. He founded four monasteries to revive Hinduism and to spread Advaita philosophy.

These monasteries are at Sringeri in Karnataka in the south, Dwaraka in Gujarat in the west, Puri in Orissa in the east, and Jyotimath in Uttarakhand in the north.

Books written by Adi Shankaracharya:

Viveka Chudamani
Commentary on the Brahma Sutras
Commentary on the Brihadaranyaka Upanishad
Commentary on the Taittiriya Upanishad
Commentary on the Bhagavad Gita
Commentary on Vishnu Sahasranama
Upadesha Sahasri
Bhaja Govindam
Sivananda Lahari and Saundaryalahari

1017-1137 A.D.—Ramanujacharya

Ramanujacharya was a philosopher and a spiritual leader. He was born by name Ilaya Perumal in a Brahmin family in the village of modern day Tamil Nadu, India in 1017 A.D. The unusual lifetime of Sri Ramanujacharya is under scrutiny.

After Shankaracharya's

Advaita, another popular characteristic of revival of Hinduism started from several mystical and passionate devotional movements by twelve Srivaishnava alvars. The alvars came from a variety of social strata; their ranks comprised shudras and one woman. The strong devotionalism of their poetry and the notion that caste and sex is no obstacle to a relationship with the Divine was uncharacteristic to classical Vedic thought.

At the same time, Vedanta school of philosophy focused on the explanation and clarification of speculative and philosophical Vedic commentaries known as the Upanishads. The Advita or non-dualist interpretation of Vedanta developed by Adi Shankaracharya was spreading. Advita argued that the Brahman presented in the Upanishads is the static and is undistinguished absolute reality. Therefore, false perception of difference is due to avidya or ignorance.

Ramanuja was a disciple of Yadavaprakasha, an Advatic scholar. Although Yadavaprakasha was impressed with Ramanuja's analytical skills, he was concerned about Ramanuja's emphasis on bhakti. According to some sources, after some clashes over interpretation, Yadavaprakasa understood Ramanuja was becoming a threat and plotted a way to kill him. However, Ramanuja discovered the plot and escaped. Another version is that one of Yadavaprakasa's students planned to kill Ramanuja to please his teacher. Ramanuja's previous mentor, Kanchipurna, suggested him to meet Yamunacharya who was a proponent of Vishishtadvaitha school of thought. But, Yamunacharya had died by the time Ramanuja reached his place and saw that Yamunacharya's three fingers were curled. Ramanuja interpreted the meaning of curled fingers as —

- Teach the doctrine of Sharanagati
- Write a commentary on Brahma Sutras based on Vishishtadvaita,
- Continue to remember the glories of Parashara, the author of Vishnu Purana, and Satakopa Nammalwar, the author of four works called Divya Prabandams

(Tiru Vaai Mozhi, Tiru Virutham, Tiru Aasiriyam and Periya Tiru Andaadi

Ramanuja started travelling and having philosophical debates with the custodians of various Vishnu temples. Many of them became his disciples after losing the debates. Ramanuja standardised liturgy at these temples and increased the membership of the Srivaishnava school of thought. Ramanuja, who was a Srivaishnavite, might have faced threats from some Shaivite Chola rulers who were religiously intolerant. Ramanuja and his followers moved to the Hoysala kingdom in Karnataka, ruled by a Jain king Bittideva and queen Shantala Devi. When Ramanuja cured Bittideva's daughter from some illness, Bittideva converted to Srivaishanavism and changed his name to Vishnuvardhana.

Ramanujacharya's Vishishtadvaita Philosophy (Qualified Monism)

Ramanuja's philosophy is recognised as Vishishtadvaita because it unites Advaita (oneness of God) with Vishesha (attributes).

Ramanuja's system of philosophy interprets that the Lord (Narayana) has two inseparable attributes, namely, the matter and the souls. They are related to Him as the body is related to the soul. They have no existence apart from Him. They are inherent in him as attributes in a substance. Matter and souls constitute the body of the Lord. The god is their indweller. He is the controlling Reality. Matter and souls are the subordinate elements. They are termed as *Viseshanas*, attributes. God is the *Viseshya* or that which is qualified.

Ramanuja has written nine books:

- Shri Bhashya or Brahma Sutra Bhashya
- Gadhya Thraya (three prose hymns. All three are important works in Srivaishnava philosophy:
- Vaikunta Gadyam
- Sriranga Gadyam
- Saranagati Gadyam
- Vedartha Sangraha

- Vedanta Saara (essence of Vedanta)
- Vedanta Deepa (the light of Vedanta),
- Gita Bhashya (commentary on the Bhagavad Gita)
- Nithya Grantham (About the daily activities to be performed by all Sri Vaishnavas)

1238–1317 A.D.—Madhvacharya

Shri Madhvacharya was the proponent of Tattvavada (Philosophy of Reality), popularly known as Dvaita philosophy or Dualistic school and promoted bhakti movement. It is one of the three most influential Vedanta philosophies of India.

Madhvacharya

On the philosophical side, Buddhism and Jainism were getting stronger as a reaction to excessive ritualism of the Vedas. Sri Shankara's Advaita (monism) was advocating the notion of mayavada (theory of illusion), which claimed the whole world is unreal and the Atman or Brhaman alone is real.

Mdhvacharya's Dwaita Philosophy (Dualism)

In the philosophical system of the Madhvacharya, tattvas or categories of reality are primarily two: svatantra-tattva (Independent reality) and asvatantra-tattva (dependent reality). According to Madhavacharya, God who creates the universe is the Independent reality; the entire universe created by him is the dependent reality. He emphasises monotheism (One God) alone is the quintessence of Vedic literature and not polytheism (Many Gods). All names of God are only epithets or nicknames. There is no sound or word, in any language of the world, which is not essentially a name of God.

According to the Madhva, souls are eternally distinct. In his theory, god saves souls completely by his grace without which even the strong devotion and strict morality are of no use. But on those souls who live righteous lives with perseverance, grace will be bestowed. Evil souls by their bad karma will hopelessly go down and they will never rise up and will be expelled from the universe to a state of eternal damnation, which is regarded as infinite isolation from God.

The inconscient world has five-features: five elements, five elemental essences, five sheaths, five sense-organs and so on. That is why it is called as "pra-pancha" or with five elements. Thus Madhwacharya distinguishes five-fold differences also in this world:

1. Jiva-jada bheda
2. Jada-Jada bheda
3. Jiva-Jiva bheda
4. Jiva-Isha bheda
5. Jada-Isha bheda

1. Difference between matter and spirit
2. Difference between matter and matter
3. Difference between one spirit and another spirit
4. Difference between spirit and God
5. Difference between the matter and God

This difference is not temporary. It is a constant and natural property of everything. It is called Pancha Bhedas in Dvaita philosophy.

The philosophy of Madhva:

- Vishnu is the highest God
- The world is real
- The concept of Pancha Bhedas is an eternal fact
- All living beings are dependent upon Vishnu for their existence
- There is a hierarchy amongst living beings that is eternal (without beginning or end)

- Salvation lies in the soul experiencing its intrinsic joy
- Salvation can be attained only through pure and faultless love of God (combined with knowledge of his greatness)
- Vishnu is to be perceived in his nature through the holy scriptures

Madhwacharyas's Works

Commentaries on the Gita

- Gita Bhashya
- Gita Tatparya

Commentaries on the Brahmasutras

- Brahmasutra Bhashya
- Anu Bhashya
- Anu Vyakhyana
- Nyaya Vivarana

Commentaries on the Upanishads

- Ishavasya Upanishad Bhashya
- Kena Upanishad Bhashya
- Kathopanishad Upanishad Bhashya
- Mundaka Upanishad Bhashya
- Satprashna Upanishad Bhashya
- Mandukya Upanishad Bhashya
- Aitareya Upanishad Bhashya
- Taittireya Upanishad Bhashya
- Brihadaranyaka Upanishad Bhashya
- Chandogya Upanishad Bhashya

Commentaries on the Vedas, Puranas and Mahabharata

- Bhagavata Tatparya
- Mahabharata Tatparya Nirnaya
- Rig Veda Bhashya

Works related to Tattvavada (Philosophy of Truth)

- Pramana Lakshana
- Katha Lakshana
- Upadhi Khandana
- Prapanch Mithyatva-anumana Khandana
- Mayavada Khandana
- Tattva Samkhyana
- Tattva Viveka
- Tattvoddyota
- Karma Nirnaya
- Vishnu Tattva Vinirnaya

Other works

- Yamaka Bharata
- Narasimha Naka Stuti
- Dvadasha stotra
- Krishnamruta Maharnava
- Sadachara Smruti
- Tantra Sara Sangraha
- Yati Pranava Kalpa
- Krishna Jayanti Nirnaya
- Kanduka Stuti

Religious Establishments

The main image of Lord Krishna was established by Madhvacharya in Udupi. The eight monasteries of Udupi founded by Madhvacharya are following his philosophy since then. The Eight monasteries (Ashta Mathas) are Krishnapura Matt, Pejavara Mutt, Puttige Mutt, Sodhe Mutt, Kaniyooru Matt, Adamaru Matt, Shiruru Matt and Palimaru Matt.

1132-1196 A.D.—Basaveshwara

Basaveshwara was a philosopher, revolutionary, and a social reformer, who fought against caste system, gender inequalities and blind beliefs, besides increasing honor to work culture. His teachings and preachings are universal

and go beyond all belief systems.He was a great mystic of his time and started a literary revolution through Vachana Sahitya in Kannada language. Basaveshwara fought against the inhuman practice of caste system, which discriminated people based on their birth. He spread social awareness through his poetry, popularly known as Vachanas. These are rational and progressive social thoughts including established perception of God in Hindu society. Basaveshwara did not preach people the intricate aspects of spirituality; but, he taught how to live happily in a rational social order, later came to be known as Veerashaiva Dharma or Lingayata Dharma. The Anubhava Mantapa founded by Basaveshwara promoted social democracy. Basaveshwara believed that man becomes noble not by his birth but by his action in the society. He declared that all individuals are laborers. Some may be intellectual laborers and others may be manual laborers. He also taught the dignity of manual labor by maintaining the work as worship. Basaveshwara arranged people's committees representing various professions such as agriculture, horticulture, tailoring, weaving, dyeing, and carpentry. All vocations were regarded with equal value and its members belonged to all types of professions.

Basaveshwara taught his followers a lesson of self-purification. He tried to improve the moral level of the public life in the country, and insisted that the same rules of conduct to be applied to the administrators as well as the individual members of the society.

Basaveshwara's chief teaching to mankind is:

Do not steal, do not kill, do not utter lies
Do not lose your temper, do not detest others

Do not glorify yourself, do not blame others
This alone is purity within, this alone is purity without;
And this alone is the way to please our Lord Kudalasangamadeva

Basaveshwara created controversy by his radical actions and actively ignoring the social rules associated with the caste system, which he always wished to abolish. He allowed untouchables to have lunch at his residence and praised the marriage of a Brahmin woman and an untouchable man which made orthodox Hindus very furious. He was a great humanitarian and preached a new way of life regardless of gender, belief, tradition, religion, caste, social status.

3

Mughal Empire

Until about the 10th century, Indians enjoyed the Indian Civilization without any interruption. All previous invaders Greek, Persians, Yueh-chis (Kushans), and Huns had been absorbed into Indian life and culture and digested the customs and tradition, and completely ceased to exist as separate entities.

Muslim domination in India started when the Turks appeared on the scene of history. In 986 A.D. Amir of Ghazni Sabuktagin attacked India and defeated the Hindu ruler, Raja Jaipal of Bathindah in Punjab. Muslims destroyed the areas under their control and instilled terror in the hearts of Hindus.

At the end of 13th century, the Slave Dynasty was replaced by Turko-Afghan Khiljis, who extended their empire southward. Early in the fourteenth century, Ala-uddin crossed the Vidhya Mountains and entered into the Deccan and started to conquest the peninsula. Hindu states were unable to unite themselves against the foreign invaders and ultimately, the whole of India plunged under the wave of the Turko-Afghan conquerors.

The Moghal period started from 1556 A.D. with the ascent of Jalaluddin Mohammad Akbar, known as Akbar the Great. During the period, the Mughal Empire had a highly centralized administration connecting different provinces. All of the important monuments of the Mughals are distinguished by Persian cultural influence with exceptional literary, artistic, and architectural innovations.

The name *Mughal* is derived from the original Central Asian plains conquered by Genghis Khan known as Moghulistan, the Land of Mongols.

For centuries thereafter, generation after generation of Hindus saw the Muslim conquests.

Amaury de Reincourt writes the pitiful condition of Indians during that period:

"The breakdown of the Universal Empire of Mauryas left India with a Universal Society, not a Universal State. That was the final political and social form in which its life stream was gloomy and survived until alien civilisations challenged and overpowered it. Its political philosophy was never attempted to overcome the pessimism and distrust of Kautilya's Arthashastra. In India politics is considered as a replica of the lawless world of the jungle. Most of the rulers followed Kautilya's harmful, malicious, mischievous traits. This attitude of indifference toward all worldly matters was mainly responsible for the collapse of the Indian world into an anarchic combination of unstable and quarreling states. When their country was conquered by aliens, Indians did not care. They turned their attention inward selfishly, and intellectual communities completely submerged in the religious mysticism and ceremonies neglecting the world of politics and history.

"Alberuni described the Hindus' pride and their unwillingness to communicate their culture and knowledge to foreigners. He wondered at their religious tolerance and lack of systematic and rational study of religion among pandits, and their reluctance to risk their lives for their ideals. Indians did not concern about the events taking place west of Hakra River, the historical boundary between Sind and Hind. For all practical purposes, the area occupied by the Arabs remained unholy ground to the Hindus, and mainland of India moved on living unconcerned. It is only in the days of Mahmud of Ghazni's invasion, the Hindu hostility began. For centuries thereafter, generation after generation, Hindus wept as they heard the pitiful tale of the Muslim conquests, and then drying their tears, and went to work for their Muslim masters losing their identification."

971-1030 A.D.—Mahmud of Ghazni

Mahmud was a son of a Turkish slave. At the age of 27, he became a ruler of Ghazni in 998 A.D. He demonstrated remarkable administrative capability and rulership.

It is said that Mahmud took oath to invade India every year and made 17 attempts to conquer India. The first campaign began in 1001 A.D. and the last campaign ended in 1026 A.D.

His main opponent in northern India was Jaipal, the ruler of Punjab. When in 1001 Mahmud rallied against India with 15,000 horse troops, Jaipal confronted him with 12,000 horse troops, 30,000 foot soldiers, and 300 elephants. In a battle near Peshawar, the Indians, though superior in numbers and equipment, were defeated under the attack of the Muslim horses, leaving 15,000 soldiers dead. As Raja Jaipal could not endure his defeat, climbed to his own funeral pyre and ended his life.

His son Anandpal with the help of other Indian kings waged war against Mahmud. In the middle of aggressive fight, Anandpal's panic-stricken elephant, departed from the battle field. The Indian army believing that their leader was returning back ran away from the battlefield. This unexpected victory enabled Mahmud to move forward into the center of India. After annexing the Punjab, he returned with enormous booty.

On April 30, 1030, Mahmud caught malaria and died in Ghazni at the age of 59. The Ghaznavid Empire was ruled by his successors for another 157 years.

Alberuni

Alberuni was regarded as one of the famous scholars of the medieval Islamic period and was knowledgeable in mathematics, astronomy, physical and natural sciences, and also renowned geographer, historian, chronologist and linguist. He made a thorough study of Sanskrit and Hindu literature and wrote a profound description of India in his famous work Tahkik-i-Hind (An Enquiry into India). In this document one can find a mine of information about India and its people.

The book "Indica of Alberuni" provides us a rare insight to the habits, customs, beliefs, religion, philosophy, literature, geography, laws, chronology, astronomy, and astrology of Hindu India as Alberuni saw it in 1030 A.D.

He accompanied Mahmud of Ghazni to India around 1010 A.D. and stayed in Punjab for many years and studied the Sanskrit language very deeply.

His earliest biographer informs that "he never had a pen out of his hand, or his eye ever off a book, and his thoughts were always directed to his studies, with an exception of two days in a year." He was beyond comparison, superior to every man of his time in the art of composition, in scholar like accomplishments, and in the knowledge of geometry and philosophy, and above all he had "most firm regard for truth."

He considered Hindus as excellent philosophers and felt strong affection towards Hindu philosophy. He was considered as impartial writer on custom and creeds of various nations.

Alberuni explains that art and science require the protection of kings. "For they alone could free the minds of scholars from the daily anxieties for the necessities of life, and stimulate their energies to earn more fame and favour, the yearning for which is the pith and marrow of human nature."

To Alberuni the Hindus were excellent philosophers, good mathematicians and astronomers, although he considered himself superior to them. He never concealed whatever he considered wrong and unpractical with them, but he duly appreciated their mental achievements and took maximum care to correct his views. Whenever he ran into something that was noble and grand both in science and in practical life, he never failed to place it before his readers with warm-hearted words of admiration. Speaking of the construction of the ponds at holy bathing-places, he said, "In this they have attained a very high degree of art, so that our people (the Muslims), when they see them, wonder at them, and are unable to describe them, much less to construct anything like them."

Alberuni felt a strong affection towards Indian philosophy. Probably he thought that the philosophers both in ancient Greece and India are ignorant, image-loving crowd. Eventually he realised that in reality that they have very same ideas as his own, that is pure monotheism. He realised that originally all people were alike, pure and virtuous, worshipping one sole Almighty God. But, in the course of time, that the dark passions of the group of people had given rise to the difference of religion, of philosophical and political persuasions, and of idolatry. "The first cause of idolatry was the desires of commemorating the dead and of consoling the living; but on this basis it has developed, and has finally become a foul and pernicious abuse".

He contrasted the democratic equality of people in his country with the castes of India, the matrimonial law of Islam with degraded forms of it in India, the cleanliness and decency of Muslims with filthy customs of the Hindus. With all this, his recognition of Islam was not without a hidden secret. He dared not to attack Islam, but he attacked the Arabs. In his work on chronology he criticises the ancient Muslims having destroyed the civilisation of Iran, and makes us to understand that the earlier Arabs were certainly no better than the Zoroastrian Iranians. Whenever he spoke of a dark side in Hindu life, he turned round sharply to compare the manners of the ancient Arabs, and declared that they were quite as bad, if not worse. This could only be meant as a hint to the Muslim reader not to be too arrogant towards the poor bewildered Hindu, trodden down by the savage hordes of King Mahamud, and not to forget that the founders of Islam were not angels.

He was a strict judge both of himself and of others. He himself was perfectly sincere and it was the same sincerity he demanded from others. Whenever he did not fully understand a subject, or only understood a part of it, he would tell the reader accordingly, either asking the reader's pardon for his ignorance, or promising to continue his hard work and to publish its results in time, as if he were acting under a moral responsibility to the public.

He did not like those who hate to admit their ignorance by frankly saying, "I do not know", and he was provoked to strong annoyance whenever he encountered a lack of sincerity.

If Brahmagupta teaches two theories of the eclipses, (1) the popular about the Rahu consuming the luminous body, and (2) the scientific one, Alberuni considers Brahmagupta committed the sin against conscience by undue concessions to the priests of the country. It was the fear of a fate like that which happened to Socrates when he came into conflict with the beliefs of the majority of his countrymen.

In the works of Varahamihira, he found honest scientific work sentences which sound to him "like the ravings of a madman", but he gently suggested that behind those passages, perhaps there may be an esoteric meaning, unknown to him. However, when Varahamihira seems to exceed all limits of common sense, Alberuni regarded that "to such things silence is the only proper answer."

He sincerely hated the verbosity of Indian authors or rhyme writers, who used lots of words where a single one would be sufficient. He called it "mere nonsense—a means to keep people in the dark and throw an air of mystery about the subject. This superficial and abundance of words offer painful difficulties to those who want to learn knowledge resulting in absolutely waste of time".

When a man from Kanoj came and lectured on chronology, the serious scholar smiled and remarked, "I used great care in examining every single one of them, in repeating the same questions at different times in a different order and context. But Lo! What different answers did I get! God is omniscient."

He did not blindly accept the traditions of former ages; he wanted to understand and criticise them. He wanted to filter the wheat from the chaff, and discard everything that alleviates against the laws of nature and of reason.

He criticised manuscript tradition like a modern philologist. Sometimes he doubted that the text to be corrupt, and inquired the cause of the corruption and proposed to make corrections. He criticised different translations and complained the carelessness and ignorance of the copyists. He was aware that Indian works, badly translated and carelessly copied by the successive copyists will be very soon degenerate to such a degree that an Indian author would hardly recognise his own work, if it were presented to him in such a garb.

He wrote, "My book is nothing but a simple historic record of facts. I have already translated two books into Arabic, one about the origins and a description of all created beings, called Samkhya, and another about the emancipation of the soul from the shackles of the body by Patanjali."

In the book "Alberuni's India", he covered the following subjects with broad knowledge. Mere the title of the chapters give us a clue how deeply he studied Sanskrit and Indian philosophy.

1. On the Hindus in general, as an introduction to our account of them.
2. On the belief of the Hindus in God.
3. On the Hindu belief as to created things, both "intelligibilia" and "sensibilia".
4. From what cause action originates, and how the soul is connected with matter.
5. On the state of the souls, and their migrations through the world in the metempsychosis.
6. On the different worlds, and on the places of retribution in paradise and hell.
7. On the nature of liberation from the world, and on the path leading thereto.
8. On the different classes of created beings, and on their names.
9. On the castes, called "colours" (varna), and on the classes below them.
10. On the source of their religious and civil law, on prophets, and on the question whether single laws can be abrogated or not.
11. About the beginning of idol-worship, and a description of the individual idols.
12. On the Veda, the Puranas and other kinds of their national literature.
13. Their grammatical and metrical literature.
14. Hindu literature in the other sciences—astronomy, astrology, etc.
15. Notes on Hindu metrology, intended to facilitate the understanding of all kinds of measurements which occur in this book.
16. Notes on the writing of the Hindus, on their arithmetic and related subjects, and on certain strange manners and customs of theirs.

17. On Hindu sciences which prey on the ignorance of people.
18. Various notes on their country, their rivers, and their ocean—itineraries of the distances between their several kingdoms, and between the boundaries of their country.
19. On the names of the planets, the signs of the zodiac, the lunar stations, and related subjects.
20. On the brahmanda.
21. Description of earth and heaven according to the religious views of the Hindus, based upon their traditional literature.
22. Traditions relating to the pole.
23. On mount meru according to the belief of the authors of the puranas and of others.
24. Traditions of the puranas regarding each of the seven dvýpas.
25. On the rivers of India, their sources and courses.
26. On the shape of heaven and earth according to the Hindu astronomers.
27. On the first two motions of the universe (that from east to west according to ancient astronomers, and the precession of the equinoxes) both according to the Hindu astronomers and the authors of the puranas.
28. On the definition of the ten directions.
29. Definition of the inhabitable earth according to the Hindus.
30. On lanka, or the cupola of the earth.
31. On that difference of various places which we call the difference of longitude.
32. On the notions of duration and time in general, and on the creation of the world and its destruction.
33. On the various kinds of the day or nychthemeron, and on day and night in particular.
34. On the division of the nycrthemeron into minor particles of time.

35. On the different kinds of months and years.
36. On the four measures of time called mana.
37. On the parts of the month and the year.
38. On, the various measures of time composed of days, the life of Brahman included.
39. On measures of time which are larger than the life of Brahman.
40. On the samdhi, the interval between two periods of time, forming the connecting link between them Definition of the terms "kalpa" and "chaturyuga", and an explication of the one by the other.
41. On the division of the chaturyuga into yugas, and the different opinions regarding the latter.
42. A description of the four yugas and of all that is expected to take place at the end of the fourth Yuga.
43. On the manvantaras.
44. On the constellation of the great bear.
45. On Narayana, his appearance at different times, and his names.
46. On Vasudeva and the wars of the Bharata.
47. An explanation of the measure of an akshauhiný.
48. A summary description of the eras.
49. How many star-cycles there are both in a "kalpa" and in a "chaturyuga".
50. An explanation of the terms "adhimasa", "unaratra", and the "aharganas", as representing different sums of days.
51. On the calculation of "ahargana" in general, that is, the resolution of years and months into days, and, vice versa, the composition of years and months out of days.
52. On the ahargana, or the resolution of years into months, according to special rules which are adopted in the calendars for certain dates or moments of time.
53. On the computation of the mean places of the planets.
54. On the order of the planets, their distances and sizes.

55. On the stations of the moon.
56. On the heliacal risings of the stars, and on the ceremonies and rites which the Hindus practice at such a moment.
57. How ebb and flow follow each other in the ocean
58. On the solar and lunar eclipses.
59. On the parvan.
60. On the dominants of the different measures of time in both religious and astronomical relations, and on connected subjects.
61. On the sixty years-samvatsara, also called "shashtyabda".
62. On that which especially concerns the Brahmins, and what they are obliged to do during their whole life.
63. On the rites and customs which the other castes, besides the Brahmins, practice during their lifetime.
64. On the sacrifices.
65. On pilgrimage and the visiting of sacred places.
66. On alms, and how a man must spend what he earns.
67. On what is allowed and forbidden in eating and drinking.
68. On matrimony, the menstrual courses, embryos, and childbed.
69. On lawsuits.
70. On punishments and expiations.
71. On inheritance, and what claim the deceased person has on it.
72. About what is due to the bodies of the dead and of the living (that is, about burying and suicide).
73. On fasting, and the various kinds of it.
74. On the determination of the fast-days.
75. On the festivals and festive days.
76. On days which are held in special veneration, on lucky and unlucky times, and on such times as are particularly favorable for acquiring in them bliss in heaven.

77. On the karanas.
78. On the yogas.
79. On the introductory principles of Hindu astrology, with a short description of their methods of astrological calculations.

The Hindus believe that there is no country but theirs, no nation like theirs, no kings like theirs, no religion like theirs, no science like theirs... They are by nature niggardly in communicating that which they know, and they take the greatest possible care to withhold it from men of another caste among their own people, still much more, of course, from any foreigner... Their haughtiness is such that, if you tell them of any science or scholar in Khorasan and Persis, they will think you to be both an ignoramus and a liar. If they traveled and mixed with other nations, they would soon change their mind, for their ancestors were not as narrow-minded as the present generation is."

Edward Sachau observes: "To al-Beruni the Hindus were excellent philosophers, good mathematicians and astronomers, though [out of a certain self-confidence] he believes himself to be superior to them, and disdains to be put on a level with them. He does not conceal whatever he considers wrong and unpractical with them, but he duly appreciates their mental achievements ... and whenever he hits upon something that is noble and grand both in science and in practical life, he never fails to lay it before his readers with warm-hearted words of approbation. Speaking of the construction of the ponds at holy bathing-places, he says: "In this they have attained a very high degree of art, so that our people (the Muslims), when they see them, wonder at them, and are unable to describe them, much less to construct anything like them."

1175-1206-Muhammad of Ghur

The Muhammad of Ghur was born in Afghanistan. He established the first great Muslim Empire in Northern India, stretching from the Punjab to Bengal. Muhammad Ghazni was the younger brother of Ghiyas ud-Din, who for most of his life was Sultan of Ghur, one of the thirty provinces of Afghanistan.

Muhammad Ghur was assassinated on March 15, 1206 on his way back to Ghazni after crushing a revolt at Lahore.

1221-1327 A.D—Mongol invasion

In the 13th century, the Sultanates were successful in protecting the Indian subcontinent from the destruction by the Mongol invasion from Central Asia. Nevertheless, the invasion of Timur in 1398 A.D. radically destabilized the Delhi Sultanate. The Delhi Sultanate recovered briefly under the Lodis before it was conquered by the Mughal emperor Babar in 1526 A.D.

THE SULTANATES

1210-1526 A.D.—The Delhi Sultanate

The Delhi Sultanate refers to the various Muslim dynasties that ruled India between 1206 and 1526. They were Islamic Sultanates from Turkic origin and they were replaced by Mughal Dynasty. The five dynasties were the Mamluk Dynasty, Khilji Dynasty, Tughlaq Dynasty, Sayyid Dynasty and Lodi Dynasty.

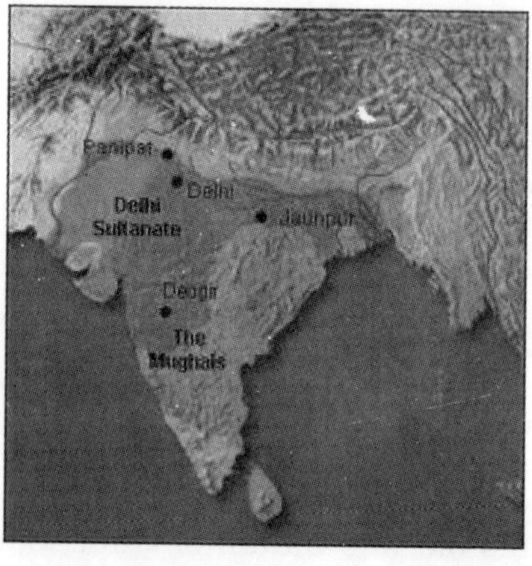

1206-1290 A.D.—Mamuluk (Slave) Dynasty

Mamuluk Dynasty were known as people who developed the techniques of war to a high degree. Muhammad of Ghor from Afghanistan extended his state southwards up to Lahore and a great part of Punjab. He appointed Qutub-ud-din Aibak, his slave (Mamluk) as a governor of that part. Qutub-ud-din Aibak became independent after the death of his master. The Mamuluk Dynasty is also known as the Slave Dynasty. Aibak started to build the Qutub Minar in 1193 and it was completed by his successor and son-in-law Iltutmish in 1197. Iltutmish was succeeded by Razia Sultana, his daughter, who was a good administrator and the first female ruler in the Muslim world. Balban followed her and ruled until 1286 A.D. Confronting with rebels by occupied regions and rival families, the Mamluk Dynasty came to an end in 1290 A.D.

1290-1320 A.D.—Khilji Dynasty

The Khilji Dynasty took control of the Empire in a coup which removed the last of the Maumluks. Jalaluddin Khilji was the first king of Khilji Dynasty who made Delhi as his capital in 1290 A.D.

From 1296 to 1316 A.D., Alauddin Khilji dominated the Delhi sultanate with many achievements. Soon after becoming the Sultan of Delhi, he conquered Gujarat state. Then he won Chittor in 1303 A.D. by defeating Rana Ratan Singh. Alauddin Khilji conquered Mandu, Chander, Ujjain, Dhar and Malwa in 1305 A.D. Malik Kafur who was the general of Alauddin Khilji played a significant role in winning over the major portions of Southern India.

The Khiljis continued their voyage to the south of Narmada River and up to Tamil Nadu. The Vijayanagara Empire united southern India and seized the Delhi Sultanate's expansion until 1565 A.D.

1320-1413 A.D.—Tughlaq Dynasty

The Tughlaqs were also from Turkish origin and around 1321 A.D. Ghazni Tughlaq climbed the throne with a title

Ghiyath al-Din Tughlaq. The Tughlaq dynasty was able to retain its rule due to their strong allies like Turks, Afghans and the Muslim world.

The Tughlaq Dynasty existed nearly one hundred years. It produced two popular Sultans: Muhammad-Bin Tughlaq and Firoz Shah Tughlaq. Muhammad bin Tughlaq shifted his capital in 1326 A.D. from Delhi to Devgiri (Daulatabad) to rule strategically from centrally located capital. A highway between Delhi and Devagiri was built. Because of lack of facilities, he shifted the capital again back to Delhi. During the Qarachil journey, he lost the Empire and died in 1351.

Mohammad bin Tughlaq was succeeded by Firoz Shah Tughlaq who was known for his reformations. He gave a number of important concessions to religious people. He tried to ban some practices of orthodox Muslim people considering they were un-Islamic. Also he prohibited the practice of Muslim women going to worship at the graves of saints.

Firoz Shah Tughlaq instituted economic policies to increase material welfare of his people. Many rest houses, gardens and tombs were built. A number of Madrasas were opened to encourage literacy. He opened hospitals of free treatment for poor and encouraged physicians to develop Unani medicine. He built hundreds of villages and constructed five major canals for irrigation bringing more land under cultivation. For administration of his empire, he much depended on Malik Maqbul (Gannama Nayaka), formerly a commander of Warrangal fort[1].

Firoz Shah encouraged translation of Hindu religious works from Sanskrit to Persian. He had a large personal library of manuscripts in Persian, Arabic, and other languages.

Firoz Shah brought thousands of slaves from all over the country and trained them in various arts and crafts.

1. In 1323 A.D. after the fall of Warrangal, located in Andhra Pradesh, the Kakatiya king Prataparudra and his trusted minister and commander Gannama Nayaka were captured and taken to Delhi. King Prataparudra committed suicide by drowning himself in the river Narmada. Gannama Nayaka was converted to Islam and given the name Malik Maqbul.

He was the first Muslim sultan who strictly imposed Jazya tax on Brahmins. He is reported to have demolished many Hindu temples. Surprisingly, as a man of humanitarian actions, Firoz was intolerant towards non-Muslims. Within the Muslim community also, he honored only the Sunnis, not the Shias.

Firoz Shah Tughlaq was responsible for the down-fall of the Tughlaq dynasty.

1414-1451 A.D.—Sayyid Dynasty

After the Tughlaq dynasty disintegrated, the Sayyid Dynasty ruled Delhi Sultanate of India from 1414 to 1451. They succeeded the Tughlaq Dynasty and controlled the Sultanate until they were superseded by the Lodi Dynasty. This family claimed to be Sayyids or descendants of the Prophet Muhamad.

This dynasty had four major rulers: Khizr Khan, Mubarak Shah, Muhammad Shah and Alam Shah.

1451-1526 A.D.—Lodi Dynasty

Bahlul Lodi, the founder of Lodi Dynasty replaced the Sayyid Dynasty. Sikander Lodi was considered the best leader of the dynasty. The last ruler of this dynasty Ibrahim Lodi was defeated and killed by Babar in the battle of Panipat in 1526. The defeat of Ibrahim ended the Lodhi Dynasty and marked the beginning of Mughal rule in India.

In the middle of the 14th century, the Sultanate introduced an economic system in their provinces and districts establishing a network of market centers. State revenues were based on successful agriculture. This revenue enabled them to promote digging wells in villages, offering seeds to peasants, and encouraging commercial crops like sugarcane and rice.

1347–1527 A.D.—Bahamani Sultanate

The Bahmani Sultanate was a Muslim state of the Deccan in southern India and one of the great medieval Indian kingdoms.

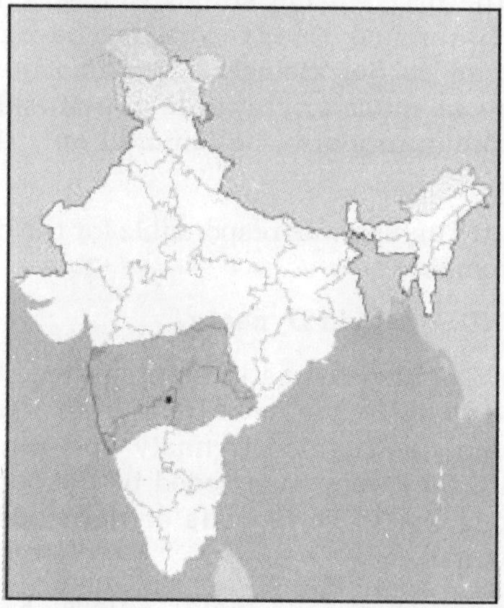

Bahmani Sultanate, 1347 – 1527 A.D.

The Bahamani Sultanate was founded by governor Ala-ud-Din Hassan Bahman Shah, a persian, who revolted against the Muhammad bin Tughlu, Sultan of Delhi, on 3 August 1347 A.D. He established an independent state on the Deccan within the Delhi Sultanate's southern provinces. Between 1347 and 1425, the Bahmani capital was Ahsanabad (Gulbarga) Later, it was moved to Muhammadabad (Bidar).

The Bahmani confronted the Vijayanagara Empire in the south. After 1518 A.D. the Bahamani sultanate broke up into five states: Ahmednagar, Berar, Bidar, Bijapur, and Golkanda known as Deccan Sultanates.

The Bahmani dynasty believed that they descended from Bahman, the legendary king of Iran. They were supporters of Persian language, culture and literature. Some personalities of the dynasty were favmiliar with the language and composed literature.

The Deccan Sultanates

The Deccan sultanate, which broke up from Bahamani Sultanates consisted five Muslim kingdoms of Central and

South India: Ahamadnagar, Berar, Bidar, Bijapur and Golconda.

Deccan Sultanates

1490–1636 A.D.—Ahmadnagar Sultanate

After conquering the Bahmani Sultanate army, Malik Ahmed Shah Bahri, the governor of Junnar, declared independence on 1490 A.D. and founded the Nizam Shahi Dynasty rule on the sultanate of Ahmadnagar. This dynasty was ruled by fourteen rulers.

1490-1574 A.D.—Berar Sultanate

After the breakdown of Bahmani sultanate, Fath-ullah Imad-ul-Mulk, governor of Berar declared independence in 1490 A.D. and established the Imad Shahi Dynasty of Berar sultanate. This dynasty was ruled by five rulers.

1492–1619 A.D.—Bidar Sultanate

Bidar sultanate was one of the Deccan sultanates in south India. Its founder, Qasim Barid joined the service of the Bahamani sultan Muhammad Shah III. He started his profession as a Commander-in-Chief, but later became the Prime Minister of the Bahmani sultanate. After his death in 1504 A.D., his son Amir Barid controlled the administration of the Bahmani sultanate. In 1528 A.D, due to the last Bahmani ruler Kalimullah from Bidar, Amir Barid became independent. This dynasty was ruled by nine rulers.

1490–1686 A.D.—Bijapur Sultanate

The Bijapur sultanate was ruled by the Adil Shahi Dynasty. The Adil Shahis were initially regional rulers of the Bahamani Sultanate. After the breakup of the Bahmani states, Ismail Adil Shah founded a sovereign sultanate as one of the five Deccan sultanates.

1518-1687 A.D.—Golconda Sultanate

The Qutb Shahi Dynasty was ruling sultanate of Golconda in southern India. They were Shia Muslims and belonged to Turkic ethnic group.

The dynasty's founder Sultan Quli Qutub-ul-Mulk served Bahmani sultan Mohammad Shah. After the disintegration of the Bahmani sultanate, he conquered Golconda and became the Governor of Telangana area and founded Qutb Shahi Dynasty of Golconda. Mughal Emperor Aurangzeb's army occupied Golconda in 1687 A.D.

Cultural contributions of Deccan Sultanates

All five Deccan sultanates have contributed tremendously in the fields of art, music, literature and architecture.

Deccan sultanates developed Dakhni Urdu language, copying resources from Arabic-Persian, Marathi, Kannada and Telugu. It helped administrative purposes as well as literary development. The Deccani miniature painting flourished in the courts of Ahmadnagar, Bijapur, and Golconda making major cultural contribution by the Deccan Sultantaes. The architectural grandeur of Deccan, like Char Minar and Gol Gumbaz, belongs to this period. The religious tolerance demonstrated by the Nizam Shahi, Adil Shahi and Qutb Shahi rulers is admirable.

The major architectural activities of the Barid Shahi rulers are the garden tombs. The tomb of Ali Barid Shah is most famous monument in Bidar, in Karnataka state.

The Adil Shahi rulers contributed greatly in the fields of art, architecture, literature and music. Bijapur developed into a cosmopolitan city, and attracted numerous artists, musicians, scholars, and Sufi saints from Rome, Iran, Iraq, Turkey, and Turkestan.

Other major architectural works in Bijapur sultanate is the unfinished Jami Masjid. The greatest monument in Bijapur is Gol Gumbaz, the tomb of Muhammad Adil Shah.

Fortified city of Golconda is one of the architectural achievements of the Qutb Shahi Dynasty. Muhammad Quli Qutb Shah constructed one of the unique monuments in Deccan, the Char Minar.

The Qutb Shahi rulers were great supports of literature and invited many scholars, poets, historians and Sufi saints from Iran to settle in their sultanate. Ibrahim Quli Qutb Shah supported Telugu literature also. Muhammad Quli Qutb Shah was not only a great patron of art and literature, but also a poet by himself. He wrote in Dakhani, Persian and Telugu. In addition to praise of God and the Prophet, he wrote on nature, love and contemporary social life. The Qutb Shahi rulers invited Persian artists to their court, which left a profound impact of different phases of Iranian art on the miniature paintings in this period.

1526-1530 A.D.—Babar

Zahir ud-din Muhammad Babar from Central Asia rose to power at Kabul, the modern day Afghanistan. He established the Mughal Empire in India after defeating Ibrahim Lodhi in the Battle of Panipat in 1526 A.D.

Babar crossed the mountains and came to India. After waging aggressive battles against the Rajputs and Lodhis, Babar took possession of Delhi and Agra. Afterwards he gradually spread his territory and conquered most of Indian sub-continent and Afghanistan.

He invaded India five times. In the fifth invasion he encountered with Ibrahim Lodhi in the first battle of Panipat in April 1526 A.D. Babar's army was better equipped with military than Lodhi's army. Babar had guns while the Ibrahim Lodhi relied on elephants. The most successful innovation of Babar was the introduction of gunpowder. Gunpowder artillery along with other new tactics gave Babar a greater advantage. Babar's strategy won the war and Ibrahim Lodhi died fighting in the battle.

Babar died in Agra, India on December 26, 1530 when he was 48 years old.

1530-1556 A.D.—Humayun

Nasir ud-din Muhammad Humayun was a son of Babar and the second Mughal Emperor who ruled modem day Afghanistan, Pakistan and some parts of northern India. For fifteen years in the middle of his reign, from 1540-1555, he lost his kingdom, but he regained it again by Persian help. In a very short time, Humayun expanded his Empire conquering central plateau around Delhi and left a significant legacy for his son Akbar.

He died in 1556 and his 13 year old son Akbar succeeded him.

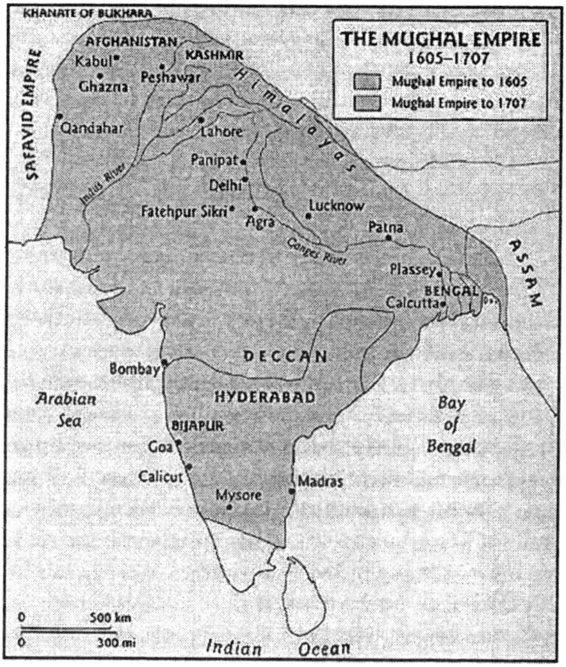

1556-1605 Akbar

Jalaluddin Muhammad Akbar was the third Mughal Emperor. At the end of his magnificent reign in 1605 A.D., the Mughal Empire covered most of the northern and central India.

Humayun died in 1556 AD. His son Akbar was thirteen years old when he ascended the Mughal throne in Delhi. During his leadership, he eradicated military fear from powerful Pashtun descendant of Sher Shah Suri and in the Second Battle of Panipat, he defeated the Hindu king Hemu. Within two decades, he consolidated his power and brought all parts of northern and central India under his rule.

Akbar was a great conqueror, but an idealistic one. Completing the work started by Babar, he strengthened his control over northern India, and made allies with Rajputs. Preoccupied by the dream of an All-India Empire, marched towards Sultanates of the Deccan and integrated the peninsula to his Empire. Akbar was an astonishing ruler, who not only consolidated the political power of his Empire, but also significantly influenced the artistic and cultural life of India.

During the early years of his rule, Akbar had intolerant attitude towards Hindus and the other religions. He had committed cruel atrocities on Hindus and massacred Hindus and destroyed temples. But later, he became tolerant of other races and religions. All discrimination against Hindu religion was banned and the tax on unbelievers of Islam was eliminated. From the beginning of the Islamic intrusion, a special tax was imposed on non-believers of Islam. This special tax, called the *jizya*, was obnoxiously opposed by all during the Muslim rule in India. Besides, they levied a pilgrimage tax on unbelievers travelling to various Hindu pilgrimage centers. Akbar eliminated this tax in 1564 A.D. He encouraged marriages between Mughals and Hindu women.

Akbar was curious to understand the various manifestations of human mind, mainly through the religions of the Hindus, Parsees, and Christians, anticipating to understand the ultimate truth. In a special building, called the "Home of Worship", he organised discussions on religion and philosophy. In 1582 A.D he proclaimed a new religious system, called "Din Idaho", the "Divine Faith". But the new religion of Akbar never became popular.

Akbar regularly held debates and discussions with Jain scholars and was intensely impressed by their teachings. Convinced by their logical arguments about vegetarianism and non-violence preached by the Jain monks, he stopped eating meat and became vegetarian, prohibited slaughter of animals and birds on Jain festival, and gave up fishing and hunting.

Early in the Akbar's rule, Hindus could not construct temples without the emperor's permission. In the beginning, his army was responsible for the demolition of rich Hindu temples, which had gold deities in the Doab region between Ganga and Yamuna rivers. Later, he eventually made amendments to his policy by donating a golden umbrella to cover the deity at a temple which had been demolished, and allowed the reconversion of a mosque into Hindu temple at Kurukshetra.

Akbar's rule largely influenced art and culture in the country. He was a great supporter of art and architecture. Since he had huge interest in painting, he decorated the walls of his palaces with murals. Akbar promoted a lively literary culture and encouraged translations from Sanskrit to Persian and Persian to Sanskrit and Hindi. Also, religious literature was translated into Persian language from other languages, like Chaghatai Turkish, Sanskrit and Arabic.

Akbar suffered from stomach ailment and died on 27 October 1605.

1605-1627 A.D.—Jahangir

After the death of Akbar, his son Jahangir strengthened the Mughal Empire in India. Jahangir was born on August 31, 1569 and was named as Nuruddin Salim Jahangir. Nuruddin, which means "light of faith", has been derived from Arabic language and Jahangir, which means "world conqueror" is derived from Persian language.

Jahangir ended a century long struggle with the state of Mewar. With a tremendous loss of life and property, Rajputs surrendered to Jahangir.

Jahangir was fascinated with art and architecture. Paintings created under his administration were neatly listed, filed, and dated providing scholars with accurate ideas about the time and occasion of their creation as well as their aesthetic qualities.

Jahangir died on the way back from Kashmir in 1627 A.D.

1592–1666 A.D.—Shah Jahan

Shah Jaahan ascended the throne after his father Jahangir's death in 1627 A.D. His initial name was Prince Shihab-ud-din Muhammad Khurram given by his grandfather Akbar. Khurram means "joyful" in Persian language. Similar to Akbar, he was keen to expand his Empire.

The period of Shah Jahan rule was the golden age of Mughal architecture. Shah Jahan constructed many magnificent monuments; the most famous one was Taj Mahal at Agra in commemoration of his wife, Mumtaz Mahal. Other memorable constructions are Pearl Mosque in Agra, Red Fort and the Maja Masjid Mosque in Delhi, mosques in Lahore, and mosque in Thatta. The famous Peacock Throne dates from his time.

He was imprisoned by his son Aurangzeb when he fell ill in 1658 A.D. He died in 1666 A.D.

1618-1707 A.D.—Aurangzeb

Aurangzeb was the son of Shah Jahan and Mumtaz. From the beginning of his ascendance to throne, Aurangzeb engaged in constant war. He advanced towards north-west up to Punjab and Afghanistan. In south, he conquered three

Muslim kingdoms: Nizams of Ahmednagar, Adilshahis of Bijapur and Qutbshahis of Golconda.

Soon after his succession, Aurangzeb reportedly deserted the liberal religious views of his predecessors. He brought untold miseries on Hindu population and their sacred places imposing cruel policies. In Storia do Mogor, an Italian traveller Manucci describes the consequences of Aurangzeb's 1668 A.D. verdict on music. Aurangzeb's instructions to administrators particularly on music were grave:

"In India, both Moguls and Hindus are very fond of listening to songs and instrumental music. He therefore ordered the same official to stop music. If in any house or elsewhere he heard the sound of singing and instruments, he should forthwith hasten there and arrest as many as he could, breaking the instruments. Thus was caused a great destruction of musical instruments. Finding themselves in this difficulty, their large earnings likely to cease, without there being any other mode of seeking a livelihood, the musicians took counsel together and tried to appease the king in the following way: About one thousand of them assembled on a Friday when Aurangzeb was going to the mosque. They came out with over twenty highly-ornamented biers (coffin stand), crying aloud with great grief and many signs of feeling, as if they were escorting to the grave some distinguished defunct. From afar Aurangzeb saw this multitude and heard their great weeping and lamentation, and, wondering, sent to know the cause of so much sorrow. The musicians redoubled their outcry and their tears, fancying the king would take compassion upon them.

Lamenting, they replied with sobs that the king's orders had killed Music; therefore they were bearing her to the grave. Report was made to the king, who quite calmly remarked that they should pray for the soul of Music, and see that she was thoroughly well buried. In spite of this, the nobles did not cease to listen to songs in secret. This strictness was enforced in the principal cities." This implies he not only placed a prohibition on music, but actively crushed any resistance to his policies.

Another significantly heinous statement against Aurangzeb was his policy of temple destruction. Mentioning about Aurangzeb's atrocities towards Indians and Hindu temples, Manucci recorded the emperor's failure on this count:

> "In this realm of India, although King Aurangzeb destroyed numerous temples, there does not thereby fail to be many left at different places, both in his empire and in the territories subject to the tributary Princes. All of them are thronged with worshippers; even those that are destroyed are still venerated by the Hindus and visited for the offering."

After Emperor Aurangazeb's death in 1707 A.D., the empire fell into succession of crisis.

1720–1782 A.D— Hyder Ali

Hyder Ali was a monarch of the kingdom of Mysore, India. He was a wise leader. He effectively challenged British military attacks during two Anglo-Mysore wars.

Hyder Ali was born in Budikote, Karnataka. He was a

fifth son of Fatah Muhammad, who served Raja Wadeyar of Mysore as a Naik (chief). He entered military service along with his brother Shahbahz after their father died in a battle. Hyder worked under Shahbahz controlling 100 cavalry and 2,000 infantry. By 1755 A.D., he controlled 3,000 infantry and 1,500 cavalry and increased his strength by loot and steal.

Hyder Ali possessed remarkable memory and numerical expertise. His Chief Financial Assistant Khande Rao established an accounting system to manage Hyder's finances so that all his goods, income by earned or booty was accounted without fraud. This financial management made Hyder to rise to highest power dramatically.

Hyder had friendly relations with Christians in Mangalore. His army hired Catholic soldiers and allowed Christians to build a church at Srirangapatnam.

Hyder Ali developed war rockets with an important change: the use of metal cylinders to contain the combustion powder. Although the hammered soft iron he used for making cylinder was crude, the bursting strength of the container of black powder was much higher than the earlier paper construction.

Military rocket innovations

Although the Rocket technology was already in use when Hyder's father served Mysore, it was Hyder who enhanced them further and significantly expanded their use in the military. Technological innovations included the use of high-quality iron casting for the combustion chamber, enabling the use of higher powered explosive charges. He also organized bands of rocket men who were proficient in aiming rockets based on the size of the rocket and the distance to the target. Rockets could also be mounted on carts that improved their mobility and enabled to fire a large numbers of them simultaneously. Professor Roddam Narasimha in his lecture on the curious history of rockets mentions:

"The Mysore rockets of this period were much more advanced, than what the British had seen or known, chiefly because of the use of iron tubes for holding the propellant; this enabled higher bursting pressures in the combustion chamber and hence higher thrust and longer range for the missile. The rockets consisted of a tube (about 60 rom[2] diameters and 200 rom long), fastened to a sword or 3 m bamboo pole, and had a range of 1-2 km. In the famous battle of Pollilur (1780) in which the British were defeated a scene celebrated on the walls of Darya Daulat Bagh in Srirangapatna—a strong contributory cause is thought to have been the explosion of Colo Baillie's ammunition tumbrils[3], touched off by Mysore rockets. Rockets were used in the 3rd and 4th Anglo-Mysore Wars as well; although they caused much confusion and fear especially when used against massed troops or cavalry, they were too inaccurate to tilt decisively the fortunes of battle in favour of Tippu."

Hyder Ali engaged in wars constantly to increase his power: (1) First war with the Marathas, (2) First Anglo-Mysore War, (3) Second war, with Marathas, and (4) Second Anglo-Mysore war.

Hyder died at Chittor on December 6, 1782 A.D.

1750–1799 A.D.—Tippu Sultan

Tippu Sultan was a son of Hyder Ali and was born in Devanahalli near Bangalore, Mysore state. He had many honorary names as Sultan Fateh Ali Khan Shahab, Tipp Saheb or Bahadur Khan Tippu Sultan.

During Tippu's childhood, his father Hyder Ali rose to power in Mysore and Tippu assumed the

2. Rom = range of motion.
3. Tumbrils = A two-wheeled cart.

leadership of the kingdom after Hyder Ali's death. He was a successful ruler, a scholar, a soldier, and a poet. He was proficient in many languages. He was a pious Muslim, but the majority of the people were Hindus. He used French trained army in many of his battles. On request of French, he built a first church in Mysore.

He completed the construction of Lal Bagh in Bangalore, which was started by his father Hyder Ali. Hyder Ali wished to build Mughal type Botanical Garden. Later his son, Tippu included horticultural wealth to the garden by importing trees and plants from several countries.

He built roads, public buildings, and ports on the Kerala seashore. His trade extended to countries which included Sri Lanka, Afghanistan, France, Turkey, and Iran.

Unlike his father, Tippu hated Christians. He treated Mangalore Catholics in very heinous manner.

These experiments led the Royal Woolwich Arsenal to begin rocket research and development program in 1801 based on the Mysorean technology. According to William Congreve's report in Notes and Records of the Royal Society:

"The Indian war rocket that inspired his efforts was a product of military reform in the armies of Mysore, India, during a period of prolonged war. From 1767 to 1799 the armies of Hydar Ali and his son Tippu Sultan fought the British, who sought to extend their dominion over southern India after gaining control of the east at the battles of Plassey and Buxar.

The use of military rockets, or *baana*, had flourished in India since the reign of the Mughal emperor Akbar in the second half of the sixteenth century. Under Haidar and Tipp, production expanded in Mysore, probably in the fort of Tirthahalli, in the northern part of their kingdom. Rockets consisted of bamboo sticks or woods steel blades attached to iron cases, about eight inches long and weighing from six to twelve pounds, charged with one to two pounds of gunpowder. Rocket making was skilled work, undertaken by specialised artisan castes, whose expertise reflected long

Indian traditions of working the high-quality iron ores and saltpetre[4] deposits found in India. By the end of Tippu's reign, some 5000 Mysorean troops fired off huge volleys of rockets against the enemy, although, as in Britain, rockets served other functions besides the military. Like McCartney, Tippu deployed his best technologies as diplomatic gifts, sending rockets to the Ottoman sultan, Abdülhamid I, on an embassy to Constantinople in 1783 (unlike the Chinese emperor, the sultan was impressed and sent a tiger throne to Tippu in return). Rockets were also used as a measuring unit in India, and in Mysore they were subject to the princely practice of 'name-changing', whereby the prince signaled his power by creating new names for things. To *Mir Miraan,* the commanding officers of his armies, Tippu 'presented dresses of gold embroidery... and jeweled gorgets. About this time the sultan changed the names of the different arms, as for instance... a *ban,* or rocket, *Shuhab.*'

He engaged in wars constantly to increase his power, which includes : (1) Second Mysore War, (2) Third Mysore War, (3) Fourth Mysore War apart from several other minor wars. Like his father, Tippu sultan used rockets in military extensively with improved technology.

During Fourth Mysore War, Tippu Sultan died defending his capital on May 4, 1799. Tippu was buried on next afternoon, near the tomb of his father. In the midst of his burial, a great storm broke with massive winds and rains. Lieutenant Richard Bayly of the British 12th regiment wrote on May 5, 1799:

"...I must relate the effects and appearance of a tremendous storm of wind, rain, thunder, and lightning that ensued on the afternoon of the burial of Tippu Sahib. I had returned to camp excessively indisposed. About five o'clock a darkness of unusual obscurity came on and volumes of huge clouds were hanging within a few yards of the earth, in a motionless state. Suddenly, a rushing wind, with irresistible force, raised pyramids of sand to an amazing height, and

4. Potassium mitrate or the mineral niter, the important oxidising component of gunpowder and also of food preservative.

swept most of the tents and marquees in frightful eddies far from their site. Ten Lascars, with my own exertions, clinging to the bamboos of the marquee scarcely preserved its fall. The thunder cracked in appalling peals close to our ears, and the vivid lightning tore up the ground in long ridges all around. Such a scene of desolation can hardly be imagined; Lascars struck dead, as also an officer and his wife in a marquee a few yards from mine. Bullocks, elephants, and camels broke loose, and scampering in every direction over the plain; every hospital tent blown away, leaving the wounded exposed, unsheltered to the elemental strife. In one of these alone eighteen men who had suffered amputation had all the bandages saturated, and were found dead on the spot the ensuing morning. The funeral party escorting Tippu's body to the mausoleum of his ancestors situated in the Lal Bagh Garden, where the remains of his warlike father, Hyder Ali, had been deposited, were overtaken at the commencement of this furious whirlwind, and the soldiers ever after were impressed with a firm persuasion that his Satanic majesty attended in person at the funeral procession. The flashes of lightning were not as usual from far distant clouds, but proceeded from heavy vapors within a very few yards of the earth. No park of artillery could have vomited forth such incessant peals as the loud thunder that exploded close to our ears. Astonishment, dismay, and prayers for its cessation were our solitary alternative. A fearful description of the Day of Judgment might have been depicted from the appalling storm of this awful night. I have experienced hurricanes, typhoons, and gales of wind at sea, but never in the whole course of my existence had I seen anything comparable to this desolating visitation. Heaven and earth appeared absolutely to have come in collision, and no bounds set to the destruction. The roaring of the winds strove in competition with the stunning explosions of the thunder, as if the universe was once more returning to chaos. In one of these wild sweeps of the hurricane, the poles of my tent were riven to atoms, and the canvas wafted forever from my sight. I escaped without injury, as also my exhausted Lascars, and casting myself in an agony of despair on the sands, I fully expected instant annihilation. My hour was not,

List of Mughal Emperors

Emperor	*Reign Period*	*Notes*
Zaheeruddin Muhammad Babar	1526-1530 A.D.	Founder of the Mughal Dynasty
Nasiruddin Muhammad Humayun	1530-1540 A.D.	Reign broke up by Suri Dynasty
Sher Shah Suri1	1540–1545 A.D.	Overthrew Humayun and established the Suri Dynasty
Islam Shah Suri	1545–1554 A.D.	Second and last ruler of Suri Dynasty.
Nasiruddin Muhammad Humayun	1555–1556 A.D.	Reinstated the leadership again
Jalaluddin Muhammad Akbar	1556–1605 A.D.	Akbar significantly expanded the Mughal Empire. Though he was intolerant towards other religions initially, later he tried to unify all non-believers of Islam
Nooruddin Muhammad Jahangir	1605–1627 A.D.	He signed a treaty with the British East India Company promising to give preferential treatment to their merchants
Shahabuddin Muhammad Shah Jahan	1627–1658 A.D.	During his leadership, Mughal art and architecture flourished. He was responsible to construct Taj Mahal, Jama Masjid, Red Fort, Shalimar Gardens in Lahore and Jahangir Mausoleum
Mohiuddin Muhammad Aurangzeb Alamgir	1658–1707 A.D.	He deserted the liberal religious views of Akbar and reinstated the Islamic law

Emperor	*Reign Period*	*Notes*
Bahadur Shah I	1707–1712 A.D.	After his rule, the beginning of the end of Mughal Empire started
Jahandar Shah	1712–1713 A.D.	Ruled India for a brief period of time
Farrukhsiyar	1713–1719 A.D.	In 1717 he granted an order or decree to the English East India Company granting them duty free trading rights for Bengal and confirmed their position in India
Rafi Ul-Darjat	1719 A.D.	Ruled India for a brief period of time
Shah Jahan II	1719 A.D.	Ruled India for a brief period of time
Nikusiyar	1719 A.D.	Ruled India for a brief period of time
Muhammad Ibrahim	1720 A.D.	Ruled India for a brief period of time
Muhammad Shah	1719–1720 A.D. 1720–1748 A.D.	Encountered the invasion of Nadir-Shah of Persia in 1739
Ahmad Shah Bahadur	1748–54 A.D.	Mughal forces massacred by the Maratha during the Battle of Sikandarabad
Alamgir II	1754–1759 A.D.	He was a weak ruler and was murdered by Ghazi-ud-Din
Shah Jahan III	In 1759 A.D.	Ruled India for a brief period of time
Shah Alam II	1759–1806 A.D.	Ahmed-Shah-Abdali in 1761 defeated the Marathas during the Third Battle of Panipat The fall of Tip Sultan of Mysore in 1799

Emperor	*Reign Period*	*Notes*
Hyder Ali	1761-1782 A.D.	Hyder Ali's rule of Mysore was characterised by frequent warfare with his neighbours and rebellion within his territories. He was a shrewd leader, and left to his son Tippu Sultan a kingdom that was significantly larger than when he first took it over. He organised his military along European lines, and was a pioneer in the military use of Rocket artillery
Tippu Sultan	1782-1799 A.D.	He engaged in attacks against his neighbours, and harshly crushed rebellions within his territories. He remained a merciless enemy of the British. He sent embassies to foreign states, including the Ottoman Empire and France, in an attempt to rally opposition to the British. In the Third Anglo-Mysore War Tippu was forced into a humiliating peace, losing a number of previously conquered territories, such as Malabar and Mangalore. In the Fourth Anglo-Mysore War the combined forces of the British East India Company and the Nizam of Hyderabad defeated Tippu and he was killed on 4, May 1799, defending the fort of Seringapatam.

Emperor	*Reign Period*	*Notes*
and		He introduced a number of administrative military innovations to Mysore including the expansion of rocket technology, introduced and promoted a more widespread use of Persian and Urdu languages in southern India
Akbar Shah II	1806–1837 A.D.	Hypothetical figurehead under British protection
Bahadur Shah Zafar	1837–1857 A.D.	The last Mughal emperor who was overthrown by the British and exiled to Burma in 1857.

however, come. Towards morning the storm subsided; the clouds became more elevated, the thunder and lightning ceased, and nature once more resumed a serene aspect. But never shall I forget that dreadful night to the latest day of my existence. All language is inadequate to describe its horrors. Rather than be exposed to such another scene, I would prefer the front of a hundred battles...."

Influence of Mughal Rule on India

The Mughal period is famous for its multiple cultural developments. The Timurids had a great cultural tradition. Their ancestral kingdom at Samarkand was the meeting place of the cultural traditions of Central and West Asia. The Mughals brought with them Muslim cultural traditions from Turko-Iranian areas, which eventually stimulated the evolution of the Indo-Muslim culture, a combination of two cultures: Central-West Asia and Turko-Iranian cultures.

The Turks were supporters of arts and education. They had poets, amateur painters, calligraphers, singers, and instrumentalists. The Turks were fine warriors, capable of handling a sword as a pen. They loved palaces, gilded tents, fine clothing and rich garnishes. They were collectors of books and paintings eagerly seeking new kind of luxury always.

Major contributions of Mughals to India are their exceptionally ingenious architecture. A number of monuments were built by the Muslim emperors throughout their Indian occupation. Particularly Shaha Jahan's contributions to architecture and painting are outstanding. His most monumental work include Taj Mahal, which is regarded as World Heritage Site. Other World Heritage Sites include the Humayun's Tomb, Fatehpur Sikri, Red Fort, Agra Fort, and Lahore Fort.

The palaces, tombs, and forts built by Mughal Dynasty are situated in Delhi, Aurangabad, Fatehpur Sikri, Agra, Jaipur, Lahore, Kabul, Sheikhupura, and many other places of India, Pakistan, Afghanistan, and Bangladesh.

Mughal's influence on political and cultural could be found in areas like :

- Smaller kingdoms were brought together under centralised and stately government system
- New trade routes were built to Arab and Turkic lands
- Persian art and culture combined with Indian art and culture
- Mughal cuisine was introduced to Indian subcontinent. For example, Aloo ka Raita, various kinds of korma, Chole or Chana masala, Tikkas, Naan, Palak Paneer, Kababs, Tandoori, Biryani, Pulao, Keema, Malai Kofta, Navratan korma, Samosa, Barfi, Gulabjamun, Kalakand, Kulfi, Sheer korma, Badam Halva, etc.
- Magnificent gardens
- Mughal miniature paintings

Urdu language

Even though Persian language was the leading official language of the Empire, the language of the elite developed into a form of Hindustani known as Urdu. Compared with Hindi, the Urdu language derives more vocabulary from Persian and Arabic than from Turkic languages. Hindi derives its vocabulary from Sanskrit profoundly. Modern Hindi uses Sanskrit-based vocabulary along with Urdu borrowed words from Persian and Arabic, and it is mutually understandable with Urdu.

Astronomy

Mughal astronomers made improvement in observational astronomy and produced about hundred Zij[5] treatises.

The instruments and observational techniques used at the Mughal observatories were primarily derived from the Islamic tradition. Two most remarkable Mughal Celestial

5. *Zij* is the generic name applied to Islamic astronomical books that tabulate parameters used for astronomical calculations of the positions fo the Sun, Moon, stars, and planets. The name is derived from the middle Persian term *zih* or *zig*, meaning cord. The term is known to refer the arrangement of threads in weaving as the arrangement of rows and columns in tabulated data.

seamless Globes were invented during Mughal's rule. The second celestial globe exhibits 1018 star positions marked by inlaid silver points and 48 constellation figures drawn in outline apartment from usual circles. The interesting feature of this globe is that it is bilingual. It includes the names of the Zodiac signs, lunar mansions, and other constellation in both Arabic and Sanskrit scripts. The graduations are also numbered in two systems. The ecliptic is graduated in single degrees and each fifth is labelled in Arabic and Sanskrit numerals.

Another remarkable work is a metallurgical seamless Globe invented in Kashmir by Ali Kashmiri ibn Luqman in 998 A.D. Another famous seamless celestial globe was produced using a lost-wax casting method in the Mughal Empire around 1630 A.D. with Arabic and Persian inscriptions. Mughal metallurgists established the method of wax casting to produce seamless globes.

Celestial Globe in brass dated 1630 A.D. The globe is hollow and was cast in one seamless piece

Technology

Fathullah Shirazi, a Persian-Indian Engineer who worked for Akbar the Great in the Mughal Empire, invented a multi-barrel gun with gun poweder. Unlike polybolos and repeating crossbows used in ancient Greece and China, Shirazi's gun was a rapid-firing gun, which had multiple gun barrels that fired hand cannons loaded with gunpowder. He also invented primitive auto cannon.

Tippu Sultan of Mysore, the Nawab in the south of India, experimented with war rockets, invented iron-cased and metal-cylinder rocket artillery.

1799–1849 A.D.—Sikh Empire

Sikhism is a distinct political body, which begun after the death of the fifth Sikh Guru, Guru Arjan Dev in 1606 A.D. Sikhs ruled mainly in areas of Punjab on both sides of India and Pakistan. They were able to establish an independent Empire under Maharaja Ranjit Singh in 1799 A.D.

Sikhism was founded by Guru Nanak Dev, a religious leader and a social reformer during the 15th century in Punjab territory. The religious practice was consecrated by Guru Gobind Singh.

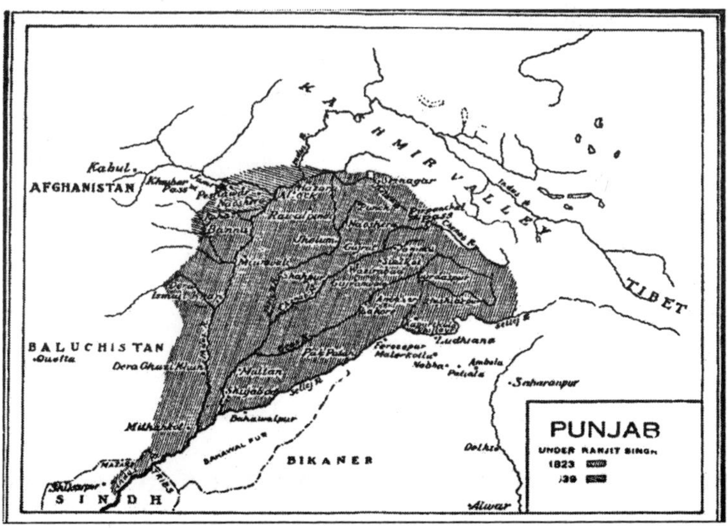

The Sikh Empire covered a region between the western Tibet and Afghanistan, including the modern day regions such as Punjab, Pakistan, Haryana, Himachal Pradesh, Chandigarh, New Delhi, Jammu, North West Frontier Province, and Parts of North-Eastern Afghanistan.

Guru Gobind Singh sanctified five persons from different social backgrounds to form Khalsa, a military order of "saint-soldiers". He deliberately initiated Five Ks: Kara (an iron bracelet), Kesh (uncut hair), Kanga (a wooden coomb), Kirpan (a curved sword), Kachera (a specific style of cotton underware), which must be used by all Sikhs.

Initially Sikhism had peaceful relations with other religions. However, Sikhs started facing religious persecution during the reign of Jahangir. Prominent Sikh Gurus were murdered by Mughals for opposing some Mughal emperors' harassment. Consequently, Sikhism militarised their group to oppose Mughal domination. The Sikh Empire's secular administration integrated innovative military, economic and governmental reforms.

After the death of Ranjit Singh 1839, the Empire was very badly weakened by internal divisions and political mismanagement. The British Empire used this opportunity to launch the Anglo-Sikh wars.

The Sikh Empire was finally defeated by British after a chain of wars. After Second Anglo-Sikh War in 1849, separate princely states and British province of Punjab were formed. Ultimately, a Lieutenant Governorship was formed in Lahore as a direct representative of the British Crown.

It is said that Sikhs have developed their own instruments: Rabab (a kind of string instrument), Dilruba, Taus (a bowed string instrument), Jori and the Sarinda (a stringed instrument). The Sarangi was also encouraged by Guru Har Gobind. The Taus was invented by Guru Har Gobind. It is said that he heard a peacock singing and wanted to create similar instrument that could mimic peacock's sounds. Taus is the Persian word for peacock. The Dilruba was made by Guru Gobind Singh at the request of his people.

When marching towards battle, the Sikhs used drumming to boost their morale and to become excited. This was called the Ranjit Nagaara (Drum of Victory). Nagaaras

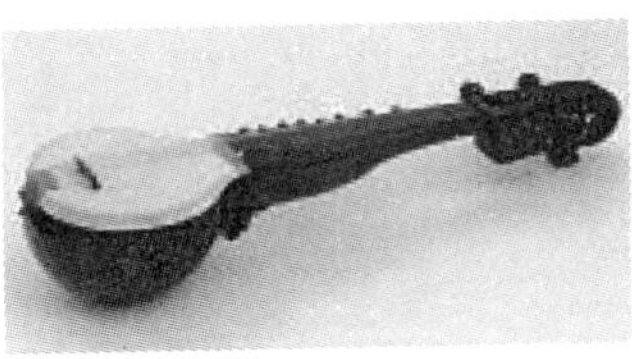

Rabaab

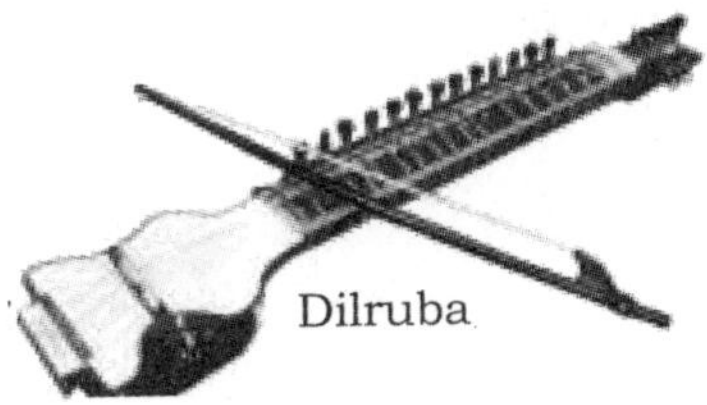

Dilruba

Jori

Taus

Sarinda

Sarangi

are large war drums, making a thundering sound and measuring about 2 to 3 feet in diameter, and are played with two sticks. While the Sikhs spirit was boosting, the opposing forces were losing morale.

The shabd is typically played in accordance with that particular raag. This style of singing is known as Gurmat Sangeet.

Sikh art and culture is special to the Punjab region. Sikh Architecture is a style of architecture that is characterized with values of progressiveness, exquisite intricacy, luster, beauty and logical flowing lines. Sikh culture is heavily influenced by martial patterns. So majority of Sikh artifacts have a military theme. Bhangra and the Giddha are two forms of indigenous Punjabi folk dancing that have been adapted and groomed by Punjabi Sikhs.

Arjan Dev was responsible for building the Darbar/ Harimandir Sahib (also called the Golden Temple).

He compiled the Sikh sacred text book known as the 'Adi Granth' and included the writings of the first five gurus and other enlightened Hindu and Muslim saints.

1674-1818 A.D.—Maratha Empire

1642-1680 A.D.—Chatrapati Shivaji

Chatrapati Shivaji established the Hindu Maratha kingdom in the Deccan against all adverse situations, fighting against the mighty Mughals. He inspired and united the common man to fight against the dictatorship of Mughal ruler Aurangzeb by instilling a sense of pride and nationality in them.

The Maratha Empire was an Indian imperial power. At some point, the Empire comprised a large part of South Asia. The Empire was founded and united by Shivaji Maharaj. He established an independent Maratha kingdom with Raigad as its capital, and successfully fought against the Mughals to protect his kingdom. The Maratha Empire declared war for 27 years with the Mughals from 1681 to 1707. Shivaji initiated Shiva Sutra, which describes strategic factors like demographics, speed and focused attack to defeat his enemies.

Shivaji's genius is most evident in his military organization, which lasted till the demise of the Maratha Empire. Shivaji was responsible for many significant changes in military organisation. They include:

- A standing army belonging to the state called *paga*
- All war horses belonged to the state; responsibility for their upkeep rested on the Sovereign
- Creation of part time soldiers from peasants who worked for eight months in their fields and supported in war for four months for which they were paid
- Highly mobile and light infantry and cavalry were his innovations and they excelled in commando tactics
- The introduction of a centralised intelligence department

- A potent and effective navy
- Introduction of field craft viz. Guerrilla warfare, commando actions, swift flanking attacks
- Innovation of weapons and firepower, innovative use of traditional weapons like tiger claw or 'Vaghnakh'. 'Vita' was a weapon invented by Shivaji
- Militarisation of almost whole society, including all classes with entire peasant population of settlements and villages near forts to actively involve in their defense.

Shivaji understood the importance of having a secure coastline and protecting the western Konkan coastline from attacks. He strategically built a strong navy army to protect and strengthen his kingdom. He was also worried about the growing dominance of British India naval forces in Indian waters and vigorously resisted them.

Venkoji, Shivaji's half-brother established Thanjavur Maratha Kingdom in South India.

Shivaji's grandson, Shahu became a ruler of Maratha Empire. During this period he appointed Peshwas, the prime ministers of the Maratha Empire. After the death of Mughal Emperor Aurangzeb, the Maratha Empire expanded largely under the rule of the Peshwas. The Empire at its climax stretched from Tamil Nadu in the south to Attock (modern-day Pakistan) on the Indus River, and advanced expeditions in Bengal. In 1761 A.D, the Maratha army lost the Third Battle of Panipat with Mughals that halted Maratha's expansion.

Ten years after the battle of Panipat, Madhavrao Peshwa reestablished the Maratha authority over North India. In order to effectively manage the Maratha states of the large Empire, Confederacy of Maratha was created. They became known as Gaekwads of Baroda, the Holkars of Indore and Malwa, the Scindias of Gwalior and Ujjain, Bhonsales of Nagpur. In 1775 A.D. the British East India Company intervened in a succession struggle in Pune which became the First Anglo-Maratha War. Marathas continued the paramount power in India until their defeat in the Second and Third Anglo-Maratha Wars (1805–1818) which made Britain to control a large portion of India.

Most of the Maratha Empire was on coastline, which was protected by a powerful navy under commanders. Securing and protecting the coastal areas and building land-based fortifications were vital aspects of the Maratha's defensive strategy.

Shivaji was a descendent of royal Bhosle family, who were well acquainted with Sanskrit and promoted it. He named his forts based on Sanskrit language. He named the Ashta Pradhan (council of ministers) as per Sanskrit classification like Nyayadhish, Senapati etc.

A noteworthy aspect of Shivaji's rule was his effort to revive ancient Hindu political tradition and court principles. He introduced Marathi in place of Persian as the court language, revived Sanskrit administrative method and compiled a dictionary of official terms such as The Rajya Vyavahar Kosh.

Sambhaji composed a *danapatra* (donation plaque), which is in Sanskrit. He writes about his father as:

1. Yavanarambha gritat mlechakshaydiksha: "Shivaji had taken a sacred oath and was on mission to defeat foreign invaders".
2. Dillindraman pradhvanspatu: "One who has defeated the Mughal Emperor of Delhi".
3. Vijayapuradhishwar prathtarmanya bhujchachayay: "One whose help was sought by Adilshahi King of Vijaypur".

Religion

Shivaji was a staunch Hindu and respected all religions. Shivaji had great respect for other contemporary saints, most notably Tukaram and saints, like Sufis. He had met Samarth Ramdas and accepted him as his mentor. Shivaji allowed his subjects freedom of religion and opposed forced conversion.

4

Colonial India

1510–1947 A.D.—Colonial India

India had experienced numerous invasions over thousands of years of its long historical existence. But all of them had come by land routes, coming down into the Indo-Gangetic plains from the rugged mountain passages of the northwest, which was the only defenseless border of a land. Otherwise, India is perfectly isolated from the rest of the world. All kinds of invaders–Aryans, Yueh-chis, Kushans, Huns brought no culture of their own with them, but all were gradually absorbed into Hindu society. Then Muslims came and retained their separate identity up to a point. But, for the first time in the 15th century, an entirely different type of invader arrived from the sea, a tiny European group and made their landfall on India's shores.

The first European power, which came to India, was the army of Alexander the Great in 327-326 B.C. His established satraps in the northwest were collapsed after he left. Later, trade was conducted between Indian states and the Roman Empire by Greeco-Roman and Egyptian sailors reaching India by sail on the Red and Arabian Seas. The spice trade between India and Europe was one of the main driving forces of the world economy in those periods.

In 1498 A.D., a Portuguese sailor Vasco da Gama's three small ships and hundred and sixty men landed in the spacious harbour of Calicut.

European culture that was started around tenth century

was bursting with energy, creative imagination and constructive visions. Europeans were inspired by a strong feeling of historical destiny that was unknown to other civilisation. They had an unshakable belief in the perfectibility of man and of human conditions. Compared with the refined Asians, they were crude and rough: but they had tremendous vitality and faith, and a bold determination to make their views available to all human races. They believed that life and creation has a purpose, humans are on earth to make sure that the message was delivered, and they were going to ensure that it would be fulfilled

Many Asians understood that these strange Europeans who came from other side of the globe had some inner mainspring which gave them mysterious power, a kind of psychological strength. It was a personal skill and individual initiative, a strength and continuity of purpose that made the difference.

Unlike early invaders in India, European's purpose to come to India was trade. So, one company after another came into being: The English East India Company secured a trading monopoly from 1600 A.D. Portuguese East India Company (*Companhia da Índia Oriental)* came into existence in 1628. The United East India Company of Netherlands was incorporated in 1602; The Danish came in 1616; the French East India Company was formed in 1664; Austrian Ostend East-India Company was established in 1722; the Swedish East India Company was followed in 1722.

Colonial India refers to regions of the Indian Subcontinent and Maharajahs under European power through trade and conquest.

The search for the wealth and prosperity of India by Europeans led the discovery of Americas by Christopher Columbus. But, at the end of the 15th century Portuguese sailor Vasco da Gama arrived India by circumnavigating Africa and re-established direct trade links after Roman period.

Trading competition brought other European powers to

India. Because Mughal Empire collapsed in the early 18th century, and then the Maratha Empire was destabilised after the third battle of Panipat, the unstable Indian states were progressively controlled by the Europeans through dependent Indian rulers.

1510-1961 A.D.—Portuguese

The closing of the traditional trade routes in western Asia by the Ottomans and enmity with the Italian states, pushed Portugals in search of an alternate sea route to India. After the decline of the Roman Empire's sea-borne trade with India, the Portuguese were the next Europeans to arrive for the purpose of trade. The first successful voyage to India was made by Vasco da Gama. In 1498, he arrived at Calicut, now in Kerala. Portugal's Northern Province included settlements at Daman, Diu, Chaul, Goa, Baçaim, Salsette, and Mumbai. Bombay (Mumbai) was given to the British crown in 1661 as part of the dowry to Catherine of Braganza.

Vasco da Gama lands at Calicut, May 20, 1498

First in India, Colonial Era began in 1502 AD when the Portuguese established the first European trade centre at Kollam, Kerala. In 1510 Afonso de Albuquerque, viceroy of India, introduced a policy of marrying Portuguese soldiers and sailors with local Indian girls. He offered lands and subsidies to Portuguese men who would marry native women. Portuguese family names such as Silva, Sousa, and Pereira are so common in India. Another aspect of the Portuguese presence was the intention to evangelise and promote Catholicism in India. In this process the Jesuits played an important role. The Jesuit Missionary Saint Francis Xavier is strongly revered among the Catholics of India.

After India's independence from British in 1947, Portugal refused to agree to India's request to hand over the control of its Indian territories. In December 1961, India invaded and occupied Goa, Daman and Diu ending 450 years of Portuguese rule in India.

1605–1825 A.D.—Dutch

Dutch trading ships on the Coromandel Coast 1680

The Dutch East India Company founded trading stations on different parts along the Indian coast. For some time they controlled the Malabar southwest coast, the Coromandel southeastern coast and Surat from 1616-1795. They conquered Ceylon (Sri Lanka) from Portuguese. The Dutch also established trading centers in Travancore and coastal Tamil Nadu, Rajshahi in modern day Bangladesh, Pipely, Hugli-Chinsura, Murshidabad in modern day West Bengal, Balasore in Orissa, Ava, Arakan, Syriam in Myanmar (Burma). Later Dutch colonies were occupied by Britain.

1620-1869 A.D.—Danish

Denmark was a small colonial power that existed in India. It established trading centres in Tranquebar (Travancore) in Tamil Nadu (1620); Serampore in West Bengal (1755) and the Nicobar Islands (1750s). Their last Danish settlement was sold to the British in 1845 A.D.

1674-1954 A.D.—French

Following the Portuguese, Dutch and Danish, the French also established trading places in India. In 1674, they established their establishment in Pondicherry on the Coromandel Coast in southeastern India. Later French settlements are Chandernagore in Bengal, Yanam in Andhra Pradesh, Mahe, and Karaikal. The French were continuously in war with the Dutch, and later on mainly with the British in India. At the peak of French power in the mid-18th century,

Dupleix meeting the Soudhabar of the Deccan, Murzapha Jung

the French occupied large areas of southern India, northern Andhra Pradesh and Orissa. Between 1744 and 1761, the British and the French repeatedly attacked one another and conquered each other's forts and towns. Eventually, British decisively defeated the French in Bengal in the Battle of Plassey in 1757 and in the southeast in 1761 in the Battle of Wandiwash. Then the British East India Company became the supreme military and political power in Southern India and in Bengal. The territories of Pondicherry, Karaikal, Yanam, Mahé and Chandernagore were returned to France in 1816. Later they were integrated with the Republic of India after its independence in 1947.

1612–1947 A.D.—British India

By the middle of the 19th century, the British had achieved direct or indirect control over almost all of India. India was the most populous and valuable colony of the British Empire. The important characteristics of the colonial world were the overwhelming importance of India in the whole scheme of European imperialism with and without the British Empire. India, with its great resources, hundreds of millions of human beings, and high standards of civilisation, weighed twice as much as all other colonies put together. In order to protect themselves on the Indian subcontinent, the British were ambitious to conquer the entire India. Then, in order to protect this whole political complex, the British were motivated to absorb India's neighbours–Ceylon, Burma, some Himalayan states, the northwestern part of the Pathans and Baluchistan. Also they sent military expeditions to Afghanistan and Tibet and brought them within the British realm of influence. The British was determined to occupy a great part of the coast of Arabia, the Persian Gulf, and southern half of Persia. And then moving towards the east coast of Africa, they occupied Zanzibar and its African surrounding, and established themselves securely in South Africa in order to protect one of the routes of India. In the east, they occupied Malaya and Singapore, and some parts of Borneo, the whole of it attached to the huge continent of Australia. The huge Indian Ocean itself had become a British lake becoming a steely triangle of South Africa, India and Australia. Then approaches to the Indian Ocean had to be guarded: the British clung tenaciously to Gibraltar, and Malta, acquired Cyprus and occupied Egypt, and control of the Suez Canal. In this whole scheme the central position of India was so well acknowledged that most consular and many diplomatic posts in the Orient were employed by and financed by British India. It became the "Jewel of the Crown" to British.

In 1857, a local rebellion by an army of sepoys escalated into the Rebellion of 1857. Many Indians were unhappy with the East India Company. Its economic policies made most people poor. British-run police and law courts were inadequate or corrupt. Within their army, the British officers had little respect for their Indian soldiers or sepoys, and in some cases they promoted conversion to Christianity. One incident triggered the massive revolt. A new type of greased cartridge was issued for the sepoys rifles. Word spread that the grease was beef and pork fat. To load a cartridge, sepoys had to bite off the greased tip. The sepoys refused to use them: Hindus because they considered the cow as sacred; the Muslims because they considered the pig as unclean. The sepoys rebelled against British and mutinied, attacking and killing their British officers.

The Rebellion took six months to suppress with heavy loss of life on both sides. As a result, British government assumed direct control over India. The new British Raj appointed governor-general administered India and Queen Victoria was crowned Empress of India. The East India Company was dissolved in 1858.

This mutiny changed the shape of the British Empire.

The Act for the Better Government of India is an Act of the parliament of the United Kingdom (21 & 22 Vict. c. 106) passed on August 2, 1858. Its provisions called for the liquidation of the British East India Company (who had up to this point been ruling British India under the auspices of Parliament) and the transmission of its functions to the British Crown. Lord Palmerston, then-prime minister of the United Kingdom, introduced a bill for the transfer of control of the Government of India from the East India Company to the Crown, to correct the grave defects in the existing system.

The main provisions of the bill were :

- The Company's territories in India were to be vested on the Queen, the Company should cease to exercise its power and control over these territories. India should be governed in the Queen's name.
- The Queen's Principal Secretary of State received the powers and duties of the Company's Court of Directors. A council of fifteen members was appointed to assist the Secretary of State for India. The council became an advisory body in Indian affairs. For all the communications between Britain and India, the Secretary of State became the real channel.
- The Secretary of State for India was empowered to send some secret dispatches to India directly without consulting the Council. He was also authorized to constitute special committees of his Council.
- The Crown was empowered to appoint a Governor-General and the Governors of the Presidencies.
- Provision for the creation of an Indian Civil service under the control of the Secretary of State.

- All the property of the East India Company was transferred to the Crown. The Crown also assumed the responsibilities of the Company as they related to treaties, contracts, and so forth.

The Act guided in a new period of Indian history bringing about the end of Company rule in India. The era of the new British Raj existed until independence was given to India and Pakistan in August 1947.

Through the contact with European ideas and institutions, gradually a slow reform movement developed into the Indian Independence Movement. This independence movement accomplished its objective with the independence of India on August 15, 1947.

British India and the Native States

The British India included regions directly administered by Britain, in addition to the princely states administered by individual kings under the sovereignty of the British Crown. In its Interpretation Act of 1889, the British Parliament implemented the following definitions:

The expression *British India* shall mean all territories and places within Her Majesty's dominions were governed by Her Majesty through the Governor-General of India, or through any Governor or other officer subordinate to the Governor-General of India.

The expression *India* shall mean British India together with any territories of a Native Prince or Chief under the paramount authority of Her Majesty; exercised through the Governor-General of India, or through any Governor or other officer subordinate to the Governor-General of India. (52 & 53 Vict. cap. 63, sec. 18)

Major provinces

At the end of the 20th century, British India consisted of eight provinces that were ruled either by a Governor or a Lieutenant-Governor. The following table lists their areas and populations.

Minor provinces

In addition, there were a few minor provinces that were administered by a Chief Commissioner.

Princely States

A Princely State, also called Native State or Indian State, was a sovereign entity of British rule in India that was not directly governed by the British, but by an Indian king or ruler under a form of indirect rule. Military, foreign affairs, and communications power were under British control. In August 1947, when India became independent from Britain, there were 565 princely states.

Dalhousie vigorously encouraged the extension of irrigation canal systems and railways. During his administration, construction of approximately 500 miles of the Ganges Canal, a source of irrigation water for a vast area was completed.

Laying telegraph lines linking to the main centers of India was completed during Dalhousie's term. Rapid transmission of information on politics, security, trade, and industry, and for personal messages of individuals was implemented encompassing around 4,500 miles of lines.

Province of British India	*Area (in thousands of square miles)*	*Population (in millions)*	*Chief Administrative Officer*
Burma	170	9	Lieutenant-Governor
Bengal (including present-day Bangaladesh, West Bengal, Bihar and Orissa)	151	75	Lieutenant-Governor
Madras	142	38	Governor-in-Council
Bombay	123	19	Governor-in-Council
United Provinces (present-day Uttar Pradesh and Uttarakhand)	107	48	Lieutenant-Governor
Central Provinces (including Berar)	104	13	Chief Commissioner
Punjab	97	20	Lieutenant-Governor
Assam	49	6	Chief Commissioner

Minor Province	*Area (in thousands of square miles)*	*Population (in thousands)*	*Chief Administrative Officer*
North West Frontier Province	16	2,125	Chief Commissioner
British Baluchistan (British Administered territory)	46	308	British Political Agent in Baluchistan served as *ex-officio* Chief Commissioner
Coorg	1.6	181	British Resident in Mysore served as *ex-officio* Chief Commissioner
Ajmer-Merwara	2.7	477	British Political Agent in Rajputana served as *ex-officio* Chief Commissioner
Andaman and Nicobar Islands	3	25	Chief Commissioner

The Governor-Generals and Viceroys—Events/Accomplishments

Viceroy	*Period of Tenure*	*Events/Accomplishments*
Charles Canning	1 Nov 1858 - 21 Mar 1862	• 1858 reorganisation of British Indian Army • Construction begins (1860): University of Bombay, University of Madras, and University of Calcutta • Indian Penal Code passed into law in 1860 • Upper *Doab* famine of 1860–61 • Indian Councils Act 1861 • Establishment of Archaeological Survey of India in 1861 • James Wilson, financial member of Council of India reorganised customs, imposes income tax, and created paper currency • Indian Police Act of 1861. Creation of Imperial Police later known as Indian Police Service
Lord Elgin	21 Mar 1862- 20 Nov 1863	• Dies prematurely in Dharamsala
Sir John Lawrence	12 Jan 1864- 12 Jan 1869	• Anglo-Bhutan Duar War (1864–1865) • Orissa famine of 1866 • Rajputana famine of 1869 • Creation of Department of Irrigation • Creation of Imperial Forestry Service in 1867 • Possession of Nicobar Islands in 1869
Lord Mayo	12 Jan 1869- 8 Feb 1872	• Creation of Department of Agriculture • Major extension of railways, roads, and canals • Indian Councils Act of 1870 • Creation of Andaman and Nicobar Islands as a Chief Commissionership (1872) • Assassination of Lord Mayo in the Andamans

Viceroy	*Period of Tenure*	*Events/Accomplishments*
Lord Northbrook	3 May 1872- 12 Apr 1876	• Mortalities in Bihar famine of 1873–74 prevented by importation of rice from Burma • Gaikwad of Baroda dethroned for inefficient government; dominions continued to a child ruler • Indian Councils Act of 1874 • Visit of the Prince of Wales, future Edward VII in 1875–76
Lord Lytton	12 Apr 1876- 8 Jun 1880	• Baluchistan established as a Chief Commissionership • Queen Victoria (in absence) proclaimed Empress of India at Delhi Durbar of 1877 • Great Famine of 1876–78: 5.25 million dead; reduced relief offered at expense of Rs.8 crore • Creation of Famine Commission of 1878–80 under Sir Richard Strachey • Indian Forest Act of 1878 • Second Anglo-Afghan War. 1878-1880
Lord Ripon	8 Jun 1880- 13 Dec 1884	• End of Second Anglo-Afghan War Repeal of Vernacular Press Act of 1878. Compromise on the Ilbert Bill • Local Government Acts extend self-government from towns to country • University of Punjab established in Lahore in 1882 • Famine Code promulgated in 1883 by the Government of India • Creation of the Education Commission • Creation of indigenous schools, especially for Muslims • Repeal of import duties on cotton and other tariffs • Railway extension
Lord Dufferin	13 Dec 1884- 10 Dec 1888	• Passage of Bengal Tenancy Bill • Third Anglo-Burmese War • Joint Anglo-Russian Boundary Commission appointed for the Afghan frontier

Viceroy	Period of Tenure	Events/Accomplishments
		• Russian attack on Afghans at Panjdeh (1885). The Great Game (conflict between British and Russian Empires) in full play • Report of Public Services Commission of 1886-87 • Creation of Imperial Civil Service • University of Allahabad established in 1887 • Queen Victoria's Jubilee, 1887
Lord Lansdowne	10 Dec 1888- 11 Oct 1894	• Strengthening of NW Frontier defense • Creation of Imperial Service Troops consisting of regiments contributed by the princely states • Gilgit Agency leased in 1899 • British Parliament passes Indian Councils Act of 1892 opening the Imperial Legislative Council to Indians • Revolution in princely state of Manipur and subsequent reinstatement of ruler • High point of The Great Game. Establishment of the Durand Line between British India and Afghanistan • Railways, roads, and irrigation works begun in Burma • Border between Burma and Siam finalized in 1893 • Fall of the Rupee, resulting from the steady depreciation of silver currency worldwide (1873–93) • Indian Prisons Act of 1894
Lord Elgin	11 Oct 1894- 6 Jan 1899	• Reorganisation of Indian Army (from Presidency System to the four Commands) • Pamir agreement Russia, 1895 • The Chitral Campaign (1895), the Tirah Campaign (1896–97) • Indian famine of 1896–97 beginning in Bundelkhand • Bubonic plague in Bombay (1896)

Viceroy	*Period of Tenure*	*Events/Accomplishments*
		• Bubonic plague in Calcutta (1898) • Riots in wake of plague prevention measures • Establishment of Provincial Legislative Councils in Burma and Punjab
Lord Curzon	6 Jan 1899- 18 Nov 1905	• Creation of the North West Frontier Province under a Chief Commissioner (1901) • Indian famine of 1899–1900 • Return of the bubonic plague, 1 million deaths • Financial Reform Act of 1899 • Gold Reserve Fund created for India • Punjab Land Alienation Act • Inauguration of Department of Commerce and Industry • Death of Queen Victoria (1901) • Dedication of the Victoria Memorial Hall, Calcutta as a national gallery of Indian antiquities, art, and history • Coronation Durbar in Delhi (1903) • Edward VII (in absence) proclaimed Emperor of India • Francis Younghusband's British expedition to Tibet (1903–04) • North-Western Provinces (previously Ceded and Conquered Provinces) and Oudh renamed as United Provinces in 1904 • Reorganisation of Indian Universities Act (1904) • Systemisation of preservation and restoration of ancient monuments by Archaeological Survey of India with Indian Ancient Monument Preservation Act. • Inauguration of agricultural banking with Cooperative Credit Societies Act of 1904 • Partition of Bengal (1905). New province of East Bengal and Assam under a Lieutenant-Governor

Viceroy	*Period of Tenure*	*Events/Accomplishments*
Lord Minto	18 Nov 1905- 23 Nov 1910	• Creation of the Railway Board • Anglo-Russian Convention of 1907 • Government of India Act of 1909 (also Minto-Morley Reforms) • Appointment of Indian Factories Commission in 1909 • Establishment of Department of Education in 1910
Lord Hardinge	23 Nov 1910- 4 Apr 1916	• Visit of King George V and Queen Mary in 1911 • Commemoration as Emperor and Empress of India at last Delhi Durbar • King George V announces creation of new city of New Delhi to replace Calcutta as capital of India • Indian High Courts Act of 1911 • Indian Factories Act of 1911 • Construction of New Delhi, 1912-1929 • World War I, Indian Army in: Western Front, Belgium, 1914; German East Africa (Battle of Tanga), 1914; Mesopotamian Campaign (Battle of Ctesiphon), 1915; Siege of Kut, 1915-16; Battle of Galliopoli, 1915-16 • Passage of Defense of India Act 1915
Lord Chelmsford	4 Apr 1916- 2 Apr 1921	• Indian Army in: Mesopotamian Campaign (Fall of Baghdad, 1917); Sinai and Palestine Campaign (Battle of Megiddo, 1918) • Passage of Rowlatt Act, 1919 • Government of India Act of 1919 (also Montagu-Chelmsford Reforms) • Jallianwala Bagh Massacre, 1919 • Third Anglo-Afghan War, 1919 • University of Rangoon established in 1920
Lord Reading	2 Apr 1921- 3 Apr 1926	• University of Delhi established in 1922 • Indian Workers Compensation Act of 1923
Lord Irwin	3 Apr 1926- 18 Apr 1931	• Indian Trade Unions Act of 1926 • Indian Forest Act, 1927

Viceroy	*Period of Tenure*	*Events/Accomplishments*
		• Appointment of Royal Commission of Indian Labour, 1929 • Indian Constitutional Round Table Conference, London, 1930-32 • Gandhi-Irwin Pact, 1931
Lord Willingdon	18 Apr 1931 -18 Apr 1936	• New Delhi inaugurated as capital of India, 1931 • Indian Workmen's Compensation Act of 1933 • Indian Factories Act of 1934 • Royal Indian Air Force created in 1932 • Indian Military Academy established in 1932 • Government of India Act of 1935.· Creation of Reserve Bank of India
Lord Linlithgow	18 Apr 1936- 1 Oct 1943	• Indian Payment of Wages Act of 1936 • Burma administered independently after 1937 with creation of new cabinet position, Secretary of State, for India and Burma • Indian Provincial Elections of 1937 • Cripps' mission to India, 1942 • Indian Army in Middle East Theatre of World War II (East African campaign, 1940, Anglo-Iraqi War, 1941, Syria-Lebanon campaign, 1941, Anglo-Soviet invasion of Iran, 1941) • Indian Army in North African campaign (Operation Compass, Operation Crusader, First Battle of El Alamein, Second Battle of El Alamein) • Indian Army in Battle of Hong Kong, Battle of Malaya, Battle of Singapore • Burma Campaign of World War II begins in 1942
Lord Wavell	1 Oct 1943- 21 Feb 1947	• With 2.5 million men Indian Army becomes the largest all-volunteer force in history • World War II: Burma Campaign, 1943-45 (Battle of Kohima, Battle of Imphal) • Bengal famine of 1943

Viceroy	*Period of Tenure*	*Events/Accomplishments*
		• Indian Army in Italian campaign (Battle of Monte Cassino) • British Labor Party wins UK General Election of 1945 with Clement Attlee as prime minister • 1946 Cabinet Mission to India • Indian Elections of 1946
Lord Mountbatten	21 Feb 1947- 15 Aug 1947	• India Office changed to Burma Office, and Secretary of State for India and Burma to Secretary of State for Burma • Indian Independence Act 1947 of the British Parliament enacted on 18 July 1947 • Radcliffe Award, August 1947 • Partition of India

The cable linking Britain and India was laid in 1865. The first attempt was made to put underwater cable across the Hooghly in Calcutta in 1839.

In 1854, a government postal service was established in India. Mail could be sent any distance within the country at the low cost. This facility served not only individuals, but also people in remote villages also.

Dalhousie significantly improved the technological infrastructure that transformed the everyday life of both state and people in many ways.

The revolt of 1857 did not reverse the improvements in public services.

The British felt disappointed with Indian reaction to social change. Until the rebellion, they enthusiastically implemented social reforms, like the ban on *sahagamana* tradition by Lord William Bentinck. They experienced that traditions and customs in India were too strong and too rigid to be changed easily. As a result, British did not make further social interventions, especially regarding religion.

British Life

After 1770 A.D., the British people developed garden suburbs marked with large Palladian mansions. Although English residents in Indian cities, often consisting of wealthy officers with elaborate lavish lifestyle, lack of resistance to tropical disease had succumbed to early death. In places like Park Street Cemetery, Calcutta, they erected towering monuments to announce their dominance.

Two settlements were created between European and "natives". One was a settlement of Anglo-Indians, near the railway stations. Anglo-Indians were often seen as an embarrassment to the British, but a place for them was established in railway employment because their loyalty could be trusted. The second colony was with Bengalis, whose numbers grew in upscale cities and towns as their literacy provided them an advantage in government employment.

Beyond their separate urban residential areas, the

British went further from disease-infested land escaping to the Himalayas in the north and Nilgiri Hills in the south. In 1865, John Lawrence as a viceroy made Simla the regular summer capital of British India.

Eventually, missionaries and princes created "hill stations" of their own in such places as Missouri and Kodaikanal, Ootakamund, Murree and Mount Abu. Women and children often came to the hills for several months while men stayed behind, visiting whenever they could. Fear of specific disease was an important concern than a range of anxieties about the dangers of life in India. The hills were meant to reproduce England. Lord Lytton arrived Ootakamund in 1870's in a rainy season as a viceroy. He was excited to see such a beautiful English rain and such a delicious English mud. English cottages and country houses were built on the hills. In places of civil stations in the plains there were gardens of English flowers, English fruits and vegetables, a bandstand, and a mall. The buildings of half-timbered were built to reproduce an English country town. There were many hill schools. But, European children were sent home for schooling whenever funds permitted. The colonial British themselves returned home after their retirement.

There were many developments by the early 1880s. A new middle-class of Indian people had arisen and increased in number across the country. This hope came from the success in education and its benefits such as employment in the Indian Civil Service. Queen Victoria's proclamation of 1858 in which she declared, "We hold ourselves bound to the natives of our Indian territories by the same obligation of duty which bind us to all our other subjects" also boosted hope in Indian educated class. More importantly, the encouragement came from the works of contemporaneous Oriental scholars like Monier-Williams and Max Muller, who were portraying ancient India as a great civilisation.

On December 28, 1885, professionals and intellectuals from this middle-class—many educated Indians at the new British established universities in Bombay, Calcutta, and

Alan Octavian Hume

Madras, and familiar with the ideas of British political philosophers—founded the Indian National Congress in Bombay. Alan Octavian Hume was one of the founders of the Indian National Congress—a political party that was later led the Indian Independence Movement. He called for more Indian participation in provincial legislative councils and improved Indian access to civil service jobs.

After retiring from the civil services, Hume felt that the people of India had developed a sense of hopelessness and decided to do something.

Hume attempted to start an organisation by reaching out to selected alumni of the University of Calcutta. He wrote his inspiring thoughts in his letter on 1883,

> "If only fifty men, good and true, can be found to join as founders, the thing can be established and the further development will be comparatively easy ... And if even the leaders of thought are all either such poor creatures, or so selfishly wedded to personal concerns that they dare not strike a blow for their country's sake, then justly and rightly are they kept down and trampled on, for they deserve nothing better. Every nation secures precisely as good a Government as it merits. If you picked men, the most highly educated of the nation, scorning personal ease and selfish objects, make a resolute struggle to secure greater freedom for yourselves and your country, a more impartial administration, a larger share in the management of your own affairs, then we, your friends, are wrong and our adversaries right, then are Lord Ripon's noble aspirations for your good fruitless and visionary, then, at present at any rate all hopes of progress are at an end and India truly

neither desires nor deserves any better Government than she enjoys. Only, if this-be so, let us hear no more factious, peevish complains that you are kept in leading strings and treated like children, for you will have provided yourself such. Men know how to act. Let there be no more complaining of Englishmen being preferred to you in all important offices, for if you lack that public spirit, that highest form of altruistic devotion that leads men to subordinate private ease to the public weal – that patriotism that has made Englishmen what they are – then rightly are these preferred to you, rightly and inevitably have they become your rulers. And rulers and task-masters they much continue let the yoke gall your shoulders never so sorely, until you realize and stand prepared to act upon the eternal truth that self-sacrifice and unselfishness are the only unfailing guides to freedom and happiness."

Also he published a poem in Calcutta in 1886 summarising his feeling :

Sons of Ind, why sit ye idle,
Wait ye for some Deva's aid?
Buckle to, be up and doing!
Nations by themselves are made!

Are ye Serfs or are ye Freemen,
Ye that grovel in the shade?
In your own hands rest the issues!
By themselves are nations made! ...

Awakening the Consciousness of Indian People

Slowly, Indian people started to recognise their inability to defend themselves. As a consequence, activities to protest British government began in many parts of India.

Even though the *swadeshi* clothes were more expensive and less comfortable than its Lancashire clothing, they were worn by people throughout India as a sign of national pride. The movement also encouraged indigenous industrial progress in India. As a result, the Tata Iron and Steel Company were founded in Jamshedpur, Bengal in 1907.

The Arya Samaj supported Cow Protection Societies in their campaign, and also organised reconversion events for the purpose of welcoming Muslims back to Hinduism.

The Morley-Minto Reforms were a landmark. Gradually, the elective principles were introduced for membership in Indian legislative councils and the electorate was limited to a small group of upper-class Indians. These elected members increasingly became an opposition group in the official government. Afterwards, the communal electorates were extended to other communities, and made politics of Indian tendency by group identification through religion.

In 1915, Mohandas Karamchand Gandhi returned to India from South Africa. Gandhi followed the advice of his mentor Gopal Krishna Gokhale. Undertaking the challenge of holding the community together and confronting the colonial authority, Gandhi created a technique of non-violent resistance called *Satyagraha.* He opposed the British government through Ahimsa or non-violence to obtain the freedom.

In 1920, when British government resisted, Gandhi started his campaign of non-cooperation, provoking many Indians to return British awards and honors, to resign from civil service, and to boycott British goods. Besides, Gandhi reorganised the Congress, converting it into a mass movement and opening its membership to the poorest Indians also.

Gandhi started the Quit India movement in August 1942, demanding the immediate withdrawal of the British from India or face nationwide civil disobedience. Along with other Congress leaders, Gandhi was imprisoned and the country exploded in violent demonstrations conducted by students and after by peasant political groups in Bihar and Bengal.

Widespread agitation forced Britain to make decision about India's independence.

The Plan for Partition: 1947

Exhausted by recently concluded World War II and

realising that no consent at Britain, any international support, and increasing restlessness in India, the Labour government in Britain decided to end the British rule in India. In early 1947, Britain announced its intention of transferring power.

On August 14, 1947, the new Dominion of Pakistan came into existence. Muhammad Ali Jinnah sworn in as Pakistan's first Governor General in Karachi. The following day, August 15, 1947, India became an independent country. In New Delhi, Jawaharlal Nehru assumed the office of the Prime Minister.

English Education

The awakening of India's head and heart took place at a time when India was firmly under British control. This awakening was ignited by the association between European culture and India's solidified civilisation. Indians were impressed by recognising that European culture was in full development and had generated the Industrial Revolution.

The awakening took place in an Anglo-Indian atmosphere and expressed itself in a relatively new linguistic medium: English replaced Persian as the universal language of India (before Persian had replaced Sanskrit); the local vernaculars developed an entirely new group of autonomous literatures in various provinces.

A Company civil servant, Charles Grant, thought an idea of establishing a new educational network to teach English and impart European culture to Indians, thinking that the old Indian education was responsible for India's apparent decadence. Christian missionaries followed up his suggestion, and many great educational establishments started to teach English in humble fashion. Subsequently, any effort made by the Anglo-Indian government to encourage Indian learning was opposed by enlightened Indians. Chief among them was Raja Ram Mohan Roy, whose powerful protest against the establishment of a Sanskrit College in Calcutta is considered as a classic. Reiterating this decision in a petition to Governor General Lord Amherst, he wrote that "The Sanskrit system of education would be the best calculated to keep this country in darkness if such had been the policy of British legislature. But as the improvement of the native population is the object of the Government, it will consequently promote a more liberal enlightened system of instruction, embracing mathematics, natural philosophy, chemistry and anatomy....."

Englishmen were aware of the dangers of a new English education system. They always feared that to train the Indians the new civilisation of the West in English with its newly attained and progressively developing mastery over the forces of nature was extremely threatening to their existence. They believed that keeping Indians in dark within the narrow boundaries of their traditional culture is the secured way of longevity of the British Empire in India. Sir Richard Temple compared the potential discontent in the hearts of the educated natives and contrasted it with the loyalty of the uneducated Indians.

As a consequence, Missionaries like Alexander Duff, administrators like Lord Bentinck established the Medical College in Calcutta. From 1835 onwards, European learning through the medium of English language was revolutionised the whole educational system of India. The result was a great gap between the small English-educated classes and the great illiterate or vernacular-educated masses. The gap was also widened between the Hindu middle classes and the Hindu upper classes, who remained faithful to their traditional learning, and the Indian Muslims, who remained aloof from Western education altogether. To a large extent, this awakening of India was due to the result of evolution of liberalism in Europe itself—historic changes in Britain, such as, the Catholic Emancipation Act (1829), the Reform Bill (1832), the Abolition of Slavery (1833), and the New Poor Law (1834) had passed.

The other side of the benefit was that it gave India something it had missed since the days of Ashoka: cultural unification and linguistic unity. Although English influence affected about only one per cent of the population, it enabled these small elite to have free intellectual communication. Future Indian Nationalists to come were born in English language atmosphere. The Indian press in English had already developed to a remarkable extent in the nineteenth century and early in the twentieth century. More than thousand books in English were published each year. All major discussions and controversies on technical or political took place in English.

Three points must be made about this early group of the English educated.

First, English educated were representatives of the old professional elites in each region. It had a long-term consequence throughout the country on non-elites, for example, non-Brahmins in the west and south. Best and highest opportunities were afforded to the small percentage of Brahmins who had acquired western education.

Secondly, English connected people across India. It was a necessary component for creating political ties and movements because English was the cosmopolitan language throughout the world. A large portion of the English-educated men and women had experience in the areas like government, law, and journalism.

Thirdly, the English-educated people better understood the new phrases of liberal politics and provided competition to the traditional notables. When electoral politics were introduced, frequently they took part in election.

The gap between the British-educated upper classes and the rest of the population increased gradually. Yet, it is this education and the use of the English tongue that gave real rational unity to India. If this had not happened, if the British had concentrated on developing the vernaculars, there would not have been one Indian nationalism, but many; local loyalties of Bengalis and Punjabis, Marathas and Gujaratis, Tamils and Telugus, Kannadas would have taken the upper hand and destroyed the fabric of all-Indian unity. Regardless of the whole thing, modern India was shaped by this European education and strongly united by the use of English.

Rabindranath Tagore gave a remarkable description of the alteration in sentiment that had taken place in his generation: "As I look back on the vast stretch of years that lie behind me, I am struck by the change that has taken place... our direct contact with the larger world of men was linked up with the contemporary history of the English people . . . the educated of those days had recourse to English language and literature, their days and nights were eloquent with the stately declamations of Burke, with Macaulay's long rolling sentences, discussions centered upon Shakespeare's drama and Byron's poetry and above all upon the large-hearted liberalism of the nineteenth century English politics. At the time, though tentative attempts were being made to gain our national independence, at heart we had not lost faith in the generosity of the English race..."

The true expression of modern India flourished in the vernacular languages, before it was commonly used for oral communication and poetic expression. Here again, the leader was Raja Ram Mohan Roy, who promoted European culture and yet made Bengali a literary language. Even the vernaculars made strong imprint on English models and patterns rapidly blooming to life by the impact of English culture. One after another, the vernaculars became alive during the nineteenth century, offering new mediums of expression to scholars, novelists, dramatists, philosophers – the novelist Bankim Chandra Chattopadhyay, the dramatist Dinabandhu and the poet Rabindranath Tagore in Bengali and many more in Marathi, Gujarati and so on. It dragged the new Indian middle classes out of their lethargy.

Certainly, these vernaculars literature began to invigorate the sleeping nationalism of the Indians. One advantage in this awakening of nationalism was to kindle Indian interest in history.

The women began to play a role as writers and promoters of social reform. One outspoken woman princely ruler, the Begum of Bhopal, covered from head to foot in the garment *burqa* travelled extensively to encourage education for girls. Pandita Ramabai, educated in Sanskrit classics, travelled throughout India to campaign women's education and social reform, and wrote articles about her views. Widowed at age twenty-five, she travelled to England to learn English and pursued medical studies, and got converted to Christianity. In 1888, she established a home school for widows in Bombay and Poona. A Deccan Brahmin woman, Gangabai, established one of the most successful female institutions, the "Mahakali Pathshala" in Calcutta in 1893, intended to instill Hindu religious and moral principles. A Bengali Muslim, Begum Rokeya Sakhawat Hossain, set up schools for girls, condemned extreme seclusion, and wrote extensively, including a brilliant skit, *Sultana's Dream* in which the roles of men and women were reversed.

Social Reformers

Earlier civilisations who invaded India were able to assimilate Indian culture and were not able to preserve their separate identity for a long time. But, the British wanted to maintain their identity separately. The most intelligent Indians were profoundly puzzled at the view of British Empire whose heart was located at the other end of the earth, and kept pumping new blood into the imperial arteries to avoid a fatal dilution.

British organised with remarkable efficiency of the whole banking system, the new transportation network of rail and road, the extraction of minerals, the erection of power plants, the building of dams and digging of irrigation canals, while the Indian world went on weaving its endless and purposeless dreams, undisturbed with this western impact.

But while the more concrete-minded, practical people of the Far East felt the physical impact of Western power with agonizing keenness in the 19th century, the Indians felt the cultural impact with the same agonising keenness, only much earlier. In those days, every scheme of British was overwhelmed by the thoughtful Indians with a sense of the absolute superiority of the West: its complete monopoly of scientific knowledge in basic research and in technological application, the exuberant artistic creations, the vigorous literature, the dynamic outlook on life that contrasted so sharply with the complete stagnation that had solidified India's old Civilisation. A few farsighted Indians, who began the process of India's awakening started to promote full integration of India. The awakening took two different but complementary aspects: first an awakening of the head, and then an awakening of the heart – corresponding respectively to the two revolutionary activities of Raja Ram Mohan Roy and Ramakrishna. The keynote in both cases, philosophical and religious, intellectual and emotional, was the required agent of a fusion between East and West.

The general view of India during the Colonial Era was widespread. Even though it sounds erotic, it demonstrates the reality in some situations and circumstances. 18th century social reformers worked hard to change this view considerably.

- Indians are inherently incapable of adventurous behavior and do not venture beyond the boundaries of the Indian subcontinent (Kaalapaani syndrome).
- Indians are incapable of original, rational and creative ideas.
- Indians are incapable of independent thinking and are unquestioning in their adherence to authoritarian dogmas such as those in the Vedic texts, and are only capable of rote learning.
- Indians fundamentally have no intention in making progress and advancing in the modern world, and are lost in an ancient mind set.
- Everything good and worthwhile in the Indian subcontinent has been imported by the invaders, and the only indigenous characteristics are those like caste is natural to the Indian civilisation.
- Indian is pessimistic and will not make an effort to change his destiny which is written in stone the moment he is born.
- Caste system is an artifact of the Indian religious belief system, and that the India is inherently opposed to egalitarian ideas and is wedded to the racial and ethnic stratification of its own society.
- Indian is egregious in the manner in which he exploits his fellow Indian.
- Indian is lazy and sluggish.
- India has no sense of history and is even poorer at keeping records of his historical past.
- Religious beliefs of Indians are the root cause of their misfortunes.
- As a consequence of the above, the India is socially backward, morally corrupt, and always dependent upon west to reform the problems in Indian society.

Even though it sounds erotic, it demonstrates the reality in some situations and circumstances. 18th century social reformers worked hard to change this view considerably.

Macaulay argued that Indians could be transformed

through the systems of law, free trade, and education. He believed that Britain's mission was not to create just a class of Indians sufficiently well versed in English to help the British to rule the country, but to create the Indians with English in taste, in opinions, in morals and in intellect. As a result, he visualised, Indians would become independent and exemplify the imperishable empire of English arts, their morals, their literature and their laws in time.

1772–1833 A.D.—Raja Ram Mohan Roy

Raja Ram Mohan Roy was a writer, educationist, journalist, philosopher, politician, social reformer, theologian and humanist. He fought to liberate India from darkness, superstition and ignorance.

The great awakening was introduced by Raja Ram Mohan Roy late in the 18th century. His fantastic knowledge and amazing life symbolised this blend of East and West for which he worked hard all his life. Sunken in both Hindu and Muslim cultures, fluent in Arabic, Persian, Sanskrit, English, Hebrew, Greek and Latin languages, expelled by caste and family, lived for years thereafter in Benares and Tibet. He finally returned home in 1796. Campaigning vigorously against the monstrous distortions of centuries of sloth, corruption and inertia, which had inflicted on Hinduism, he tackled every social, political and cultural problem of his time.

Raja Ram Mohun Roy was an Indian religious, social, and educational reformer who questioned traditional Hindu culture and suggested different alternative methods of progress for Indian society during British rule. Influenced by the European Liberalism, he concluded that radical reform was necessary in Hinduism and in the social practices of the Hindus. Therefore, along with Dwarkanath Tagore and other Bengalis, he founded the Brahma Samaj, an influential Indian socio-religious reform movement to fight against social evils. "There is only one God, None equals Him. He has no end. He is present in all living beings" is the message of Brahma Samaj. It emphasised the idea of universal brotherhood. It did not acknowledge the differences of caste, creed, or nationality. Also it believed that in order to worship Him fixed place or time is not necessary.

Raja Ram Mohun Roy fought for the reformation of Hindu Law, conducted the protest against restrictions on the press, rallied against the oppressive land lords, and favored the English system of education in India.

His influence on politics, public administration, education, and religion was widely popular. He worked tirelessly to abolish the practice of sati, the Hindu funeral practice in which the widow immolates herself on her husband's funeral pyre. He demanded property inheritance rights for women.Roy published magazines in English, Hindi, Persian, and Bengali. He published Brahmanical Magazine in English in 1821. One notable magazine of his was the *Sambad Kaumudi*, published in 1821. In 1822, another publication was *Mirat-ul-Akbar* in Persian language.

1836-1886 A.D.—Ramakrishna Paramahamsa

Ramakrishna Paramahamsa was a famous mystic of 19th-century India. His religious school of thought led to the formation of the Ramakrishna Mission by his main disciple Swami Vivekananda. Both were prominent persons in the Bengal Renaissance and Hindu renaissance during the 19th and 20th century.

Ramakrishna was born in a poor Brahmin Vaishnava family in rural Bengal. He became a priest of the Dakshineswar Kali Temple, which had the influence of Bengali bhakti tradition. He began to look upon the image of the goddess Kali as his mother and the mother of the universe.

His first spiritual teacher was an ascetic woman expert in Tantra and Vaishnava bhakti. Later, an Advaita Vedanta teacher taught him non-dualistic meditation, and according to Ramakrishna, he experienced nirvikalpa samadhi under his supervision. He did his *sadhana* under teachers of Tantra, Vedanta and Vaishnava. Ramakrishna also experimented with other religions, mainly Islam and Christianity and realized that they all lead to the same God. Traditionally, he was not educated, but he attracted the attention of the middle class as well as Bengali intellectuals.

Ramakrishna met the influential Brahma Samaj leader Keshab Chandra Sen. Keshab Sen already had accepted Christianity and had separated from the Adi Brahma Samaj. Initially, Keshab had rejected idolatry, but under the influence of Ramakrishna he accepted Hindu polytheism and established the "New Dispensation" Nava Vidhan religious movement to preach a mixture of Hindu philosophy and Christian theology based on Ramakrishna's principles.

Following Keshab, other Brahma Samaj followers like Vijaykrishna Goswami began to respect Ramakrishna and propagated his ideals. As such, Ramakrishna succeeded in uniting several faiths and in reforming the character of some youths.

Ramakrishna always used to test his disciples before accepting them. He used some techniques, such as study of their chest (the redness, which disclosed the significant marks of ecstasies), their breathing capacity, and soundness of their nervous structure and circulation – all of which had to be excellent before they could undertake the exercises of deep concentration. One among of his chosen disciples was a remarkable man Swami Vivekananda, who eventually transformed Ramakrishna's mission into the language of service and brought his master's greatness to the attention of the world.

Ramakrishna interacted with Debendranath Tagore, the

father of Rabindranath Tagore, and Ishwar Chandra Vidyasagar, a prominent social worker. He had also met Swami Dayananda.

Ramakrishna's teachings made a strong impression on Calcutta's intellectuals and his spiritual movement indirectly aided nationalism as it rejected caste distinctions and religious prejudices.

Mahatma Gandhi, Jawaharlal Nehru, Sri Aurobindo, Max Muller and Leo Tolstoy have acknowledged Ramakrishna's contribution to humanity.

1863-1902 A.D.—Swami Vivekananda

Swami Vivekananda was the chief disciple of Sri Ramakrishna Paramahamsa and the founder of Ramakrishna Order. He introduced Hindu philosophy of Vedanta to America and Europe and raised Hinduism to the status of a major world religion during the end of the 19th century. Vivekananda is regarded as a major force in the restoration of Hinduism in modern India. He is best known for his inspiring speech starting with "Sisters and Brothers of America" introducing Hinduism at the Parliament of the World's Religions held at Chicago, USA in 1893 A.D. Narendranath Dutta, later Swami Vivekananda, was born in 1863 to an aristocratic Bengali family of Calcutta. His parents influenced his thinking: father by his rational mind and mother by her religious nature. While searching for a master who could directly demonstrate the reality of God, he came to Ramakrishna and became his disciple. Ramakrishna taught him Advaita Vedanta (non-dualism) and that all religions are true and they all lead to same goal, and service to humanity is the most efficient way to worship God.

Vivekananda

On his way to Chicago, Vivekananda visited Japan in 1893.

It was a period of military build-up in Japan, which led to the Sino-Japanese War and the Russo-Japanese War. Noticing ongoing preparations in Japan, Vivekananda wrote,

> "The Japanese seem to have fully awakened themselves to the necessity of the present times. They have a thoroughly organized army equipped with guns that one of their own officers has invented and which is said to be second to none. Then, they are continually increasing their navy."

About the industrial progress he observed,

> "The match factories are simply a sight to see, and they are bent upon making everything they want in their own country."

Vivekananda's philosophy of life started to widen gradually as he travelled all over India like a wandering monk. Wherever he went, he became increasingly conscious of the need for modernisation, for breaking with the past and for awakening the dormant potentials rather than destroying them. Inevitably, something new emerged in him, a crying need for a new dimension of human understanding that had always been sorely lacking in Indian consciousness: historical consciousness, the bold facing of historical reality – not just the prophetic instinct, but the detached, objective and scientific precision with which western culture was in the process of reusing mankinds history

Contrasting the speedy development of Japan with the situation back in India, he appealed his countrymen to come out of their narrow holes and have a look abroad as following:

> "Only I want that our young men should pay a visit to Japan and China every year. Especially to the Japanese, India is still the dreamland of everything high and good. And you, what are you? .. talking twaddle all your lives, vain talkers, what are you? Come, see these people, and then go and hide your faces in shame. A race of dotards, you lose your caste if you come out! Sitting down these hundreds of years with an ever-increasing load of crystallized superstition on your heads, for hundreds of

years spending all your energy upon discussing the touchable or untouchableness of this food or that, with all humanity crushed out of you by the continuous social tyranny of ages—what are you? And what are you doing now?.. promenading the sea-shores with books in your hands—repeating undigested stray bits of European brainwork, and the whole soul bent upon getting a thirty rupee clerkship, or at best becoming a lawyer—the height of young India's ambition—and every student with a whole brood of hungry children cackling at his heels and asking for bread! Is there not water enough in the sea to drown you, books, gowns, university diplomas, and all?"

After his memorable work in the west, Swamy Vivekananda arrived at Colombo on January 15, 1897. While in the west he gave speeches on India's spiritual tradition. On return to India, his speeches were about upliftment of the masses, eradication of superstition and caste virus, promotion of studies in science, industrialisation of the country, removal of poverty, and the end of the colonial rule. His speeches are well recorded in his fabulous book "Lectures from Colombo to Almora". These lectures have nationalistic passion and spiritual ideology. His speeches had tremendous influence on the Indian leaders as well as common people.

After visiting America (Lectures from Colombo to Almora):

"On the other hand my mission to America was not to the Parliament of Religions. That was not only something by the way, it is only an opening an opportunity, and for that we are very thankful to the members of the Parliament; but really, our thanks are due to the great people of the United States, the American nation, the warm hearted hospitable, great nation of America, where more than anywhere else, the feeling of brotherhood has been developed. An American meets you for five minutes on board, a train, and you are his friend, and the next moment he invites you as a guest to his home and opens the secret of his whole living there. That is the character of the American race, and we highly appreciate it. Their kindness to me is passed all narration; it would take me years yet to tell you how I have been treated by them most kindly and most wonderfully."

After visiting England (Lectures from Colombo to Almora):

"No one ever landed on English soil with more hatred in his heart for a race than I did for the English, and on this platform are present English friends who can bear witness to the fact; but the more I lived among them and saw how the machine was working—the English national life—and mixed with them, I found where the heart-beat of the nation was, and the more I loved them. There is none among you here present, my brothers, who loves the English people more than I do now. We have to see what is going on there, and you have to mix with them. As the philosophy, our national philosophy of the Vedanta, has summarised all misfortunes, all misery, as coming from that one cause, ignorance, here in also we must understand that the difficulties that arise between us and the English people are mostly due to that ignorance; we do not know them, they do not us."

Vivekananda asked Indian people to shun superstitions and follow true Hinduism in his "Lectures from Colombo to Almora".

"At the same time we must not forget that what I mean by the conquest of the world by spiritual thought is the sending out of the life-giving principles, not the hundreds of superstitions that we have been hugging to our hearts for centuries. These have to be weeded out even on this soil, and thrown aside, so that they may die for ever. These are the causes of the degradation of the race and will lead to softening of the brain. That brain which cannot think high and noble thoughts, which has lost all power of originality, which has lost all vigor, that brain which is always poisoning itself with all sorts of little superstitions passing under the name of religion, we must beware of.

"I would rather see every one of you rank atheists than superstitious fools, for the atheist is alive and you can make something out of him. But if superstition enters, the brain is gone, the brain is softening, and degradation has seized upon the life. Avoid these two. Brave, bold men, these are what we want. What we want is vigour in the blood, strength in the nerves, iron muscles and nerves of steel, not softening namby-pamby ideas.

"Come, be men! Kick out the priests who are always against progress, because they would never mend, their hearts would never become big. They are the offspring of centuries of superstition and tyranny. Root out priest craft first. Come, be men! Come out of your narrow holes and have a look abroad. See how nations are on the march! Do you love man? Do you love your country? Then come, let us struggle for higher and better things; look not back, no, not even if you see the dearest and nearest cry. Look not back, but forward!"

He spoke numerous times at the Parliament on topics connected to Hinduism. All his speeches at the Parliament stressed religious tolerance.

1828 A.D.—Brahma Samaj

Brahma Samaj was established by Dwarakanath Tagore and Raja Ram Mohan Roy in order to reform Brahmanism's practices. This caused the Bengal Renaissance in 19th century and revolutionised all religious, social and educational advance of the Hindu community in Bengal.

Actually, Brahma Samaj is an assembly of all kinds of people without distinction, meeting publicly for the moderate, orderly, religious and devout worship of Eternal and Immutable Being.

Excerpts of Trust Deed of 1830 about the basic principles of Brahma Samaj are:

1. A place of public meeting of all sorts and descriptions of people without distinction as shall behave and conduct themselves in an orderly sober religious and devout manner,

2. The worship and adoration of the Eternal Unsearchable and Immutable Being who is the Author and Preserver of the Universe, but not under or by any other name designation or title peculiarly used for and applied, to any particular being or beings by any man or set of men whatsoever,
3. That no graven image statue or sculpture, carving, painting, picture, portrait or the likeness of anything shall be admitted within the said messages, building, land, tenements, hereditaments and premise,
4. That no sacrifice, offering, oblation of any kind of thing shall ever be permitted therein, and that no animal or living creature shall within or on the said message building, land, tenements, hereditaments and premises be deprived of life either for religious purposes or for food,
5. That no eating or drinking (except such as shall be necessary by any accident for the preservation of life) feasting or rioting be permitted therein, or thereon,
6. That in conducting the said worship and adoration, no object, animate or inanimate, that has been, or is, or shall hereafter become or be recognised as an object of worship by any man or set of men shall be reviled or slightingly or contemptuously spoken of or alluded to, either in preaching, prayer or in the hymns or other mode of worship that may be delivered or used in the said message or building,
7. That no sermon, preaching, discourse, prayer or hymn be delivered, made or used in such worship but such as have a tendency to the promotion of the contemplation of the Author and Preserver of the Universe, to the promotion of charity, morality, piety, benevolence, virtue and the strengthening the bonds of union between men of all religious persuasions and creeds,
8. Also that a person of good repute and well known for his knowledge, piety and morality be employed by the said Trustees or the survivors or survivors of them or the heirs of such survivor or their or his assigns

as a resident superintendent and for the purpose of superintending the worship so to be performed as in hereinbefore stated and expressed,

9. That such worship is performed daily or least as often as once in seven days.

The members used to meet every Saturday. Hymns from Vedas and Upanishads were chanted by scholars. Religious discussions were held and Raja Ram Mohan Roy recited the religious poems composed by him. These meetings were open to all Brahmins and there was no formal organisation. Christian and Muslim boys sang songs in English and Persian. Many Hindus and foreigners used to attend these meetings.

Brahma Samaj remained at all times high-level organisation catering to intellectuals, strongly influenced by the British schools and colleges, and Christian institutions set up in India. Consequently, it was able to influence directly the British Government of India in its legislative reforms. But in spite of its large-scale social work, the Brahma-Samaj remained quite remote from the India masses.

In all fields of social reform, including abolition of the caste system, dowry system, and emancipation of women and improving the educational system, the Brahma Samaj reverberated the ideologies of the Bengal Renaissance.

It also supported social reform movements of Pandit Iswar Chandra Vidyasagar's widow re-marriage movement.

Doctrine

The following doctrines, as noted in Renaissance of Hinduism, are common to all varieties and offshoots of the Brahma Samaj:

- Brahma Samaj has no faith in any scripture as an authority
- Brahma Samaj has no faith in Avatars
- Brahma Samaj denounces polytheism and idol-worship
- Brahma Samaj is against caste restrictions

- Brahma Samaj believes in the doctrines of Karma and Rebirth optional

1869 A.D.—The Arya Samaj

The Arya Samaj was established by Swami Dayanand Saraswati as a reaction against the principles augmented by Raja Ram Mohun Roy. It attacked the Brahma Samaj for its pro-European and pro-Christian attitude. A great Sanskrit scholar Swami Dayanand wanted to revive the Vedic ideals and promoted Brahmacarya and Sannyasa. He believed implicitly in the ancient scriptures, rejecting Puranic Hinduism in favor of Vedic Hinduism. He emphasised that the Puranic texts have no Vedic sanction. Vedas alone are authoritative. God and the human soul are two distinct entities, different in nature and attributes, though they are inseparable from each other. They are synonymous to pervader and the pervaded. The doctrine of Karma and Samsara was accepted by the Arya Samaj. One of its main activities of Arya Samaj is Suddhi, a purification ceremony by which non-Hindus are converted to Hinduism. The depressed classes and Harijans are entitled to be provided with the sacred thread and are given equal status with other Hindus. The Arya Samaj also reclaimed many Hindus who had converted to Islam and Christianity previously. Sanghatan, organization of the Hindus for self-defence is one of the main principles of the Arya Samaj.

The Vedic Schools represented the first practical application of Swami Dayanand's vision of religious and social reform. Students were not allowed to perform traditional idol worship (murthipuja) at the school, but they were expected to perform *Sandhyavandana* and participate in *Agnihotra* twice a day. The study of Sanskrit was opened to non-Brahmins also. The important feature of the School was that only those texts which accepted by the authority of the Vedas were to be taught.

The ten Principles of the Arya Samaj:

Principle One: God is the original source of all that is true knowledge and all that is known by physical sciences.

Principle Two: God is existent, Conscious, All Beautitude, Formless, Almighty, Just, Merciful, Unbegotten, Infinite, Unchangeable, Beginningless, Incomparable, the support of All, the Lord or all, All-pervading, Omniscient and Controller of All from within, Evermature, Imperishable, Fearless, Eternal, Pure and Creator of the universe. IT alone must be worshipped.

Principle Three: The Vedas are the books of all True knowledge. It is the paramount duty of all Aryas to read them, to teach them to others, to listen to them and to recite them to others.

Principle Four: All persons should always be ready to accept the truth and renounce the untruth.

Principle Five: All acts ought to be performed in conformity with dharma (Righteousness and Duty) i.e. after due consideration of the truth and the untruth.

Principle Six: The primary object of the Arya Samaj is to do good to the whole world *i.e.,* to promote physical, spiritual and social progress of all humans.

Principle Seven: Your dealings with all should be regulated by love and due justice in accordance with the dictates of *dharma* (righteousness).

Principle Eight: *Avidyaa* (illusion and ignorance) is to be dispelled, and *Vidyaa* (realisation and acquisition of knowledge) should be promoted.

Principle Nine: None should remain satisfied with one's own elevation only, but should incessantly strive for the social upliftment of all, realise one's own elevation in the elevation of others.

Principle Ten: All persons ought to dedicate themselves necessarily for the social good and the well being of all, subordinating their personal interest, while the individual is free to enjoy freedom of action for the individual well being.

Arya Samaj also clearly condemns practices such as polytheism, idol worship, animal sacrifice, ancestor worship, pilgrimage, priest craft, the belief in avatars, the hereditary of caste system, untouchability and child marriage on the grounds that all these lack Vedic sanction.

1824–1883 A.D.—Dayanand Saraswati

Maharishi Dayanand Saraswati was an important Hindu religious scholar, reformer and the founder of the Arya Samaj. Disapproving the idolatry and ritualistic worship, which was common in Hinduism, he worked towards restoring Vedic philosophy. Among his many contributions to India are like promoting of the equal rights to women, right to education for women and reading of Indian scriptures. He translated Vedas from Sanskrit to Hindi so that the common person could be able to read the Vedas.

Many incidents in his early childhood resulted in Dayananda's questioning the traditional beliefs of Hinduism and asking inquisitive questions about God. At the age of 14, he visited a Shiva Temple for an all-night vigil. There he waited for Lord Shiva to appear and accept the offerings made to the idol. While his father and some others fell asleep, Dayanand saw a mouse eating the offerings placed before the image. He tried to find out from elders how a God, who cannot protect even his own offerings, would protect humanity. For asking questions, Dayananada was punished by his parents. He argued with his parents and requested not to worship such a helpless God.

Dayanand was disappointed with orthodox Hinduism and became a wandering monk. He learned Panini's grammar to read Sanskrit texts and understood from them that God can be found. After wandering in search of God for decades, he found his guru, Swami Virjananda, who told him to throw away all his books. He wished Dayanand to start from a clean slate and learn directly from the Vedas. After Dayanand finished his education, Virjananda mandated him to spread the knowledge of the Vedas in society as his fees. This was the lifelong mission of Dayanand Saraswati who worked for spreading the messages of Vedas.

Dayanand Saraswati started roaring against the monstrous growth of unnecessary growth and unwanted accumulation that had deformed Hinduism for thousands of years. The essence of his teachings were that only the original Vedas, as distinct from the Brahamans and Upanishads, were divine revelation, that the true Vedic teaching was monotheist that all hymns to Agni, Indira, Surya and other divinities were in reality addressed to the One God. All other doctrines like pantheism, Vedantism and Tantrism were all evil corruptions that had to be rooted out. His inspirational teachings were spread in every corner of India except in South India, where the most intolerant form of Hinduism exists and where caste distinctions are most cruelly rigid. Its immense success was not against a strong anti-Christian sentiment, but some kind of a protestant reformation, a return to the original purity of religion in its inception. Dayananda did not attack against Bible, Koran, Buddhism or Jainism, but he confronted at the Puranas, Tantra and Vedanta and particularly at the post-Buddhist Hinduism that had combined Gautama's teaching to earlier form Hinduism.

Dayanand travelled the country challenging religious scholars and priests inviting them to discuss with him and won repeatedly on the strength of his arguments. He believed that Hinduism had been corrupted deviating from the core principles of the Vedas and misled by the priesthood for the priests' self-exaggeration. Hindu priests discouraged common people from reading Vedic scriptures and encouraged rituals such as bathing in the Ganges and feeding of priests on anniversaries, which Dayanand pronounced as superstitions or self-serving. By encouraging the nation to come out of such superstitious ideas, he worked to educate the nation to go back to Vedas.

Maharishi Swami Dayanand Saraswati

Simultaneously, he encouraged the nation for adopting social reforms like untouchability, women's education, fight against system of dowry and sati. Through his teachings, preachings, sermons and writings he inspired the nation for Swarajya (self governance), nationalism and spiritualism. His book "Satyarth Prakash" inspired millions to fight for India's freedom. Consequently, hundreds of revolutionaries sacrificed their lives in the freedom struggle.

1838–1884 A.D.—Keshab Chandra Sen

Keshab Chandra Sen was a Bengali religious preacher and social reformer. He became a member of the Brahma Samaj first. Later he left Brahma Samaj and established his own "Brahma Samaj of India". In 1878, his followers deserted him after he performed his own daughter's child marriage according to Hindu tradition. Later, he was converted to Christianity influenced by its idealism and again came under the influence of Ramakrishna Paramahamsa and founded a "New Dispensation" or "Nobo bidhan" motivated by Christianity, Vaishnava bhakti, and Hindu practices. When he was in Brahma Samaj, he vehemently criticised Christianity. He traveled throughout the country lecturing and preaching that the Brahma Samaj was meant to revitalise Hindu religion employing ancient Hindu sources and the authority of the Vedas. When Keshab Chandra Sen visited Europe, he was impressed by Christianity and he thought that only Christian doctrines could bring new life to Hindu society.

When Keshab Chandra met Ramakrishna, he already had accepted Christianity and had separated from the Brahma Samaj. Previously, Keshab had abandoned idolatry. After Ramakrishna's influence, Keshab again accepted Hindu polytheism and founded a syncretic school of spiritualism named 'Nabo Bidhan' or 'New Dispensation'. In this new institution, he intended to combine the best principles of Christianity and western spiritual tradition with Hinduism, which was based on Ramakrishna's principle.

Keshab Chandra Sen's primary quest was for a universal religion. Sen adopted a number of ceremonies from both Hinduism and Christianity, calling God as Mother. He also adopted the *homa* practice and the *arati* ceremony into Brahma Samaj ritual. He found spiritual nourishment in Durga Puja and composed a hymn of praise containing 108 names of God that echoed traditional Hindu prayers.

He died on January 8, 1884.

1850–1885 A.D.—Bharatendu Harischandra

Bharatendu Harischandra is known as the "father of modern Hindi literature and Hindi theatre". Through several dramas, life sketches and travel accounts, he represented the agonies of the people, country's poverty, dependency, inhuman exploitation, the unrest of the middle class and the urge for the progress of the country. He wrote under the pen name "Rasa". In an early editorial in English entitled 'Public Opinion in India' (1872), he wrote:

"Unless there is a general desire to shake off the trammels of superstition, the regeneration of India cannot be aimed at. Let the religion of India be the religion that can govern the millions of her subjects without any permit or hindrance. Let the dark shadows of sectarianism be vanished by the rays of western civilisation... and let the unity be the basis of that grand superstructure of national improvement which every civilised nation has in its possession."

Harischandra used modern concepts of progress and national improvement to introduce an old Hinduism with new roles and new meaning.

1861-1941 A.D.—Rabindranath Tagore

Rabindranath Tagore was a Bengali poet, novelist, musician, painter, and playwright who reshaped Bengali literature and music. He was the first non-European who

has been awarded the Noble Prize for Literature in 1913 for his magnificently beautiful work "Gitanjali".

Tagore modernised Bengali art by rejecting rigid classical forms. His works including novels, stories, songs, dramas, and essays addressed political and personal topics. "Gitanjali" (Song Offerings), "Gora" (In this book Tagore narrates the story in a fascinating way ideally attacking social taboos with intention to save the society from the claws of oppression, caste system, and to uplift women's condition), and "Ghare Baire" (Battle between the ideas of Western culture and revolution against the Western culture) are his best-known works. His verses, short stories, and novels are appreciated for their lyricism, colloquialism, naturalism, and contemplation. Tagore composed the national anthem Jana Gana Mana on January 24, 1950. He also composed the national anthem of Bangladesh— "Amar Shonar Bangla".

Rabindranath Tagore started school of his ideals called Shantinikethan, an experimental school, whose main ambition was to learn in a natural environment, which is more enjoyable and fruitful. He conceived a new type of university desiring to make Shantiniketan a connecting point between India and the world, a world center for the study of humanity beyond national and geographical limits.

After he received the Nobel Prize in 1913, the school was expanded into a university.

Tagore wrote poetries, novels, essays, short stories, dramas, and songs.

Poetry

Manasi	(The Ideal One)	1890
Sonar Tari	(The Golden Boat)	1894
Gitanjali	(Song Offerings)	1910
Gitimalya	(Garland of Songs)	1914
Balaka	(The Flight of Cranes)	1916

Dramas

Valmiki Pratibha	(The Genius of Valmiki)	1881
Visarjan	(The Sacrifice)	1890
Raja	(The King of the Dark Chamber)	1910
Dak Ghar	(The Post Office)	1912
Achalayatan	(The Immovable)	1912
Muktadhara	(The Waterfall)	1922
Raktakaravi	(Red Oleanders)	1926

Fiction

Nastanir	(The Broken Nest)	1901
Gora	(Fair-Faced)	1910
Ghare Baire	(The Home and the World)	1916
Yogayog	(Crosscurrents)	1929

Memoirs

Jivansmriti	(My Reminiscences)	1912
Chhelebela	(My Boyhood Days)	1940

English

	Thought Relics	1921

Many of his books have been translated into English.

Tagore's political thoughts were complex. He opposed British imperialism and supported Indian nationalists. Yet, he ridiculed the Swadeshi movement. He emphasised self-help and intellectual upliftment of masses as an alternative way to acquire freedom. He urged Indians to accept that there is no use of blind revolution, but the need of steady and purposeful education to govern the country.

1872–1950 A.D.—Aurobindo Ghosh

Aurobindo Ghosh was a nationalist, freedom fighter, philosopher, and a poet. Aurobindo was born in Calcutta on August 15, 1872. He studied in London and returned to India in 1893. He worked as a Professor in Baroda College for thirteen years. During this period, he joined Indian nationalist movement and took a leading role to revolt against the British Government in India. He demanded complete independence for the country in his newspaper Bande Mataram.

Aurobindo synthesised Eastern and Western philosophy, religion, literature, science and psychology in his writings. Aurobindo works include philosophy, poetry, translations and commentaries of Vedas, Upanishad, and the Gita, plays, literary, social, political, and historical criticism; spiritual journals and three volumes of letters. His principal philosophical writings are The Life Divine and The Synthesis of Yoga. His main poetic work is Savitri. Excerpts from Sri Aurobindo Talks, Letters and Articles:

"If India is to survive, she must be made young again. Rushing and billowing streams of energy must be poured into her; her soul must become, as it was in the old times, like the surges, vast, puissant, calm or turbulent at will, an ocean of action or of force.

"We have to fill the minds of our boys from childhood with the idea of the country, and present them with that idea at every turn and make their whole young life a lesson in the practice of the virtues which afterwards go to make the patriot and the citizen. If we do not attempt this, we may as well give up our desire to create an Indian nation altogether; for without such discipline nationalism, patriotism, regeneration are mere words and ideas which can never become a part of the very soul of the nation and never therefore a great realized fact. Mere academical teaching of patriotism is of no avail.

"Our actual enemy is not any force exterior to ourselves, but our own crying weaknesses, our cowardice, our selfishness, our hypocrisy, our purblind – slow and dull - sentimentalism".

"I say, of the Congress, then, this, - that its aims are mistaken, that the spirit in which it proceeds towards their accomplishment is not a spirit of sincerity and whole-heartedness, and that the methods it has chosen are not the right methods, and the leaders in whom it trusts, not the right sort of men to be leaders; - in brief, that we are at present the blind led, if not by the blind, at any rate by the one-eyed."

The Congress reacted in a way which frightened the editors of the paper who asked Aurobindo to write about cultural themes instead of Politics. Aurobindo lost interest in these writings and his articles were discontinued.

In 1910, he withdrew from politics and went to Pondicherry and dedicated himself to his spiritual and philosophical activities.

Aurobindo

Aurobindo tried to introduce the concept of evolution into Vedantic thought. Samkhya philosophy had already proposed such a notion centuries earlier, but Aurobindo rejected the materialistic tendencies of both Darwinism and Samkhya, and proposed an evolution of spirit along with matter and implied that the evolution of matter was a result of the spirit. Scientific view of Aurobindo's vision is the evolution of human life into life divine. He writes: "Man is a transitional being. He is not final. The step from man to superhuman-being is the next approaching achievement in the evolution. It is inevitable because it is at once the intention of the inner spirit and the logic of nature's process."

Aurobindo rejected a main conception of Indian philosophy that the world is illusion and living as a sanyasi or renunciate is the only way to escape. He said that it is possible not only to transcend human nature, but also to transform and to live in the world as a free and evolved human being with a new consciousness and a new nature.

1820–1891 A.D.—Ishwar Chandra Vidyasagar

Ishwar Chandra Vidyasagar was a philosopher, academic, educator, writer, translator, printer, publisher, entrepreneur, reformer, and philanthropist. He made efforts to simplify and modernise Bangla prose significantly. He also rationalised and simplified the Bengali alphabets.

He received the title Vidyasagar (Ocean of knowledge) from the Calcutta Sanskrit College due to his excellent

performance in Sanskrit studies and philosophy.

Vidyasagar promoted schools for girls in Calcutta. In those days usually education was taught to women at home by their liberal fathers or husbands.

While Vidyasagar was working at the Sanskrit College, Secretary of the College wanted the admissions to be preserved to Brahmins only. Vidyasagar wanted the college to be opened to students from all castes. As a consequence, he had to resign the college. Later, he rejoined the College and introduced many extensive changes to the College curriculum. He vigorously promoted the idea that regardless of their caste, both men and women should receive the best education. Vidyasagar took the initiative in proposing and persuading the Widow Remarriage Act XV of 1856 in India.

He was known for his charity and philanthropy, and for his immense generosity. He always responded to distress calls of the poor, sufferings of the sick, and injustice to humanity.

When he started earning, he paid fixed sums of monthly allowances to each member of his joint family, to family servants, to needy neighbours, to villagers who needed help, and to his village hospital and school. This he continued without break even when he was unemployed, and had to borrow substantially from time to time.

1838–1894 A.D.—Bankim Chandra Chattopadhyay

Bankim Chandra Chattopadhyay, was a Bengali poet, novelist, essayist, journalist, and composer of poem "Vande Mataram" or "Bande Mataram" (National Song of India) that inspired the freedom fighters of India.

He has contributed significantly for literary renaissance

of Bengal. Some of his writings, including novels, essays and commentaries were different from traditional verse-oriented Indian writings. They provided an inspiration for authors across India.Chatterjee began his literary career as a writer of poetry. Later, he turned his direction to fiction writing.

"Durgeshnandini", his first Bengali romance novel was published in 1865. His famous novels include "Kapalkundala" (1866), "Mrinalini" (1869), "Vishbriksha" (1873), "Chandrasekhar" (1877), "Rajani" (1877), "Rajsimha" (1881), and "Devi Chaudhurani" (1884). His most famous novel was Anand Math (1882). Anand Math contained the song Bande Mataram, which was later adopted as National Song. He wanted to instigate a cultural revival of Bengal by motivating the intellect of the Bengali speaking people through literary movement. As a result he brought out monthly magazine called "Bangladarshan" in 1872. The magazine carried serialised novels, Bangadarshan stories, humorous sketches, historical and miscellaneous essays, informative articles, religious discourses, literary criticisms and reviews.

Bankim Chandra was an excellent story-teller. His novels have been translated in almost all the major languages of India. He died on April 8, 1894.

Bankhim Chandras song "Bande Mataram", set to music by Rabindranath Tagore became the informal anthem of the nationalist movement after 1905:

Mother, I bow to thee!
Rich with thy hurrying streams,
Bright with thy orchard gleams,
Cool with thy winds of delight,
Dark fields waving, Mother of might,
Mother free...
Who hath said thou art weak in thy lands,

When the swords flash out in twice seventy million hands...
To thee I call, Mother and Lord!...
Thou art wisdom, thou art law,
Thou our heart, our soul, our breath,
Thou the love divine, the awe

In our hearts that conquers death...
Every image made divine
In our temples is but thine.
Thou are Durga, Lady and Queen,
With her hands that strike and her swords of sheen,
Thou are Lakshmi lotus-throned...
Mother sweet, I bow to thee
Mother great and free!

1866–1915 A.D.—Gopal Krishna Gokhale

Gopal Krishna Gokhale was one of the social and political leaders during the Indian Independence Movement against British Empire in India. Gokhale was a senior leader of the Indian National Congress and founder of the Servants of India Society. Gokhale promoted not only independence from the British Empire, but also social reforms through the Society, the Congress and other legislative bodies in which he served. To achieve his goals, Gokhale followed two principles: avoidance of violence and reform within existing government institutions.

Gokhale was one of the first generations of Indians to receive a University education. He graduated from Elphinstone College in 1884 and his education remarkably influenced the path of his career. In addition to learning English, he was exposed to western political thought and became a great admirer of theorists such as John Stuart Mill and Edmund Burke.

Gandhi considered him as his political master. Apart from being a political leader, Gopal Krishna Gokhale was also a social reformer.Education influenced Gokhale significantly. His understanding of the English language allowed him to express himself clearly, without hesitation. His English education and knowledge of history instilled in him a respect for liberty, democracy, and the parliamentary system.

Gokhale became a member of the Indian National Congress in 1889. He was moderate in his views and attitudes and cultivated a process of dialogue and discussion with British which enabled British to respect Indian rights.

Servants of India Society

When Gokhale was elected president of the Indian National Congress, he founded "Servants of India Society", specifically to unite and train Indians of different ethnicities and religions in welfare work. This organisation worked for underprivileged, rural and tribal people, emergency relief work, the development of literacy, and other social causes. For Gokhale, true political change in India would be possible only when a new generation of Indians become educated. He believed the existing educational institutions and the Indian Civil Service were not helping sufficiently. Gokhale hoped the Servants of India Society would satisfy this need. The objective of the Society was to train Indian people for the service of India. Gokhale wrote, "The Servants of India Society will train men prepared to devote their lives to the cause of country in a religious spirit, and will seek to promote, by all constitutional means, the national interests of the Indian people." Besides involving itself in social service and educational activities, the Society co-operated with the Congress in the political sphere and helped in the collection of funds. The Society took up the cause of promoting Indian education in earnestness. Among its many projects, it organised mobile libraries, founded schools, and provided night classes for factory workers.

When Gokhale was in England, he made a good impression as a speaker. In the Women Section of the Victoria

Era Exhibition, he read a paper about the women's condition in India. He grieved about the women's condition in India and said, "A combination of enforced ignorance and overdone religion has not only made India's women willing victims of customs, but also formidable opponents of reforms."

Gokhale, though a leader of the Indian nationalist movement, he was not concerned with independence but with social reform. He believed such reform would be best achieved by working with existing British government institutions. This view of him earned the enmity of aggressive nationalists such as Bala Gangadhara Tilak. Not discouraged by such opposition, Gokhale worked directly with the British throughout his political career in order to promote his reform goals. Extremists were in the favor of self rule while the moderates thought that time are not yet ripe for such an event. This notion finally led to a split in the Congress.

Gokhale was a mentor to Mahatma Gandhi. Gandhi returned from South Africa and received personal guidance from Gokhale, including knowledge and understanding of India and the issues confronting common Indians. In his autobiography, Gandhi calls Gokhale as his mentor and guide. Gokhale was also a mentor of Muhammed Ali Jinnah, the founder of Pakistan.

Gokhale died on Feb 19, 1915 at forty-nine years of age.

Gokhale's impact on the Indian nationalist movement was vital. Through his close relationship with the British imperial government, Gokhale forced India's colonial chiefs to recognize the potentials of a new generation of educated Indians and to include them in the governing process.

1856–1920 A.D.—Bal Gangadhar Tilak

Bal Gangadhar Tilak was an Indian nationalist, educationist, social reformer and independence fighter. Tilak was a strongest advocate of Swaraj, self-rule, in Indian consciousness. His famous quote, *"Swaraj is my birthright, and I shall have it!"* is well-remembered in India even today.

Tilak was among one of the first generation of Indians to receive a college education.

Tilak believed that "Religion and practical life are not different. To take Sanyasa (renunciation) is not to abandon life. The first duty is to serve humanity and the next is to serve God". This dedication to humanity was a fundamental element in the Indian Nationalist movement.

He was a strong critic of the Western education system, feeling it demeaned the Indian students and disrespected India's heritage.

He organised the Deccan Education Society with a few of his college friends, whose goal was to improve the quality of education for India's youth. The Deccan Education Society was set up to create a new system that taught young Indians nationalist ideas through an emphasis on Indian culture.

Tilak joined the Indian National Congress in 1890. He opposed its moderate attitude. He was one of the most eminent radicals at the time.

In 1891, Tilak opposed the Age of Consent Bill. The act increased the age from 10 to 12 at which a girl could get married. The Congress and other liberals supported it, but Tilak stood against it, calling it an interference with Hinduism.

Tilak aimed at Swarajya (Independence), not slow reforms and attempted to influence the Congress to adopt his militant program. On this issue, he clashed with the moderates at the Surat session of the Congress in 1907. Taking advantage of the split in the nationalist forces, the government prosecuted Tilak on a charge of treachery and inciting terrorism and deported him to Mandalay, Burma (Myanmar), to serve a sentence of six years imprisonment.

Later, Tilak re-united with his fellow nationalists and re-joined the Indian National Congress in 1916. He helped to found the All India Home Rule League in 1916-18 with Annie Besant, G.S. Khaparde and Muhammad Ali Jinnah. Tilak travelled from village to village trying to obtain support from farmers and locals to join the movement towards self-rule.

In 1894, Tilak changed household worship of Ganesha into Sarvajanik Ganeshotsav, and made Shivaji Jayanti a social festival.

According to Tilak's theory, North Pole was the original home of Aryans during pre-glacial period. They had to leave their place due to the ice surge around 8000 B.C. and had to migrate to the Northern parts of Europe and Asia looking for lands and for new settlements. Supporting this theory, Tilak has given certain Vedic hymns, Avestic passages, Vedic chronology, and Vedic calendars with interpretations in detail in his book, "The Arctic Home in the Vedas".

Books

In 1903, he wrote the book "The Arctic Home in the Vedas". In it he argued that the Vedas could have been composed in the Arctics, and the Aryan poets brought them south after the onset of the last Ice Age. He proposed radically new way to determine the exact time of Vedas. He tried to calculate the time of Vedas by using the position of different stars, *nakshatras*. Positions of Nakshtras were described in different Vedas. Tilak also authored Shrimad Bhagawad Gita Rahasya.

1897–1945 A.D.—Subhas Chandra Bose

Subhas Chandra Bose, also known as "Netaji", was one of the most prominent leaders of the Indian Independence Movement against the British rule. He was an Indian revolutionary leader who led an Indian national political and military force against Britain and the Western powers during World War II.

Netaji believed that foreign assistance was essential to free India from British rule. In 1939, when the Second World War broke out, Subhas Chandra Bose sought assistance from Germany, Italy, and Japan as they were enemies of Britain.

He believed that young militant groups could be molded into a military soldiers for the freedom movement and could be used to achieve independence. Gandhi opposed this ideology because it directly conflicted with his policy of ahimsa non-violence. Bose sought complete independence for India at the earliest, while the All India Congress Committee wanted it in phases.

The British Government in India perceived Subhas as a potential source of danger and therefore they arrested him.

His political views and the alliances he made with Nazi and other militant regimes against war with Britain have been the cause of arguments between historians and politicians. Some accuse him for his fascist support, while others in India have been more sympathetic towards his practical and material factors rather than on ethical objectives.

He was presumed dead on August 18, 1945 in a plane crash in Taiwan although the evidence of his death in the accident has not been proved. The lack of a body has led to many theories concerning his possible survival.

1869–1948 A.D.—Mohandas Karamchand Gandhi

Gandhi studied law in London (1888–91). Unable to find work in Bombay, he practiced law in South Africa from 1893 to 1914. There he established his first ashram and while fighting for the rights of South Africa's Indian residents, devised the ideas of *Satyagraha* movement. On his return to India Gandhi made Ahmedabad as his center and launched peasant and labor protests in Bihar and Gujarat. In 1919, he conducted India-wide protest against the Rowlatt Acts. In September 1920, he obtained

support of the Indian National Congress for his strategy of non-violence and non-cooperation with the British government. In 1930, he launched the salt march to protest against salt tax. In 1931, signing the Gandhi–Irwin Pact, Gandhi represented the Congress at the second round table conference in London. He was responsible for gaining Independence through his ideas and missions. He was assassinated by a Hindu on January 30, 1948.

1889-1964 A.D.—Jawaharlal Nehru

Jawaharlal Nehru took active part in Non-Cooperation Movement. He was one of the prime leaders of Indian freedom struggle. He was the trusted disciple of Mahatma Gandhi and later he became the first Prime Minister of India in 1947. He is widely regarded as the architect of modern India.

After the independence, Jawaharlal Nehru effectively managed the difficult situations and challenges of that time like the disorders and mass exodus of minorities across the borders of India and Pakistan, the integration of princely states into the Indian Union, the forming of a new constitution, establishing the political and administrative infrastructure for a parliamentary democracy, and drafting five year plans for the development of new independent India.

Jawaharlal Nehru played an important role in building modern India. He set up a Planning Commission, encouraged development of science and technology, and launched three successive five-year plans. His policies led to a substantial growth in agricultural and industrial production. Nehru also played a major role in developing independent India's foreign policy.

To Jawaharlal Nehru, India's current existing danger was within India. Since the independence, wherever he went across the country, he appealed for the national unity. His mission was "Integrate or perish". He thought it was a historic mission to conquer the widespread challenge—a challenge that created by many major languages, each well-established in its own historic provinces, with tens of millions of speakers connected to age-old scripts. This is a challenge to a central authority to process and to conduct smooth administration in parliamentary. He feared that this critical challenge will create a problem sometime in the future and the unity achieved by opposing British will slip away.

While differences of culture and language threatened the unity of the new nation, Nehru established programmes like the National Book Trust and the National Literary Academy which encouraged the translation of regional literatures between languages. In order to unify India, he warned again and again reminding his slogan—Integrate or Perish.

Education and Social Reform

Jawaharlal Nehru was a passionate advocate of education for India's children and youth, believing it is essential for India's future upliftment. His government directed the establishment of many institutions of higher learning, including the All India Institute of Medical Sciences, the Indian Institutes of Technology, the Indian Institutes of Management, and the National Institutes of Technology. Adult education centres, vocational and technical schools were also organised for adults, especially in the rural areas.

A system of reservations in government services and educational institutions was created to eliminate the social disparities and hardships faced by the scheduled castes and scheduled tribes. Nehru also advocated secularism and religious harmony, increasing the representation of minorities in the government.

Nehru was a writer in English and wrote a several books like, The Discovery of India, Glimpses of World History, and his autobiography, Toward Freedom.

1878–1972 A.D.—Chakravarti Rajagopalachari

Chakravarti Rajagopalachari, also called "Rajaji", was a politician, Indian Independence activist, statesman and writer and also a last Governor General of India. Rajaji

staunchly opposed the use of nuclear weapons and was a proponent of world peace and disarmament.

Rajagopalachari was a follower of Mahatma Gandhi and participated in the Non-cooperation movement giving up his profession as a lawyer.

He was the first Premier of Madras Presidency from the Congress party. He made several monumental changes: Issued the Temple Entry Authorisation and Indemnity Act 1939 through which restrictions were removed on Dalits entering Hindu temples; opened the Meenakshi Temple at Madurai to the Dalits and Shanars; Issued the Agricultural Debt Relief Act in March 1938 to ease the burden of debt on the peasants of the province.

After the breakup with the Congress, Rajaji formed a new political party under the name Swatantra Party. The party was conceived by disgruntled leaders of former princely states such as the Raja of Ramgarh, Maharaja of Kalahandi and the Maharajadhiraja of Darbhanga.

Rajaji was an accomplished writer and made contributions to Indian English literature.

Contributions to Literature and Music

Rajagopalachari was a gifted writer both in Tamil and English. He was the founder of the "Salem Literary Society". Siraiyil Tavam (Meditation in jail) was a day-to-day diary about his first imprisonment.

Rajagopalachari started the "Tamil Scientific Terms Society". This society invented new words in Tamil for scientific terms connected to botany, chemistry, physics, astronomy and mathematics.

Rajaji wrote an abridged form of Mahabharata and Ramayana in English. He translated Tamil Kambar Ramayana into English. He also wrote books on the Bhagavad Gita and Upanishads in English, and translated Marcus Aurelius to Tamil from English. Rajaji regarded his literary works were the best service he made to the people. He was one of the founders of the Bharatiya Vidya Bhavan, an organisation dedicated to the promotion of education and Indian culture.

5

Independent India

1947—Independent India

All agreed that the new India will be based on democratic values with universal suffrage, freedom of press and speech. Concerned by the persisting discrimination against untouchables and other disadvantaged groups, the Congress Party took action to ensure that these groups have a voice in the new constitutional order. It appointed an untouchable leader Dr. B.R. Ambedkar to chair the drafting committee for the constitution. The new constitution outlawed untouchability, gave greater importance to the reservation of seats in the legislatures for the former untouchables and depressed forest tribes.

The Indian Constitution was written in a Westminster style of government, with a parliament comprising two houses and a prime minister selected by the majority party in the lower house, called the Lok Sabha or House of the People. First, Nehru became the Prime Minister, while the President acted as a superficial head of state. Elements of the old colonial style of governance persisted under the new order.

The draft of the Indian Constitution has been derived from constitutions of other countries. The constitution has also taken many parts from the Government of India Act, 1935. The different parts of Indian Constitution adopted from other countries' constitution are mentioned below:

1. ***British Constitution:*** Parliamentary form of government, introduction of Speaker and his role, the concept of single citizenship, the Rule of law,

procedure of lawmaking, procedure established by Law u/a 13

2. ***Irish Constitution:*** Directive principles of state policy
3. ***USA Constitution:*** The fundamental Rights are derived from the (similar to the United States Bill of Rights).
4. ***Canadian Constitution:*** A quasi-federal form of government, where the central government plays prime role in governing the country, the idea of Residual Powers
5. ***Australian Constitution:*** Freedom of trade and commerce between different states of the country, Power of the national legislature to make laws for implementing treaties
6. ***French Constitution:*** Ideals of Liberty, Equality and Fraternity
7. ***Japanese Constitution:*** Fundamental Duties u/a 51-A
8. ***Weimar Constitution:*** Emergency Provision u/a 356
9. ***Malaysian Constitution:*** The concept of the Concurrent list
10. ***Russian constitution:*** The fundamental Duties.

Ambedkar, a graduate of Columbia University in New York, had never agreed with Gandhi's idealism. Calling "Hinduism is a veritable chamber of horrors", he argued that all Gandhism has done was to "smoothen its surface and give it the appearance of decency and respectability". Before his death in 1956, Ambedkar converted to Buddhism.

Nehru's earnest wish in 1947 was that India to shed 'the burden of the past'. But the past remained contested. The sharpest divide was that between secular liberals and supporters of Hindutva. Each possessed a vision of India's past that it cherished, and attempted to propagate.

Such an idealised past had a powerful appeal in India. The liberal economist Amartya Sen writes his views in *The Argumentative Indian,* a vision of India in which the values of forethought and diversity lay at the heart of its past. His heroes included ancient Buddhist ruler Ashoka and the Mughal emperor Akbar, Gandhi and Nehru. Sen wrote, "Akbar championed 'pluralist ideals', and even 'the politics of secularism".

By contrast, the proponents of Hindutva designed a vision of India that it is fundamentally Hindu nation from ancient times. Hindutva historians devoted plenty of time towards proving that Aryan peoples were indigenous to northern India, not migrants from Central Asia, are descendants of the country's original inhabitants from time immemorial despite a good deal of evidence to the contrary. Hindutva's heroes are like Shivaji, who is portrayed as fighting for a Hindu India against a Muslim onslaught.

Objectives of Five-Year Plans

After independence, India was suffering from dwindling economy and it needed well planned strategies to boost its economy to compete with global market. In order to make it possible, the five years plan was designed, developed, executed and monitored by the Planning Commission of India. Jawaharlal Nehru was the chairman of the first Planning Commission of India.

During this time, many irrigation projects were initiated. The World Health Organization, with the Indian government, addressed children's health and reduced infant mortality, indirectly contributing to population growth.

At the end of the first five year plan period in 1956, five Indian Institutes of Technology (IITs) were started as major technical institutions and many universities were started to promote education.

Objectives of different Five Year Plans in India:

1st Five Year Plan (1951-56)

It was designed to improve the agriculture, irrigation and power and the plan projected to decrease the India's dependence on food imports, resolve the food crisis, and ease the raw material problem particularly in jute and cotton.

2nd Five Year Plan (1956-61)

It was designed to improve the agriculture programs and to meet the raw material requirements of industry, in addition to food for the increasing population.

3rd Five Year Plan (1961-66)

This Plan's main goal was to make the country self reliant in agriculture and industry. Increased the power sector allotment, promoted economic developments in backward areas; manufacturing units were increased with subsidies. The 3rd five year plan was affected by wars with China in 1962 and Pakistan 1965 and bad monsoon.

4th Five Year Plan (1969-74)

This plan emphasised on promoting education and creating employment opportunities for the minority section of the society to improve their standard of living Another goal of the plan was to create awareness about the Family planning program.

5th Five Year Plan (1974-79)

The fifth plan was designed on checking inflation and various non-economic areas like nutritional requirements, health, family planning, etc.

6th Five Year Plan (1980-85)

The 6th five year plan focused on infrastructure and agriculture.

7th Five Year Plan (1985-1989)

The plan focused on improving various segments like welfare, education, health, family planning and also encouraged employment opportunities.

Period (1989-1991)

This period was of political instability. Hence, no five year plan was implemented during the period. The country faced severe balance of payment crisis.

8th Five Year Plan (1992-1997)

The eighth plan was designed towards modernisation of industries, poverty reduction, encouraging employment, strengthening the infrastructure. Other goals and achievements were devaluation of rupees, dismantling of license prerequisite, and decreasing trade barriers.

9th Five Year Plan (1997-2002)

The ninth five year plan focused on increasing agricultural and rural income and to improve the conditions of the marginal farmer and landless labourers.

10th Five Year Plan (2002-2007)

The 10th five year plan targeted towards making India's economy as the fastest growing economy on the global level, to reduce the poverty rate, and to increase the literacy rate in the country.

11th Five Year Plan (2007-2012)

The eleventh five year plan targets to increase GDP growth, to reduce educated unemployment, to reduce infant mortality. The plan also targets to ensure electricity generation, clean drinking water to all villages, and to protect environment by planting and protecting forests and trees.

Wars between India and Pakistan

The year 1965 saw the continued tension with Pakistan. Disappointed by India's refusal to conduct a plebiscite in Kashmir, Pakistan entered its southern border of India, in the Rann of Kutch, and then sent guerilla raiders, followed by regular army troops into Kashmir. India responded by sending tanks across the Punjab plains to the borders of Lahore. After three weeks, a ceasefire was declared by the intervention of Soviet Union.

Again military encounters with Pakistan at the time of the freedom struggle in Bangladesh in 1971, and then on the snow-covered peaks of Kashmir in 1999 kept enduring tension between India and Pakistan. These events strengthened the notion that India was the dominant power in the subcontinent and Pakistan cannot win Kashmir by force of arms.

Excerpts from The Constitution of India regarding Fundamental Rights, Duties and Responsibilities of every citizen of India are reproduced here with simple format retaining the original content.

THE CONSTITUTION OF INDIA

Preamble

WE, THE PEOPLE OF INDIA, have solemnly resolved to constitute India into a SOVEREIGN SOCIALIST SECULAR DEMOCRATIC REPUBLIC and to secure to all its citizens:

JUSTICE, social, economic and political;

LIBERTY of thought, expression, belief, faith and worship;

EQUALITY of status and of opportunity;

And to promote among them all

FRATERNITY assuring the dignity of the individual and the unity and integrity of the Nation;

IN OUR CONSTITUENT ASSEMBLY this twenty-sixth day of November, 1949, do HEREBY ADOPT, ENACT AND GIVE TO OURSELVES THIS CONSTITUTION.

THE UNION AND ITS TERRITORY

Article # 1: Name and territory of the Union.—

(1) India, that is Bharat, shall be a Union of States.

(2) The States and the territories thereof shall be as specified in the First Schedule.

(3) The territory of India shall comprise—

(a) the territories of the States;

(b) the Union territories specified in the First Schedule; and

(c) such other territories as may be acquired.

Article # 2: Admission or establishment of new States.—

Parliament may by law admit into the Union, or establish, new States on such terms and conditions as it thinks fit.

Article # 2A; *[Sikkim to be associated with the Union.] Rep. by the Constitution (Thirty- sixth Amendment) Act, 1975, s. 5 (w.e.f. 26-4-1975).*

Article # 3: Formation of new States and alteration of areas, boundaries or names of existing States.—Parliament may by law—

(a) Form a new State by separation of territory from any State or by uniting two or more States or parts of States or by uniting any territory to a part of any State;

(b) Increase the area of any State;

(c) Diminish the area of any State;

(d) Alter the boundaries of any State;

(e) Alter the name of any State:

Provided that no Bill for the purpose shall be introduced in either House of Parliament except on the recommendation of the President and unless, where the proposal contained in the Bill affects the area, boundaries or name of any of the States, the Bill has been referred by the President to the Legislature of that State for expressing its views thereon within such period as may be specified in the reference or within such further period as the President may allow and the period so specified or allowed has expired.

Explanation I.—In this article, in clauses *(a)* to *(e)*, "State" includes a Union territory, but in the proviso, "State" does not include a Union territory.

Explanation II.—The power conferred on Parliament by clause *(a)* includes the power to form a new State or Union territory by uniting a part of any State or Union territory to any other State or Union territory.

Article #4: Laws made under articles 2 and 3 to provide for the amendment of the First and the Fourth Schedules and supplemental, incidental and consequential matters.—

(1) Any law referred to in article 2 or article 3 shall contain such provisions for the amendment of the First Schedule and the Fourth Schedule as may be necessary to give effect to the provisions of the law and may also contain such supplemental, incidental and consequential provisions (including provisions as to representation in Parliament and in the Legislature or Legislatures of the State or States affected by such law) as Parliament may deem necessary.

(2) No such law as aforesaid shall be deemed to be an amendment of this Constitution for the purposes of article 368.

PART II
CITIZENSHIP

Article #5: Citizenship at the commencement of the Constitution.—

At the commencement of this Constitution, every person who has his domicile in the territory of India and—

(a) who was born in the territory of India; or

(b) either of whose parents was born in the territory of India; or

(c) who has been ordinarily resident in the territory of India for not less than five years immediately preceding such commencement, shall be a citizen of India.

Article #6: Rights of citizenship of certain persons who have migrated to India from Pakistan.—

Notwithstanding anything in article 5, a person who has migrated to the territory of India from the territory now included in Pakistan shall be deemed to be a citizen of India at the commencement of this Constitution if—

(a) he or either of his parents or any of his grandparents was born in India as defined in the Government of India Act, 1935 (as originally enacted); and

(b) *(i)* in the case where such person has so migrated before the nineteenth day of July, 1948, he has been ordinarily resident in the territory of India since the date of his migration, or

(ii) in the case where such person has so migrated on or after the nineteenth day of July, 1948, he has been registered as a citizen of India by an officer appointed in that behalf by the Government of the Dominion of India on an application made by him therefore to such officer before the commencement of this Constitution in the form and manner prescribed by that Government:

Provided that no person shall be so registered unless he has been resident in the territory of India for at least six months immediately preceding the date of his application.

Article #7: Rights of citizenship of certain migrants to Pakistan.—

Notwithstanding anything in articles 5 and 6, a person who has after the first day of March 1947, migrated from the territory of India to the territory now included in Pakistan shall not be deemed to be a citizen of India:

Provided that nothing in this article shall apply to a

person who, after having so migrated to the territory now included in Pakistan, has returned to the territory of India under a permit for resettlement or permanent return issued by or under the authority of any law and every such person shall for the purposes of clause (*b*) of article 6 be deemed to have migrated to the territory of India after the nineteenth day of July, 1948.

Article #8: Rights of citizenship of certain persons of Indian origin residing outside India.—

Notwithstanding anything in article 5, any person who or either of whose parents or any of whose grandparents was born in India as defined in the Government of India Act, 1935 (as originally enacted), and who is ordinarily residing in any country outside India as so defined shall be deemed to be a citizen of India if he has been registered as a citizen of India by the diplomatic or consular representative of India in the country where he is for the time being residing on an application made by him therefore to such diplomatic or consular representative, whether before or after the commencement of this Constitution, in the form and manner prescribed by the Government of the Dominion of India or the Government of India.

Article #9: Persons voluntarily acquiring citizenship of a foreign State not to be citizens.—

No person shall be a citizen of India by virtue of article 5, or be deemed to be a citizen of India by virtue of article 6 or article 8, if he has voluntarily acquired the citizenship of any foreign State.

Article #10: Continuance of the rights of citizenship.—

Every person who is or is deemed to be a citizen of India under any of the foregoing provisions of this Part shall, subject to the provisions of any law that may be made by Parliament, continue to be such citizen.

Article #11: Parliament to regulate the right of citizenship by law.—

Nothing in the foregoing provisions of this Part shall

derogate from the power of Parliament to make any provision with respect to the acquisition and termination of citizenship and all other matters relating to citizenship.

PART III
FUNDAMENTAL RIGHTS
General

Article #12: Definition.—

In this Part, unless the context otherwise requires, "the State" includes the Government and Parliament of India and the Government and the Legislature of each of the States and all local or other authorities within the territory of India or under the control of the Government of India.

Article #13: Laws inconsistent with or in derogation of the fundamental rights.—

(1) All laws in force in the territory of India immediately before the commencement of this Constitution, in so far as they are inconsistent with the provisions of this Part, shall, to the extent of such inconsistency, be void.

(2) The State shall not make any law which takes away or abridges the rights conferred by this Part and any law made in contravention of this clause shall, to the extent of the contravention, be void.

(3) In this article, unless the context otherwise requires,—

(a) "law" includes any Ordinance, order, bye-law, rule, regulation, notification, custom or usage having in the territory of India the force of law;

(b) "laws in force" includes laws passed or made by a Legislature or other competent authority in the territory of India before the commencement of this Constitution and not previously repealed, notwithstanding that any such law or any part thereof may not be then in operation either at all or in particular areas.

(4) Nothing in this article shall apply to any amendment of this Constitution made under article 368.

Right to Equality

Article #14: Equality before law.—

The State shall not deny to any person equality before the law or the equal protection of the laws within the territory of India.

Article #15: Prohibition of discrimination on grounds of religion, race, caste, sex or place of birth.—

(1) The State shall not discriminate against any citizen on grounds only of religion, race, caste, sex, place of birth or any of them.

(2) No citizen shall, on grounds only of religion, race, caste, sex, place of birth or any of them, be subject to any disability, liability, restriction or condition with regard to—

(a) access to shops, public restaurants, hotels and places of public entertainment; or

(b) the use of wells, tanks, bathing ghats, roads and places of public resort maintained wholly or partly out of State funds or dedicated to the use of the general public.

(3) Nothing in this article shall prevent the State from making any special provision for women and children.

(4) Nothing in this article or in clause (2) of article 29 shall prevent the State from making any special provision for the advancement of any socially and educationally backward classes of citizens or for the Scheduled Castes and the Scheduled Tribes.

Article #16: Equality of opportunity in matters of public employment.—

(1) There shall be equality of opportunity for all citizens in matters relating to employment or appointment to any office under the State.

(2) No citizen shall, on grounds only of religion, race, caste, sex, descent, place of birth, residence or any of them, be ineligible for, or discriminated against in respect of, any employment or office under the State.

(3) Nothing in this article shall prevent Parliament from making any law prescribing, in regard to a class or classes of employment or appointment to an office under the Government of, or any local or other authority within, a State or Union territory, any requirement as to residence within that State or Union territory prior to such employment or appointment.

(4) Nothing in this article shall prevent the State from making any provision for the reservation of appointments or posts in favour of any backward class of citizens which, in the opinion of the State, is not adequately represented in the services under the State.

(4A) Nothing in this article shall prevent the State from making any provision for reservation in matters of promotion, with consequential seniority, to any class or classes of posts in the services under the State in favour of the Scheduled Castes and the Scheduled Tribes which, in the opinion of the State, are not adequately represented in the services under the State.

(4B) Nothing in this article shall prevent the State from considering any unfilled vacancies of a year which are reserved for being filled up in that year in accordance with any provision for reservation made under clause (4) or clause (4A) as a separate class of vacancies to be filled up in any succeeding year or years and such class of vacancies shall not be considered together with the vacancies of the year in which they are being filled up for determining the ceiling of fifty per cent. reservation on total number of vacancies of that year.

(5) Nothing in this article shall affect the operation of any law which provides that the incumbent of an office in connection with the affairs of any religious or denominational institution or any member of the governing body thereof shall be a person professing a particular religion or belonging to a particular denomination.

Article #17: Abolition of Untouchability.—

"Untouchability" is abolished and its practice in any form is forbidden. The enforcement of any disability arising out of "Untouchability" shall be an offence punishable in accordance with law.

Article #18: Abolition of titles.—

(1) No title, not being a military or academic distinction, shall be conferred by the State.

(2) No citizen of India shall accept any title from any foreign State.

(3) No person who is not a citizen of India shall, while he holds any office of profit or trust under the State, accept without the consent of the President any title from any foreign State.

(4) No person holding any office of profit or trust under the State shall, without the consent of the President, accept any present, emolument, or office of any kind from or under any foreign State.

Right to Freedom

Article #19: Protection of certain rights regarding freedom of speech, etc.—

(1) All citizens shall have the right—

(a) to freedom of speech and expression;

(b) to assemble peaceably and without arms;

(c) to form associations or unions;

(d) to move freely throughout the territory of India;

(e) to reside and settle in any part of the territory of India; and

(g) to practise any profession, or to carry on any occupation, trade or business.

(2) Nothing in sub-clause *(a)* of clause (1) shall affect the operation of any existing law, or prevent the State from making any law, in so far as such law imposes reasonable restrictions on the exercise of the right conferred by the said sub-clause in the interests of

the sovereignty and integrity of India, the security of the State, friendly relations with foreign States, public order, decency or morality, or in relation to contempt of court, defamation or incitement to an offence.

(3) Nothing in sub-clause *(b)* of the said clause shall affect the operation of any existing law in so far as it imposes, or prevent the State from making any law imposing, in the interests of the sovereignty and integrity of India or public order, reasonable restrictions on the exercise of the right conferred by the said sub-clause.

(4) Nothing in sub-clause *(c)* of the said clause shall affect the operation of any existing law in so far as it imposes, or prevent the State from making any law imposing, in the interests of the sovereignty and integrity of India or public order or morality, reasonable restrictions on the exercise of the right conferred by the said sub-clause.

(5) Nothing in sub-clauses *(d)* and *(e)* of the said clause shall affect the operation of any existing law in so far as it imposes, or prevent the State from making any law imposing, reasonable restrictions on the exercise of any of the rights conferred by the said sub-clauses either in the interests of the general public or for the protection of the interests of any Scheduled Tribe.

(6) Nothing in sub-clause *(g)* of the said clause shall affect the operation of any existing law in so far as it imposes, or prevent the State from making any law imposing, in the interests of the general public, reasonable restrictions on the exercise of the right conferred by the said sub-clause, and, in particular, nothing in the said sub-clause shall affect the operation of any existing law in so far as it relates to, or prevent the State from making any law relating to,—

(i) the professional or technical qualifications necessary for practising any profession or carrying on any occupation, trade or business, or

(ii) the carrying on by the State, or by a corporation owned or controlled by the State, of any trade, business, industry or service, whether to the exclusion, complete or partial, of citizens or otherwise.

Article #20: Protection in respect of conviction for offences.—

(1) No person shall be convicted of any offence except for violation of a law in force at the time of the commission of the Act charged as an offence, nor be subjected to a penalty greater than that which might have been inflicted under the law in force at the time of the commission of the offence.

(2) No person shall be prosecuted and punished for the same offence more than once.

(3) No person accused of any offence shall be compelled to be a witness against himself.

Article #21: Protection of life and personal liberty.—

No person shall be deprived of his life or personal liberty except according to procedure established by law.

Article #22: Protection against arrest and detention in certain cases. —

(1) No person who is arrested shall be detained in custody without being informed, as soon as may be, of the grounds for such arrest nor shall he be denied the right to consult, and to be defended by, a legal practitioner of his choice.

(2) Every person who is arrested and detained in custody shall be produced before the nearest magistrate within a period of twenty-four hours of such arrest excluding the time necessary for the journey from the place of arrest to the court of the magistrate and no such person shall be detained in custody beyond the said period without the authority of a magistrate.

(3) Nothing in clauses (1) and (2) shall apply—

(a) to any person who for the time being is an enemy alien; or

(b) to any person who is arrested or detained under any law providing for preventive detention.

(4) No law providing for preventive detention shall authorise the detention of a person for a longer period than three months unless—

(a) an Advisory Board consisting of persons who are, or have been, or are qualified to be appointed as, Judges of a High Court has reported before the expiration of the said period of three months that there is in its opinion sufficient cause for such detention:

Provided that nothing in this sub-clause shall authorise the detention of any person beyond the maximum period prescribed by any law made by Parliament under sub-clause *(b)* of clause (7); or

(b) such person is detained in accordance with the provisions of any law made by Parliament under sub-clauses *(a)* and *(b)* of clause (7).

(5) When any person is detained in pursuance of an order made under any law providing for preventive detention, the authority making the order shall, as soon as may be, communicate to such person the grounds on which the order has been made and shall afford him the earliest opportunity of making a representation against the order.

(6) Nothing in clause (5) shall require the authority making any such order as is referred to in that clause to disclose facts which such authority considers to be against the public interest to disclose.

(7) Parliament may by law prescribe—

(a) the circumstances under which, and the class or classes of cases in which, a person may be detained for a period longer than three months under any law providing for preventive detention without obtaining the opinion of an Advisory Board in accordance with the provisions of sub-

clause *(a)* of clause (4);

(b) the maximum period for which any person may in any class or classes of cases be detained under any law providing for preventive detention; and

(c) the procedure to be followed by an Advisory Board in an inquiry under sub-clause *(a)* of clause (4).

Right against Exploitation

Article #23: Prohibition of traffic in human beings and forced labour.—

(1) Traffic in human beings and *begar* and other similar forms of forced labour are prohibited and any contravention of this provision shall be an offence punishable in accordance with law.

(2) Nothing in this article shall prevent the State from imposing compulsory service for public purposes, and in imposing such service the State shall not make any discrimination on grounds only of religion, race, caste or class or any of them.

Article #24: Prohibition of employment of children in factories, etc. —

No child below the age of fourteen years shall be employed to work in any factory or mine or engaged in any other hazardous employment.

Right to Freedom of Religion

Article #25: Freedom of conscience and free profession, practice and propagation of religion.—

(1) Subject to public order, morality and health and to the other provisions of this Part, all persons are equally entitled to freedom of conscience and the right freely to profess, practise and propagate religion.

(2) Nothing in this article shall affect the operation of any existing law or prevent the State from making any law—

(a) regulating or restricting any economic, financial,

political or other secular activity which may be associated with religious practice;

(b) providing for social welfare and reform or the throwing open of Hindu religious institutions of a public character to all classes and sections of Hindus.

Explanation I.—The wearing and carrying of *kirpans* shall be deemed to be included in the profession of the Sikh religion.

Explanation II.—In sub-clause (*b*) of clause (2), the reference to Hindus shall be construed as including a reference to persons professing the Sikh, Jaina or Buddhist religion, and the reference to Hindu religious institutions shall be construed accordingly.

Article #26: Freedom to manage religious affairs.—

Subject to public order, morality and health, every religious denomination or any section thereof shall have the right—

(a) to establish and maintain institutions for religious and charitable purposes;

(b) to manage its own affairs in matters of religion;

(c) to own and acquire movable and immovable property; and

(d) to administer such property in accordance with law.

Article #27: Freedom as to payment of taxes for promotion of any particular religion.—

No person shall be compelled to pay any taxes, the proceeds of which are specifically appropriated in payment of expenses for the promotion or maintenance of any particular religion or religious denomination.

Article #28: Freedom as to attendance at religious instruction or religious worship in certain educational institutions.—

(1) No religious instruction shall be provided in any

educational institution wholly maintained out of State funds.

(2) Nothing in clause (1) shall apply to an educational institution which is administered by the State but has been established under any endowment or trust which requires that religious instruction shall be imparted in such institution.

(3) No person attending any educational institution recognised by the State or receiving aid out of State funds shall be required to take part in any religious instruction that may be imparted in such institution or to attend any religious worship that may be conducted in such institution or in any premises attached thereto unless such person or, if such person is a minor, his guardian has given his consent thereto.

Cultural and Educational Rights

Article #29: Protection of interests of minorities.—

(1) Any section of the citizens residing in the territory of India or any part thereof having a distinct language, script or culture of its own shall have the right to conserve the same.

(2) No citizen shall be denied admission into any educational institution maintained by the State or receiving aid out of State funds on grounds only of religion, race, caste, language or any of them.

Article #30: Right of minorities to establish and administer educational institutions. —

(1) All minorities, whether based on religion or language, shall have the right to establish and administer educational institutions of their choice.

(1A) In making any law providing for the compulsory acquisition of any property of an educational institution established and administered by a minority, referred to in clause (1), the State shall ensure that the amount fixed by or determined under such law for the acquisition of such property is such as would not restrict or abrogate the right guaranteed under that clause.

(2) The State shall not, in granting aid to educational institutions, discriminate against any educational institution on the ground that it is under the management of a minority, whether based on religion or language.

Saving of Certain Laws

Article #31A: Saving of laws providing for acquisition of estates, etc.—

(1) Notwithstanding anything contained in article 13, no law providing for—

(a) the acquisition by the State of any estate or of any rights therein or the extinguishment or modification of any such rights, or

(b) the taking over of the management of any property by the State for a limited period either in the public interest or in order to secure the proper management of the property, or

(c) the amalgamation of two or more corporations either in the public interest or in order to secure the proper management of any of the corporations, or

(d) the extinguishment or modification of any rights of managing agents, secretaries and treasurers, managing directors, directors or managers of corporations, or of any voting rights of shareholders thereof, or

(e) the extinguishment or modification of any rights accruing by virtue of any agreement, lease or licence for the purpose of searching for, or winning, any mineral or mineral oil, or the premature termination or cancellation of any such agreement, lease or licence, shall be deemed to be void on the ground that it is inconsistent with,

or takes away or abridges any of the rights conferred by article 14 or article 19:

Provided that where such law is a law made by the Legislature of a State, the provisions of this article shall not apply thereto unless such law, having been reserved for the consideration of the President, has received his assent :

Provided further that where any law makes any provision for the acquisition by the State of any estate and where any land comprised therein is held by a person under his personal cultivation, it shall not be lawful for the State to acquire any portion of such land as is within the ceiling limit applicable to him under any law for the time being in force or any building or structure standing thereon or appurtenant thereto, unless the law relating to the acquisition of such land, building or structure, provides for payment of compensation at a rate which shall not be less than the market value thereof.

(2) In this article,—

(a) the expression "estate" shall, in relation to any local area, have the same meaning as that expression or its local equivalent has in the existing law relating to land tenures in force in that area and shall also include—

(i) any *jagir, inam* or *muafi* or other similar grant and in the States of Tamil Nadu and Kerala, any *janmam* right;

(ii) any land held under ryotwari settlement;

(iii) any land held or let for purposes of agriculture or for purposes ancillary thereto, including waste land, forest land, land for pasture or sites of buildings and other structures occupied by cultivators of land, agricultural labourers and village artisans;

(b) the expression "rights", in relation to an estate, shall include any rights vesting in a proprietor, sub-proprietor, under-proprietor, tenure-holder, *raiyat, under-raiyat* or other intermediary and any rights or privileges in respect of land revenue.

Article #31B: Validation of certain Acts and Regulations.—

Without prejudice to the generality of the provisions contained in article 31A, none of the Acts and Regulations specified in the Ninth Schedule nor any of the provisions thereof shall be deemed to be void, or ever to have become void, on the ground that such Act, Regulation or provision is inconsistent with, or takes away or abridges any of the rights conferred by, any provisions of this Part, and notwithstanding any judgment, decree or order of any court or Tribunal to the contrary, each of the said Acts and Regulations shall, subject to the power of any competent Legislature to repeal or amend it, continue in force.

Article #31C: Saving of laws giving effect to certain directive principles.—

Notwithstanding anything contained in article 13, no law giving effect to the policy of the State towards securing [1][all or any of the principles laid down in Part IV] shall be deemed to be void on the ground that it is inconsistent with, or takes away or abridges any of the rights conferred by article 14 or article 19; [2]*and no law containing a declaration that it is for giving effect to such policy shall be called in question in any court on the ground that it does not give effect to such policy:*

Provided that where such law is made by the Legislature of a State, the provisions of this article shall not apply thereto unless such law, having been reserved for the consideration of the President, has received his assent.

Article #31D: [*Saving of laws in respect of anti-national activities.*] *Rep. by the Constitution (Forty-third Amendment) Act,*1977, *s.2 (w.e.f.*13-4-1978*).*

Right to Constitutional Remedies

Article # 32: Remedies for enforcement of rights conferred by this Part.—

(1) The right to move the Supreme Court by appropriate

proceedings for the enforcement of the rights conferred by this Part is guaranteed.

(2) The Supreme Court shall have power to issue directions or orders or writs, including writs in the nature of *habeas corpus, mandamus,* prohibition, *quo warranto* and *certiorari,* whichever may be appropriate, for the enforcement of any of the rights conferred by this Part.

(3) Without prejudice to the powers conferred on the Supreme Court by clauses (1) and (2), Parliament may by law empower any other court to exercise within the local limits of its jurisdiction all or any of the powers exercisable by the Supreme Court under clause (2).

(4) The right guaranteed by this article shall not be suspended except as otherwise provided for by this Constitution.

Article #33: Power of Parliament to modify the rights conferred by this Part in their application to Forces, etc.—

Parliament may, by law, determine to what extent any of the rights conferred by this Part shall, in their application to,—

(a) the members of the Armed Forces; or

(b) the members of the Forces charged with the maintenance of public order; or

(c) persons employed in any bureau or other organisation established by the State for purposes of intelligence or counter intelligence; or

(d) persons employed in, or in connection with, the telecommunication systems set up for the purposes of any Force, bureau or organisation referred to in clauses *(a)* to *(c)*, be restricted or abrogated so as to ensure the proper discharge of their duties and the maintenance of discipline among them.

Article #34: Restriction on rights conferred by this Part while martial law is in force in any area.—

Notwithstanding anything in the foregoing provisions

of this Part, Parliament may by law indemnify any person in the service of the Union or of a State or any other person in respect of any act done by him in connection with the maintenance or restoration of order in any area within the territory of India where martial law was in force or validate any sentence passed, punishment inflicted, forfeiture ordered or other act done under martial law in such area.

Article #35: Legislation to give effect to the provisions of this Part.—

Notwithstanding anything in this Constitution,—

(a) Parliament shall have, and the Legislature of a State shall not have, power to make laws—

(i) with respect to any of the matters which under clause (3) of article 16, clause (3) of article 32, article 33 and article 34 may be provided for by law made by Parliament; and

(ii) for prescribing punishment for those acts which are declared to be offences under this Part;

and Parliament shall, as soon as may be after the commencement of this Constitution, make laws for prescribing punishment for the acts referred to in sub-clause *(ii)*;

(b) any law in force immediately before the commencement of this Constitution in the territory of India with respect to any of the matters referred to in sub-clause (*i*) of clause (*a*) or providing for punishment for any act referred to in sub-clause (*ii*) of that clause shall, subject to the terms thereof and to any adaptations and modifications that may be made therein under article 372, continue in force until altered or repealed or amended by Parliament.

Explanation.—In this article, the expression "law in force" has the same meaning as in article 372.

PART IVA

FUNDAMENTAL DUTIES

Article #51A: Fundamental duties.—

It shall be the duty of every citizen of India—

(a) to abide by the Constitution and respect its ideals and institutions, the National Flag and the National Anthem;

(b) to cherish and follow the noble ideals which inspired our national struggle for freedom;

(c) to uphold and protect the sovereignty, unity and integrity of India;

(d) to defend the country and render national service when called upon to do so;

(e) to promote harmony and the spirit of common brotherhood amongst all the people of India transcending religious, linguistic and regional or sectional diversities; to renounce practices derogatory to the dignity of women;

(f) to value and preserve the rich heritage of our composite culture;

(g) to protect and improve the natural environment including forests, lakes, rivers and wild life, and to have compassion for living creatures;

(h) to develop the scientific temper, humanism and the spirit of inquiry and reform;

(i) to safeguard public property and to abjure violence;

(j) to strive towards excellence in all spheres of individual and collective activity so that the nation constantly rises to higher levels of endeavour and achievement.

PART XVII

OFFICIAL LANGUAGE

CHAPTER I—LANGUAGE OF THE UNION

Article #343: Official language of the Union.

(1) The official language of the Union shall be Hindi in Devanagari script.

The form of numerals to be used for the official purposes of the Union shall be the international form of Indian numerals.

(2) Notwithstanding anything in clause (1), for a period of fifteen years from the commencement of this Constitution, the English language shall continue to be used for all the official purposes of the Union for which it was being used immediately before such commencement:

Provided that the President may, during the said period, by order1 authorise the use of the Hindi language in addition to the English language and of the Devanagari form of numerals in addition to the international form of Indian numerals for any of the official purposes of the Union.

(3) Notwithstanding anything in this article, Parliament may by law provide for the use, after the said period of fifteen years, of—

(a) the English language, or

(b) the Devanagari form of numerals, for such purposes as may be specified in the law.

Article #344: Commission and Committee of Parliament on official language.

(1) The President shall, at the expiration of five years from the commencement of this Constitution and thereafter at the expiration of ten years from such commencement, by order constitute a Commission which shall consist of a Chairman and such other members representing the different languages specified in the Eighth Schedule as the President may appoint, and the order shall define the procedure to be followed by the Commission.

(2) It shall be the duty of the Commission to make recommendations to the President as to—

(a) the progressive use of the Hindi language for the official purposes of the Union;

(b) restrictions on the use of the English language for all or any of the official purposes of the Union;

(c) the language to be used for all or any of the purposes mentioned in article 348;

(d) the form of numerals to be used for any one or more specified purposes of the Union;

(e) any other matter referred to the Commission by the President as regards the official language of the Union and the language for communication between the Union and a State or between one State and another and their use.

(3) In making their recommendations under clause (2), the Commission shall have due regard to the industrial, cultural and scientific advancement of India, and the just claims and the interests of persons belonging to the non-Hindi speaking areas in regard to the public services.

(4) There shall be constituted a Committee consisting of thirty members, of whom twenty shall be members of the House of the People and ten shall be members of the Council of States to be elected respectively by the members of the House of the People and the members of the Council of States in accordance with the system of croportional representation by means of the single transferable vote.

(5) It shall be the duty of the Committee to examine the recommendations of the Commission constituted under clause (1) and to report to the President their opinion thereon.

(6) Notwithstanding anything in article 343, the President may, after consideration of the report referred to in clause (5), issue directions in accordance with the whole or any part of that report.

CHAPTER II—REGIONAL LANGUAGES

Article #345: Official language or languages of a State —

Subject to the provisions of articles 346 and 347, the Legislature of a State may by law adopt any one or more of the languages in use in the State or Hindi as the language or languages to be used for all or any of the official purposes of that State:

Provided that, until the Legislature of the State otherwise provides by law, the English language shall continue to be used for those official purposes within the State for which it was being used immediately before the commencement of this Constitution.

Article #346: Official language for communication between one State and another or between a State and the Union—

The language for the time being authorised for use in the Union for official purposes shall be the official language for communication between one State and another State and between a State and the Union:

Provided that if two or more States agree that the Hindi language should be the official language for communication between such States, that language may be used for such communication.

Article #347: Special provision relating to language spoken by a section of the population of a State –

On a demand being made in that behalf the President may, if he is satisfied that a substantial proportion of the population of a State desire the use of any language spoken by them to be recognised by that State, direct that such language shall also be officially recognised throughout that State or any part thereof for such purpose as he may specify.

CHAPTER III—LANGUAGE OF THE SUPREME COURT, HIGH COURTS, ETC.

Article #348: Language to be used in the Supreme Court and in the High Courts and for Acts, Bills, etc. —

(1) Notwithstanding anything in the foregoing provisions of this Part, until Parliament by law otherwise provides—

(a) all proceedings in the Supreme Court and in every High Court,

(b) the authoritative texts—

(i) of all Bills to be introduced or amendments thereto to be moved in either House of Parliament or in the House or either House of the Legislature of a State,

(ii) of all Acts passed by Parliament or the Legislature of a State and of all Ordinances promulgated by the President or the Governor of a State, and

(iii) of all orders, rules, regulations and bye-laws issued under this Constitution or under any law made by Parliament or the Legislature of a State, shall be in the English language.

(2) Notwithstanding anything in sub-clause *(a)* of clause (1), the Governor of a State may, with the previous consent of the President, authorise the use of the Hindi language, or any other language used for any official purposes of the State, in proceedings in the High Court having its principal seat in that State:

Provided that nothing in this clause shall apply to any judgment, decree or order passed or made by such High Court.

(3) Notwithstanding anything in sub-clause *(b)* of clause (1), where the Legislature of a State has prescribed any language other than the English language for use in Bills introduced in, or Acts passed by, the Legislature of the State or in Ordinances promulgated by the Governor of the State or in any order, rule, regulation or bye-law referred to in paragraph *(iii)* of that sub-clause, a translation of the same in the English language published under the authority of the Governor of the State in the Official Gazette of that State shall be deemed to be the authoritative text thereof in the English language under this article.

Article #349: Special procedure for enactment of certain laws relating to language—

During the period of fifteen years from the

commencement of this Constitution, no Bill or amendment making provision for the language to be used for any of the purposes mentioned in clause (1) of article 348 shall be introduced or moved in either House of Parliament without the previous sanction of the President, and the President shall not give his sanction to the introduction of any such Bill or the moving of any such amendment except after he has taken into consideration the recommendations of the Commission constituted under clause (1) of article 344 and the report of the Committee constituted under clause (4) of that article.

CHAPTER IV—SPECIAL DIRECTIVES

Article #350: Language to be used in representations for redress of grievances—

Every person shall be entitled to submit a representation for the redress of any grievance to any officer or authority of the Union or a State in any of the languages used in the Union or in the State, as the case may be.

Article #350A: Facilities for instruction in mother-tongue at primary stage—

It shall be the endeavour of every State and of every local authority within the State to provide adequate facilities for instruction in the mother-tongue at the primary stage of education to children belonging to linguistic minority groups; and the President may issue such directions to any State as he considers necessary or proper for securing the provision of such facilities.

Article #350B: (1) Special Officer for linguistic minorities.—

There shall be a Special Officer for linguistic minorities to be appointed by the President.

(2) It shall be the duty of the Special Officer to investigate all matters relating to the safeguards provided for linguistic minorities under this Constitution and report to the President

upon those matters at such intervals as the President may direct, and the President shall cause all such reports to be laid before each House of Parliament, and sent to the Governments of the States concerned.

Article #351: Directive for development of the Hindi language –

It shall be the duty of the Union to promote the spread of the Hindi language, to develop it so that it may serve as a medium of expression for all the elements of the composite culture of India and to secure its enrichment by assimilating without interfering with its genius, the forms, style and expressions used in Hindustani and in the other languages of India specified in the Eighth Schedule, and by drawing, wherever necessary or desirable, for its vocabulary, primarily on Sanskrit and secondarily on other languages.

REFERENCES

1. Amaury de Reincourt, *The Soul of India*, Harper & Bros; 1st edition (1960).
2. A.L. Basham, *Hinduism: The Concise Encyclopedia of Living Faiths*, Beacon Press, Boston, 1967.
3. A.L. Basham, *Jainism: The Concise Encyclopedia of Living Faiths*, Beacon Press, Boston, 1967.
4. A.L. Basham, *The Wonder that was India*, Sidgwick & Jackson, London, 1954.
5. Barbara D. Metcalf and Thomas R. Metcalf, *A Concise History of Modern India*, 2nd Ed. Cambridge University Press. 2006.
6. Barbara D. Metcalf and Thomas R. Metcalf, *Concise History of Modern India*, Second Edition, Cambridge University Press, 2006.
7. Bal Gangâdhar Tilak, *The Arctic Home in the Vedas*. Publishers Messrs. TILAK BROS, Gaikwar Wada, Poona City, 1903.
8. Bannanje Govindacharya (Kannada Original). 1997. *Madhvacharya.* Electronic version published by English version translated by Dr. K. Krishnamurthy and Dr. U.P.

Upadhyaya. Electronic version published by Tara Prakashana, 3, Sunberry Drive, Penfield, NY 14526 1997.

9. Clifford J. Jolly, Fred Plog, *Physical Anthropology and Archeology*, 4th Edition, Alfred A Knopf, Inc. 1987.

10. Chakravarthi Rajagopalachari, *Mahabharata*, 1954.

11. K. Chandramouli (2002-07-25). "*The City of Boiled Beans*". The Hindu, Thursday, July 25, 2002 (Chennai, India: The Hindu).

12. Constitution of India (Modified up to the 1st December 2007).

13. David Frawley, *The Myth of Aryan Invasion of India.*

14. Dr. D. Devakunjari, 2010. *Madurai Through the Ages*, Arulmigu Meenakshi Sundareswarar Thirukkoil, Madurai.

15. David M. Knipe, *Hinduism.* Harper Collins Publishers, N.Y. 1991.

16. D. Devakunjarim *Madurai Through the Ages*, Society for Archaeological, Historical and Epigraphical Research, Madras, 2010.

17. Edward James Rapson, *The Cambridge History of India*, CUP Archive, 1922, India.

18. Edward C. Sachau, 1845–1930. (Translator and Editor) 2 Vols. 1910, Kegan Paul, Trench, Trubner & Co. Ltd., London.

19. Edward C. Sachau, 1910. *Alberuni's India*, An account of the religion, philosophy, literature, geography, chronology, astronomy, customs, laws and astrology of India about A.D. 1030. (Edited with Notes and Indices by Edward).

20. The Gazetteer of India, Volume 1: *Country and people.* Delhi, Publications Division, Government of India, 1965. Chapter VIII - Religion, HINDUISM. By Dr. C.P. Ramaswami Aiyar, Dr. Nalinaksha Dutt, Prof. A.R. Wadia, Prof. M. Mujeeb, Dr. Dharm Pal and Fr. Jerome D'Souza, S.J., Dr. C.P. Ramaswami Aiyar, Dr. Nalinaksha Dutt, Prof. A.R. Wadia, Prof. M. Mujeeb, Dr. Dharm Pal and Fr. Jerome D'Souza, S.J.

21. Gregory L. Possehl, *Mehrgarh*, Period I, Period II, Period III, Craft Production in Early Periods, Periods IV–VII, Hordeum vulgare, vulgare.

22. *Harbans, Mukhia, 2004. The Mughals of India, Blackwell Publishing.*
23. I.B. Horner, Buddhism: Mahayana. Concise Encyclopedia of Living Faiths, Beacon Press, Boston, 1967.
24. I.B. Horner, *Buddhism: Theravada. Concise Encyclopedia of Living Faiths,* Beacon Press, Boston, 1967.
25. Imperial Gazetteer of India Vol. IV (1907), *The Indian Empire, Administrative,* Published under the authority of His Majesty's Secretary of State for India in Council, Oxford at the Clarendon Press. pp. xxx, 1 map, 552. (look in library).
26. Ismail ragi al Faruqi (Ed) & David E. Sopher (Ed), *Historical Atlas of the Religions of the World,* Macmillan Publishing Co., Ind. New York. 1974.
27. John Whitney Hall, Editor, *History of the World,* World Publication Group, Inc. 1988.
28. A. Jayaram. *Karnataka's Illustrious Rajput Connection,* The Hindu, May 31, 2004.
29. R. Shamasastry 1915. *Kautilya's Arthashastra.* Translated into English, Bangalore Government Press. 1915.
30. Kalyan Ray, Craftsmen Lived in South India 1.5 mn years ago: *Deccan Herald.* 26 March 11.
31. Lars Martin Fosse. *The Bhagavad Gita,* YogaVidya.com, Woodstock, New York 12498-0569 USA.
32. Maurice S. Dimand (1953). *Mughal Painting under Akbar the Great. The Metropolitan Museum of Art Bulletin* 12 (2): 46–51.
33. J.W. McCRINDLE, "Ancient India as described by Megasthenes and Arrian", Brubner & Co. London, 1877.
34. B. Pattabhi Sitaramayya (1935), *The History of the Indian National Congress,* Working Committee of the Congress.
35. S. Radhakrishnan, *Indian Philosophy,* Vol. I, George Allen & Unwin Ltd., 1923.
36. S. Radhakrishnan, *Indian Philosophy,* Vol. II, George Allen & Unwin Ltd., 1923.
37. E.J. Rapson, Ed. 1922. *The Cambridge History of India,* Vol. I, The University Press.

38. Raghunath S. Pappu, Contribution of R.B. Foote to the Indian Paleolithic Studies. Prehistoric Cultures of North East India and South East Asia, A Comparative Study, Proceedings of Robert Bruce Foote on Indian Prehistory and Protohistory, 2004.

39. Robert C. Lester, 1987. *Buddhism*, Harper & Row, Publishers, San Francisco.

40. Romalia Thaper, *Ancient Indian Social History*: Some Interpretations, Orient Blackswan, 1978.

41. Robert Sewell, Fernão Nunes, Domingos Paes. *A forgotten Empire: Vijayanagar*. Kessinger Publishing, 2004.

42. D.P. Sharma, *Prehistoric Cultures of North East India and South East Asia*, A Comparative Study, Proceedings of Robert Bruce Foote on Indian Prehistory and Protohistory, 2004.

43. Sailendra Nath Sen, *Ancient Indian History and Civilization*. New Age International, 1999.

44. A.K. Sharma, *The Prehistoric Narmada Man, Prehistoric Cultures of North East India and South East Asia*, A Comparative Study, Proceedings of Robert Bruce Foote on Indian Prehistory and Protohistory, 2004.

45. Subodh Kapoor. *The Indian Encyclopedia*, Volume 1.

46. S.R. Sarma, S.M.R. Ansar, A.G. Kulkarni, 1992. *Two Mughal Celestial Globes*. Indian Journal of History of Science.

47. Selig S. Harrison. *The Challenge to Indian Nationalism*, Vol. 34, No.4, July 1956.

48. Tilak and Gokhale: *a comparative study of their socio-politico-economic* By Mohammad Shabbir Khan.

49. Thapar, Romila (1978, reprint 1996). *Ancient Indian Social History: Some Interpretations*, New Delhi: Orient Longman.

50. Vivekananda, Lectures *from Colombo to Almora*, Advaita Ashrama, Calcutta, 13th Edition, 1992.

51. Whitefield Foy, *The Religious Quest*, Rutledge, London, 1988.

INTERNET REFERENCES

1. Wikepedia

2. Ganesh N. Devy, *Indigenous languages*: http://www.india-seminar.com/2009/600/601_ganesh_n_devy.htm
3. India forum: http://www.indiaforum.org/india/hinduism/aryan/page26.html
4. Vedas : http://www.crystalinks.com/vedas.html
5. Jainism at: http://en.wikipedia.org/wiki/jainism
6. http://www.jrank.org/history/pages/6295/Mehrgarh.html
7. htp://tamilnadumonuments.com/history.html

Appendices

Appendix I
List of Prime Ministers of India

Sl.No.	Names	Period		Part
1.	Jawaharlal Nehru	August 15, 1947	to May 27, 1964	Congress
2.	Gulzarilal Nanda	May 27, 1964	to June 9, 1964	Congress
3.	Lal Bahadur Shastri	June 9, 1964	to January 11, 1966	Congress
4.	Gulzarilal Nanda	January 11, 1966	to January 24, 1966	Congress
5.	Indira Gandhi	January 24, 1966	to March 24, 1977	Congress
6.	Morarji Desai	March 24, 1977	to July 28, 1979	Janata Party
7.	Choudhary Charan Singh	July 28, 1979	to January 14, 1980	Janata Party
8.	Indira Gandhi	January 14, 1980	to October 31, 1984	Congress
9.	Rajiv Gandhi	October 31, 1984	to December 2, 1989	Congress
10.	Vishwanath Pratap Singh	December 2, 1989	to November 10, 1990	Janata Dal
11.	Chandra Shekhar	November 10,1990	to June 21, 1991	Janata Dal
12.	P.V. Narasimha Rao	June 21, 1991	to May 16, 1996	Congress (I)
13.	Atal Behari Vajpayee	May 16, 1996	to June 1, 1996	BJP
14.	H.D. Deve Gowda	June 1, 1996	to April 21, 1997	Janata Dal
15.	Inder Kumar Gujral	April 21, 1997	to March 19, 1998	Janata Dal
16.	Atal Behari Vajpayee	March 19, 1998	to May 22, 2004	BJP
17.	Manmohan Singh	May 22, 2004	to Present	Congress

Appendix II

National Parties

A list of recognised National Parties. (Election Commission of India as of September 2009)

S.N.	*Symbol*	*Name*	*Acronym*	*Year*
1.		Bahujan Samaj Party	BSP	1984
2.		Bharatiya Janata Party	BJP	1980
3.		Communist Party of India	CPI	1925
4.		Communist Party of India (Marxist)	CPI (M)	1964
5.		Indian National Congress	INC	1885
6.		Nationalist Congress Party	NCP	1999

State

A list of recognized State Parties. (Election Commission of India as of September 2009).

S.N.	Symbol	Name	Acronym	Year	States
1.		All Jharkhand Students Union Party	AJSU	1986	Jharkhand
2.		All India Anna Dravida Munnetra Kazhagam	AIADMK	1972	Tamil Nadu, Puducherry
3.		All India Forward Bloc	AIFB	1939	West Bengal
4.		All India Trinamool Congress	AITC	1998	Arunachal Pradesh, West Bengal
5.	Lock & Key	All India United Democratic Front	AUDF	2004	Assam
6.	Elephant	Asom Gana Parishad	AGP	1985	Assam
7.		Biju Janata Dal	BJD	1997	Orissa
8.	Nangol	Bodoland People's Front	BPF		Assam
9.		Dravida Munnetra Kazhagam	DMK	1949	Tamil Nadu, Puducherry
10.	Paniharin	Haryana Janhit Congress (BL)	HJC(BL)		Haryana

S.N.	Symbol	Name	Acronym	Year	States
11.		Indian National Lok Dal	INLD	1999	Haryana
12.		Jammu & Kashmir National Conference	JKNC	1932	Jammu and Kashmir
13.		Jammu & Kashmir National Panthers Party	JKNPP	NA[D]	Jammu and Kashmir
14.		Jammu and Kashmir People's Democratic Party	PDP	1998	Jammu and Kashmir
15.		Janata Dal (Secular)	JD (S)	1999	Karnataka, Kerala
16.		Janata Dal (United)	JD (U)	1999	Bihar
17.		Jharkhand Mukti Morcha	JMM	1972	Jharkhand, Orissa
18.		Jharkhand Vikas Morcha (Prajatantrik)	JVM(P)	2006	Jharkhand
19.		Kerala Congress	KEC	1964	Kerala

S.N.	Symbol	Name	Acronym	Year	States
20.		Kerala Congress (M)	KEC (M)	1979	Kerala
21.	Bungalow	Lok Jan Shakti Party	LJSP	2000	Bihar
22.	Railway Engine	Maharashtra Navnirman Sena	MNS	2006	Maharashtra
23.		Maharashtrawadi Gomantak Party	MAG	1963	Goa
24.		Manipur People's Party	MPP	1968	Manipur
25.		Mizo National Front	MDF	1959	Mizoram
26.		Mizoram People's Conference	MPC	1972	Mizoram
27.		Muslim League Kerala State Committee	MUL	1948	Kerala

S.N.	Symbol	Name	Acronym	Year	States
28.		Nagaland People's Front	NPF	2002	Nagaland
29.		National People's Party	NPP	1997	
30.		Pattali Makkal Katchi	PMK	1989	Tamil Nadu
31.		Peoples Party of Arunachal	PPA	1978	Arunachal Pradesh
32.	Full Sun with rays	Praja Rajyam Party	PRP	2008	Andhra Pradesh
33.		Pudhucherry Munnetra Congress	PMC	2005	Puducherry
34.	Hurricane Lamp	Rashtriya Janata Dal	RJD	1997	Bihar, Jharkhand, Manipur
35.		Rashtriya Lok Dal	RLD	1974	Uttar Pradesh
36.		Revolutionary Socialist Party	RSP	1940	West Bengal
37.		Samajwadi Party	SP	1992	Uttar Pradesh
38.		Save Goa Front	SGF	NA	Goa
39.		Shiromani Akali Dal	SAD	1920	Punjab

S.N.	Symbol	Name	Acronym	Year	States
40.		Shiv Sena	SHS	1966	Maharashtra
41.		Sikkim Democratic Front	SDF	1993	Sikkim
42.	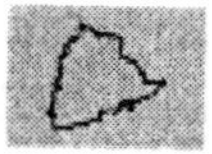	Telangana Rashtra Samithi	TRS	2001	Andhra Pradesh
43.		Telugu Desam Party	TDP	1982	Andhra Pradesh
44.		United Democratic Party	UDP	NA	Meghalaya
45.		Uttarakhand Kranti Dal	UKKD	1979	Uttarakhand
46.		Zoram Nationalist Party	ZNP	1997	Mizoram

APPENDEX III

Indian States and Union Territories

S.N.	Name	Language	Capital
1.	Andhra Pradesh	Telugu, Urdu, Hindi	Hyderabad
2.	Arunachal Pradesh		Itanagar
3.	Assam	Assamese, Bodo, Rabha dialect, Deori, Bengali	Dispur
4.	Bihar	Urdu, Bhojpuri, Maithili, Magadhi	Patna
5.	Chhattisgarh	Chattisgarhi, Hindi	Raipur
6.	Goa	Konkani, Marathi	Panaji
7.	Gujarat	Gujarati	Gandhinagar
8.	Haryana	Haryanvi(Western Hindi)	Chandigarh (shared)
9.	Himachal Pradesh	Western Hindi	Shimla
10.	Jammu and Kashmir	Kashmiri	Srinagar (summer) Jammu (winter)
11.	Jharkhand	Hindi	Ranchi
12.	Karnataka	Kannada	Bengaluru
13.	Kerala	Malayalam	Thiruvananthapuram
14.	Madhya Pradesh	Hindi	Bhopal
15.	Maharashtra	Marathi	Mumbai
16.	Manipur	Manipuri	Imphal
17.	Meghalaya	Khasi, Pnar	Shillong
18.	Mizoram	Mizo	Aizawl
19.	Nagaland	Naga	Kohima
20.	Odisha (formerly Orissa)	Odia	Bhubaneswar
21.	Punjab	Punjabi	Chandigarh (shared)
22.	Rajasthan	Rajasthani (Western Hindi)	Jaipur
23.	Sikkim	Nepali	Gangtok
24.	Tamil Nadu	Tamil	Chennai
25.	Tripura	Bengali	Agartala
26.	Uttar Pradesh	Hindi, Urdu[2]	Lucknow
27.	Uttarakhand	Western Hindi	Dehradun (interim)
28.	West Bengal	Bengali, Nepali, Santali	Kolkata

Union Territories

No.	*Name*	*Language*	*Capital*
1.	Andaman and Nicobar Islands	Bengali	Port Blair
2.	Chandigarh	Punjabi	Chandigarh
3.	Dadra and Nagar Haveli	Marathi and Gujarati	Silvassa
4.	Daman and Diu	Gujarati	Daman
5.	Lakshadweep	Malayalam	Kavaratti
6.	National Capital Territory	Hindi	New Delhi
7.	Puducherry	French and Tamil	Puducherry

APPENDIX IV
List of Indian Languages

Adi
Adiwasi Garasia
Agariya
Anal
Andaman Creole Hindi
Andh
Angami
Ao
Apatani
Arakanese
Assamese
Asuri
Balti
Bazigar
Bengali
Betta Kurumba
Bhadrawahi
Bhattiyali
Bhili/Bhilodi
Bhunjia
Biete
Birhor
Bishnupriya
Bodo
Bodo Parja
Braj Bhasha
Buksa
Car Nicobarese
Chang Naga
Changthang
Chenchu
Chokri Naga
Churahi
Dangaura Tharu
Degaru
Deori
Desiya Odia
Dhatki
Dhivehi (Mahl dialect)
Dimasa
Dogri
Dogri
Dungra Bhil
Duruwa
Eastern Magar
Eastern Muria
Eastern Tamang
English
Falam Chin
Far Western Muria
Gadaba
Gaddi
Gangte
Garo
Gondi
Gowlan
Gowli
Gujarati
Hajong
Halabi
Hmar
Ho
Hrangkhol
Idu-Mishmi
Inpui Naga
Jaunsari
Jennu Kurumba
Juang
Kabui (Rongmei)
Kachari
Kaikadi
Kalto (Nahali)
Kamar
Kanikkaran
Kanjari
Kannada
Karbi/Mikir
Kashmiri
Khandeshi
Kharia
Khasi
Khezha Naga
Khiamniungan Naga
Khirwar
Khoibu Naga
Khond/Kondh
Khowar
Kinnauri

Kisan
Koch
Kodagu
Kokborok
Kolami
Konda-Dora
Konkani
Konyak
Korku
Korra Koraga
Korwa
Koya
Kudmali
Kui
Kullu
Kumarbhag Paharia
Kurichiya
Kurukh
Ladakhi
Lamkang
Lepcha
Liangmai Naga
Limbu
Lodhi:
Lotha
Mahali
Maithili
Majhwar
Mal Paharia
Malaryan
Malavedan
Malayalam
Malto
Manna-Dora
Mao
Mara
Maram Naga
Marathi
Maring Naga
Matu Chin
Mawchi
Meitei/Manipuri
Mirgan
Mishing
Mizo
Moinba
Mudu Koraga
Mukha-Dora
Munda
Mundari
Muthuvan
Mzieme Naga
Naga Pidgin
Nepali
Nishi
Nocte Naga
Noiri
Northern Pashto
Northern Rengma Naga
Odia
Ooty, Nilgiris
Paite
Palya Bareli
Pangwali
Paniya
Pardhan
Pardhi
Pattani
Persian
Phom
Pnar
Pochuri Naga
Poumei Naga
Punjabi
Rabha
Rajput Garasia
Rana Tharu
Rathwi Bareli
Ravula
Rawang
Reli
Sakechep
Sangtam Naga
Sansi
Santali
Saurashtra
Sauria Paharia
Savara
Savara
Sema
Seraiki
Sherpa
Shina
Sholaga

Sikkimese
Sindhi
Sirmauri
Southern Rengma Naga
Spiti Bhoti
Tamil
Tangkhul
Tase Naga
Telugu
Thado
Thangal Naga
Tibetan
Tiwa
Toto
Tulu
Tutsa Naga
Ullatan
Urdu
Vaagri Booli
Vaiphei
Wancho Naga
War
Western Muria
Western Panjabi
Yimchungru Naga
Zangskari
Zeme Naga

Number of Official Languages of India

No.	State	Language
1.	Andhra Pradesh	Telugu
2.	Arunachal Pradesh	English
3.	Assam	Assamese
4.	Bihar	Maithili, Hindi
5.	Chhattisgarh	Chhattisgarhi, Hindi
6.	Goa	Konkani
7.	Gujarat	Gujarati, Hindi
8.	Haryana	Hindi
9.	Himachal Pradesh	Hindi
10.	Jammu and Kashmir	Urdu
11.	Jharkhand	Hindi, Santali
12.	Karnataka	Kannada
13.	Kerala	Malayalam, English
14.	Madhya Pradesh	Hindi
15.	Maharashtra	Marathi
16.	Manipur	Meiteilon (Manipuri)
17.	Meghalaya	English
18.	Mizoram	Mizo
19.	Nagaland	English
20.	Orissa	Oriya,
21.	Punjab	Punjabi
22.	Rajasthan	Hindi
23.	Sikkim	Nepali
24.	Tamil Nadu	Tamil
25.	Tripura	Bengali, Kokborok, English
26.	Uttarakhand	English, Hindi

Index

A

Abhidhamma Pitaka, 80
Abhijnana Shakuntala by Kalidasa, 40
Aboriginal Tribes, 110, 135, 136
Acheulian Tools, 12, 13
Aden—Mecca, 156
Adi
  Advaita Philosopher, 160
  Books written, 161
  Brahma Samaj, 247
  Granth, 212
  Shankaracharya, 160, 162
Adil
  Shahi Rulers, 189
  Shahis, 188
Administration, 105, 106, 110, 148, 157, 170, 224
  Of the Mauryan Dynasty, 119
Administration Division, 83
  Executive, 83
  Judicial, 83
  Military Functions, 83
Administrative System, 107
Advait
  Vedant, 247
  Vedantism, 160
  Philosophy, 161
Advanced Technologies, 16
Afghanistan, 122, 156, 181, 183, 189, 190
  And Pakistan, 119
  Mountains, 129
Africa, 221
Age of Consent Bill, 1891, 270
Agni, 31
Agriculture and Metallurgy, 28
Ahimsa or Non-Violence, 237
Ahsanabad (Gulbarga), Bahamani Capital, 186
Aihole
  And Badamai Territory, 145
  Inscriptions, 145
AIIMS, 274
Ajat Shatru, 83
Ajiva, 74
Ajivika Sect, 112
Akbar, 107, 190-192, 194, 278
Akbar The Great, 170, 209
Akshauhini, 42, 44
Ala-ud-Din Hasan Bahman Shah, 186
Alauddin, 170
Alauddin Khilji, 183
  Conquered Mandu—Malva, 183
Alberuni, 173-176, 181
  Books on India, 176
  Knowledge of Maths,
Astronomy, Geography—Linguist, 173
Alburquerque, Afonso de, 218
Alexander, 87, 104, 87
Alexander the Great, 96, 119, 216
All India Home Rule League, 270

Alpine Caucasians, 6
Ambedkar, Dr. B.R.,
Untouchable Leader, 276, 277
Anandpal, 172
Ancient
Culture of Mesopotamia, 19
Hymns, 8
India, 12
Indian Culture, 28
Persians, 27
Stone Tools Mining Industry, 12
Tamil Kingdom, 140
Andaman and Nicobar Islands, 143
Andamans, 4
Andhra Pradesh Coastal Rivers, 330
Andronova
Culture, 29
Sites, 29
Anga—Kamboja, 38
Angaraland Plate, 4
Anglo-Maratha
War I, 214
War III, 215
Anglo-Mysore, 196, 198
War I, 198
War II, 199
Anglo-Sikh War, 211
Anglo-Sikh War II, 211
Animal Economy, 16
Antioch, 140
Antiochus, 112
Antyajas, 148
Apabhransha Phase, 9
Aquatic Fossils, 2
Arabian—Latin Languages, 245
Arabic
And Persians Inscriptions, 208
Dravidians, Turkish, Farsi, Portuguese, Persian—Languages, 9
Arabic-Persian-Telugu, 188
Arachosia, 121
Archaeological
Excavations, 21
Survey of India, 138
Architectural Grandeur of Deccan, 188
Architecture, 116
Ari Kesari, Court Poet of Chalukyas, 76
Ariana, 121
Arjan Dev, 212
Arjun, 39, 50, 51, 148
Art of Writing, 26
Arthasastra, 88, 89, 107
On Administration, 89, 100
On Rules Regarding Labourers, 93
Artistic style and Technology, 136
Arts, 2
And Crafts, 28
And Education, 206
Arya Samaj, 237, 255
Established by Swamy Dayananda Saraswati, 255
Principles, 255-256
Aryan
Civilisation, 25
Culture and Civilisation, 28
Dharma, 27
Immigration, 138
Invaders 26
Invasion Theory, (AIT), 25, 27
Invasions, 26, 27
Leaders, 26
North Pole Original Home of, 27

Traditions, 139
Tribesmen, 25
Varna Pattern, 139
Aryans, 21, 28, 64,135
Aryans (Bharatas, Yadus, Anus and Purus), 26
Ashoka, 113, 139, 143
Buddhist Ruler, 278
Death, 123
Inscriptions, 143
Maurya's Leadership, 83
The Great, 109
Ashoka's
Activities, 111
Death, 113
Grandson Brihadratha, 113
Life, 110-112
Sons' Viceroys in Taxila and Ujjain, 112
Ashvins, 30
Asian Plate, 2
Atharva Veda, 31, 36, 56
Atharvam, Ancient Poet, 31
Athenian Buildings, 110
Attirampakkam Excavations, 12
Aurangzeb, 194, 213, 214
Death in 1707, 196, 199
Son of Shah Jahan, 194
Australia, 2
Australian Constitution, 277
Australoid Group, 20
Australoids, 6
Austrian Ostend East India Company, 217
Avalokiteshwara, 81

B

Babar, 185, 189, 192
Introduced Gunpowder (in India), 190
Mughal Emperor, 182
Bacteria, 121
Badami Chalukyas, 145
Badkshan, 16
Bahamani
Sultan Ahmad Shah, 151
Sultanate, 185, 186
Sultanate Army, 187
Bahraich and Gonda Regions (UP), 151
Baked Bricks, 19
Bal Gangadhar Tilak's Theory, 27
Baladitya, Narasimhagupta, 115
Balarama, 45
Balban, 183
Baluchistan, 221
Bana, 127
Bank of Narmada, 13
Barabar Hills, 112
Basaveshwara, 167
Founded Anubhava Mantapa, 168
Mystic, 168
Philosopher, 168
Revolutionary, 168
Social Reformer, 168
Teachings, 168
Battle
At Madurai, 153
Of Panipat, 185
Of Panipat, I, 190
Of Panipat, II, 191
Of Panipat III, 214
Of Panipat, (1526), 189
Of Plassey in 1757, 220
Of Wandiwash, 220
Bead Drilling Industry, 17
Benares, 245
Bengal, 6
Renaissance, 246, 252
Bengali
Art, 261
Bhakti Tradition, 247
Intellectuals, 237

Bentinck, Lord William, 233
Besent, Annie, 270
Bhagavad Gita, Brief, 49-52
Bhangara and Giddha, 212
Bharasila, 87
Bharat-Bahubali Ras, 77
Bharathas, 85
Bharatpur, Maharaja of-, 130
Bhima, 40, 42, 85
Bhonsales of Nagpur, 214
Bidar Sultanate, 187
Bijayapur Sultanate, 188
Bijjala, Who Destroyed
    Chalukyas, 151, 152
Bimbasara, 83
Bindusara's Son Ashoka, 109
Black Skinned Inhabitants, 6
Bodhisattavas, 81
Bolan, 21
    River, 16
Bone Industry, 16
Book Keeping and
    Registration, 106
Borneo, 221
Bose, Subhash Chandra
    (Netaji), Brief, 271
    Indian Revolutionary, 271
Braham Sutras, 162
Brahma Samaj, 246, 247,
    252, 259
    Doctrines, 254
    Established by
    Dwarkanath Tagore, 252
    Principles, 252
Brahmanical Religions, 138
Brahmanism
    And Upanishads, 258
    Of Vedas, 56
Brahmans and Upanishads,
    29
Brahmi Script, 73
Brahmins and Buddhists,
    137
British
    Awards and Honours
        (Return of), 237
    Constitution, 276
    East India Company, 220
    Empire, 211
    India, 220, 223, 224, 234
    India Naval Forces, 214
    Legislature, 239
    Life, 233
    Muhammadan Affairs,
        196
    Raj, 129, 222
    Rule, 1, 224, 271
Bronze Age, 118
Buddha, 78, 79, 81, 83
Buddha Kanakamuni, 112
Buddha's Teachings, 78, 80,
    81
Buddhism, 77-81, 109, 111,
    127, 160, 277
    And Jainism, 135, 160,
        164
    And Jainism, Emergence
        of, 8
    Jainism, Saivism,
        Vaishnavism, 38
Buddhist, 9, 149
    And Jain Missionaries,
        139
    Dharm, 80, 111
    Order, 111
    Shahis, 123
    Text, 37
    Version of Ramayana, 49
Bukka Raja I, 154
Burial of Tippu Saheb, 200
Burj Barket Marked Phase,
    16
Burma to Vietnam, 143
Butchering, 12
Button Seals, 16

C

Cable Linking Britain and India, 233
Canals, 110
Candra Dynastry, 134
Capital Punishment, 148
Caravans Sarais, 110
Carnatic Music, 66
Caste Virus, 250
Catholic Soldiers, 197
Catholics in India, 218
Caucasoid Inhabitants of India, 6
Central Asia, 5, 10, 27, 111
Central Asian Culture, 118
Central India, 5, 6
Ceramic Mehrgarh I, 16
Ceramics, 17
Ceylonese Island to India, 4
Chakra Vyuha, 42
Chalukya, 146
  Dynasty, 146
  Empire, 145
  Of Valapi Badami, 146
Chalukyas, 149, 150, 154
Chanakya, Kautilya, 86
Chandra Gupta I, (Not Chandragupta Maurya), 113
Chandragupta II, Also Called Vikramaditya, 114
Char Minar, 188
Charkhari State in Madhya Pradesh, 130
Charyapada, Buddhist Work, 132
Chatrapati Shivaji, 213
  Staunch Hindu, 215
Chattopadhayay, Bankim Chandra, 241
  Bio-Brief, 265-266
Chauhanas of Ajmer, 131
Chavundaraya Purana, 145
Chedi Dynasty, 124
Chera (s), 139, 141, 142
  Kings, 142
  Were Shaivite Hindus, 142
Chess,
  As Chaturanga, 116
  Originated during Gupta Period, 116
China, 111, 143, 156
Chola
  Dynasty, 143
  Kingdom, 152
Cholas, 139, 141, 143, 144, 149
Christian Missionaries, 238
Christianity, 259, 260
Christians Institution in India, 254
Citizenship (under Indian Constitution), 284
Civil Disorder, 237
Classical
  Sanskrit Authors, 8
  Vedic Thought, 162
Classical Language, 8
  Arabic, 8
  Greek, 8
  Hebrew, 8
  Latin, 8
  Persian, 8
Coastline, 214
Collegiate Building, 20
Colombia University, 277
Colonial India, 215-275
Coloured Pottery, 24
Commentaries of Vedas, Upanishads, Gita—Political by Ghosh A, 263
Composers of Rig-Veda, (CRV), 29
  Agasthya and Bharata, 29
  Angirasa, 29
  Atri, 29
  Bhrigu, 29
  Grtsamada, 29

Kanva, 29
Kashyapa, 29
Vasishtha, 29
Conglomerah Deposits, 13
Constitution,
Australian, 277
British, 276
French, 277
Irish, 277
Japanese, 277
Malaysian, 277
Of India, 10, 281, 282
Details, 282-308
Preamble, 282
Russian, 277
USA, 277
Weimer, 277
Copper
Melting Crucibles, 16
Plate Inscription of Maharaja Sharvanatha, 40
Coromandal Coast, 219
Coronation, 111
Cosmetics, 108
Cosmopolitan Civilisation, 20
Court of Chandragupta Maurya, 140
Cow Protection Societies, 237
Cretaceous, 2
And Tertiary Periods, 4
Cubical Buildings and Granaries, 16
Cultural and Educational Rights, 286
Culture and Philosophy, 64
Cultures, 120
Central Asia, 120
Greek, 120
India, 120
Curative Powers of Herbs and Water, 31
Customs and Practices, 74

D

Dakhni Urdu Language, 188
Dakshineswar Kali Temple, 246
Dalhousie, 224, 233
Dam Sadaat, 17
Dams, 243
Danish, 219
Dasyus, 26, 135
Dayanand Saraswati, Swami, 248, 255, 257-258
Deccan
Education Society, 270
Lava, 2
Sultanate, 186
Sultanate's Cultural Contributions, 188
Deccani Miniature Paintings, 188
Decimal System, 116
Deity Mariamma, 153
Delhi Sultanate, 182
Democracy, 1
Depressed Forest Tribes, 276
Devas and Asuras Battles, 56
Development of Modern Linguistic Science, 7
Devotional Movement, 162
Dharm Mahamatras, 112
Dharmachakra, 82
Dialects, 11
Avadhi, 11
Bagheli, 11
Bhojpuri-Maithili, 11
Braj, 11
Bundali, 11
Chhattisgarhi, 11
Kanauji, 11
Marwari, 11
Urdu, 11
Diamond Mining, 156
Dilruba, 211
Dinabandhu, Dramatist, 241

Dinosaur Fossils, 2
Disadvantaged Groups, 276
District(s)
    Coimbatore and Salem, 141
    Of Bihar—Gaya, 83
Doctrine of
    Karma, 255
    Moksha, 71
Dowry to Catherine of Braganza, 218
Drainage, 5
    System, 19
Dravidian
    Cultures, 139
    Jain Culture, 140
    Language, 138
    Social Order, 139
    Tribes, 138
Dravidians Family of Languages, (DFL), 7
    Kannada, 7
    Malayalam, 7
    Tamil, 7
    Telugu, 7
    Tulu, 7
Duryodhana, 40, 42
Dutch East India Company, 219
Dutta, Narendranath, 248
Dvaita
    Philosophy, 70, 164, 165
        Panch Vedas, 165
Dynasties, 85
    Brihadratha Dynasty, 84, 85
    Gupta, 84, 88
    Harayanka, 84
    Kanva, 84
    Maurya, 84, 85
    Nanda, 84, 85
    Pradyota Dynasty, 84, 85
    Shishunaga, 84, 85
    Sunga, 84

E

Early
    Agrarian Societies, 59
    Indian Perceptions, 1
        Religious and Theological, 1
    Stone Age, 13
East India Company, 221-223
    Austrian Ostend, 217
    British, 220
    Dutch, 219
    English, 217
    French, 217
    Of Netherlands, 217
    Portuguese, 217
    Swedish, 217
Eastern
    Afghanistan, 118
    Ganga Dynasty, 134
        Ananta Varma Chodaganga—Bhanudeva-IV, 134
    Gangas, 134
Ecological River Changes, 28
Economy, 118
Edicts of Ashoka, 106
Education, 110, 245
    Classes of India, 1
Egypt, 20
Egyptian Civilisation, 20
Eight Fold Path, 109
Emperor
    Ashoka, 109
    Augustus of Rome, 140
    Brihadratha, 85
Empire of Magadh, 119
English
    East India Company, 217
    Education, 238
Epic Period, 38
Epics and Ramayana, 8
Essence of Gita by Emerson, RW, 52

Establishment of New States, 283
Europe, 6
European
  Caucasians, 6
  Imperialism, 220
European
  Liberalism, 245
  Trade Centres at Kollam, 218
Evergreen Forest, 5
Excavations, 15

F

Fa Hien, Chinese Pilgrim, 136
Fatehpuri Sikri, 206
Fath-Ullah Imad-ul-Malik, Governor of Berar, 187
Fathullah Shirazi,
  Invented Multi Barrel Gun, 209
  Persian Indian Engineering, 209
Female Slaves, 108
Fertile Upland, 12
Firoz Shah Tughlaq, 184
Fiscal System, 107
Five Year Plan (1st) to Five Year Plan (11th), 278-280
Five Year Plans, 278
  Objectives, 278
Flexed Burials, 16
Flint Tools, 24
Folk Music, 67
Foreign
  Invasions, 128
  Universities, 28
Formation of
  Grammar and Grammatical Operations, 7
  New States, 283
Fort of Tirthahalli, 199
Fossilised Human Skill, 12
Free Trade, 245
Freedom
  Of Press and Speech, 276
  Struggles in Bangladesh, 280
French
  Constitution, 277
  East India Company, 217
Fundamental
  Duties, 301
  Rights, 287-296
Funeral Rites, 98

G

Gaekwads of Baroda, 214
Gaj Valley, 21
Gandhara, 87, 118, 119, 121
  Centre of International Commercial Activities, 118
  Grace Culture, 118
Gandhi
  And Nehru, 278
  Gita-Gospel of selfless Action, 53
  Mahatma, 51, 248
  MK (Bio-Brief), 272
  Mohandas Karamchand, 237
Gandhi's
  Idealism, 277
  Political Thinking, 52
Gandhism, 277
Ganga Dynasty of Talkad, 145
Gangaikonda Cholapuram
City, 144
Ganges, 83
  Basin, 122
  Canal, 224
Gangetic
  And Brahmputra System, 5
  Plain, 6, 24, 118, 126, 129
Genghis Khan, 171

Known as Moghulistan, 171
Geological Evolution, 2
Geology of India, 2
German Romantics, 52
Ghatotkacha, 113
Ghaznavid Empire, 173
Ghazni Tughlaq (Ghiyath-al-Din Tuqhlaq), 183
Ghosh, Aurobindo, Brief Biography, 262-264
Freedom Fighter, 262
Indian Nationalist, 262
Newspaper by him-entitled Bande Matram, 262
Philosopher, 262
Spiritual and Philosophical Activities, 264
Studied in London, 262
Writings on Life Divine Synthesis of Yoga, 262
Gita, 53
Gita's Teachings, 52
Goa, Daman, Diu, 219
God Siva, 21
Gokhale, Gopal Krishan, 237, 267, 268
Died in 1915, 269
Gandhi Called him HIS Mentor, 269
Member Indian National Congress, 268
Principles, 267
Social and Political Leader, 267
Gol Gumbuz, 188
Golden
Period of Mughal Architecture, 194
Temple, 212
Golkonda, 151
Sultanate, 188
Gondwana, 2
Govt. of India 1935 Act, 276
Gram Devata, 21
Grammar Rules, 7
Granaries, 19, 21
Grant, Charles, 238
Greased Cartridge with Beef and Pork Fats, 221
Great
Bath, 20
Civilisation, 21
Wall of China, 123
Greco-Buddhism Hybrid Culture, 120
Greco-Roman, 137
Greek(s)
And Ashoka Sources, 139
And Roman Empire, 138
And Romans, 140
Doctrines, 106
Dramas, 39
Kingdom, 111
Ground Stone Tools, 16
Guerrilla Raiders, 280
Gujarat, 122
Gupta
Administration, 115
Dynasty, 40, 113
Empire, 57, 115, 126, 128, 135
Period, 39
Period Great Scholars, (GPGS), 116
Aryabhata, 116
Kalidasa, 116
Varahamitra, 116
Vatsyayana, 116
Gurjara Pratiharas, 128, 129, 147
Army, 128
Gurjaras, 127
Bhimal, Capital, 127
Great Role in Northern India, 127

Guru
Arjan Dev, 209
Gobind Singh, 209, 211
Har Gobind, 211
Nanak, 209
Religious Leader, 209
Social Reformer, 209
Gyanakanda, 33
Aranyakas, 33
Upanishads, 33

H

Hair Style and Ornaments, 16
Hand Axe Industry, 13
Harappa and Mohanjodaro (Indus Valley Civilisation), 18, 19
Harappan
Civilisation, 18, 19-21, 26, 28
Development System, 18
Empire, 20
Religions, 21
Harbour of Calicut, 216
Harihara, 154
Harihara I, 153, 154
Harimandir Saheb (Golden Temple), 212
Harivamsa Purana, 45, 55
Harshavardhana, 126, 127
Of Kannauj, 126
Harshavardhana's Sanskrit Plays, 127
Nagananda, 127
Priyadarshika, 127
Ratnavali, 127
Health and Sanitation, 21
Hellenic Sovereigns of Egypt—Syria, 122
Hemu, Hindu king, 191
Heracles, 140, 105
Herodotus, 108
Division of Egypt Peoples, 99
Hill Stations, 234
Himalayan
Foothills, 6
Snowline, 4
System, 4, 5
Zone, 2
Hinayana (Theravada), 80
Hindi
Language, 9
Official National Language of India, 10
Hindu
And Buddhist Religions, 120
And Muslims Saints, 212
And Urdu, 10
Civilisation, Origin of-, 12
Community in Bengal, 252
Cosmology, Philosophy and Geology, 56
Dynasty, 143
Funeral Practices, 246
Gurjar Rajput Tribes, 130
Philosophy, 174, 248
Pilgrim Centres, 192
Polytheism, 247
Reforms, 71
Religious Practices, 56
Religious Works, 185
Renaissance, 246
Schools of Philosophy, (HSP), 160
Buddhism, 160
Carvaka, 160
Jainism, 160
Sankhya, 160
Vaisheshika, 160
Shahis, 123
Social System, 148
Society, 216
Temples, 185
Hinduism, 11, 56, 69, 71, 160, 237, 245, 248, 252, 255, 257, 258, 277

Hindukush, 120
Hindus Main Groups, 69
    Sakta, 69
    Shaiva, 69
    Vaishnavas, 69
Hindu—Singhalese, 8
Hindustani Music, 65
Hindutva, 278
Holkers of Indore and Malwa, 214
Homer, 39
Homonid Fossils, 13
Hospitals, 109
Hoysala
    Architecture, 154
    Kingdom, 163
    Period Philosophers, 153
        Basaveshwara, 153
        Madhvacharya, 153
        Ramanujacharya, 153
    Rule, 153
Hoysalas (Kannada Empire), 152, 153
Humayun Tomb, 206
Hume, Alan Octavian, 235
Huna Invasion and Fall of Gupta Empire, 117
Hunas, 121, 123
Huns, 115
Hunting, 24
Hunting and Gathering Societies, 58
Hyder Ali, 196, 201
    5th Son of Fatah Muhammad, 197
    Friendly Relations with Christians, 197
    King of Mysore, 196
Hymns to Agni, Indra—, 258

I

Ibrahim Lodi, 190
Ice Age, 4
Idol Worship, 71
Idolatry and Ritualistic Worship, 257
IITs, 278
Iltutmish, 183
Images of Females, 16
Immigrants of Indo-Aryan, 118
Imperial Rome, 20
Important Schools of Philosophy, 69
    Nyaya—Vedanta, 69
Independence Movement, 2, 267
India
    And Hellenistic Influences, 120
    And Pakistan, 223, 280
    Ethnic Population, 6
    Geological Formations of-, 2
    Seventh Largest Country in World, 4
    Plains, 6
    Zones, 4
        Central India, 4
        East India, 4
        North-East India, 4
        Northern India, 4
        Southern India, 4
        West India, 4
India's
    Neighbour, 221
    Spiritual Traditions, 250
Indian
    And Pakistan Wars, 279
    And Pakistan, 209
    Armies at Ganges River, 119
    Army, 173
    Caucasians, 6
    Civil Services, 234, 267
    Civilisation, 32, 55, 119, 137, 276
    Culture, 2, 8, 19

Elephants, 18
Imperial Power, 213
Independence, 1
Independence Movement, 223, 235, 271, 274
Institutes of Managements, 274
Languages, 322-324
Legislature Councils, 237
Music, 64
Mythology, 8
National Congress, 235, 267
National Movement, 269
Nationalist Movement, 262, 269
Ocean, 5
Peninsula, 2
Philosophy, 38, 52, 69, 174
Social, Religious Reform Movement, 246
Society, 244
States and Union Territories Details, 320, 321
Waters, 214

Indica of Alberuni, 173
Indigo to Persia, 156
Indo-Aryan
- Languages, 9
- Linguistic Family, 6, 7
- Origin of Language, 9

Indo-European
- And Dravidians, 28
- Family, 9
- Family of Languages, 6
  - Assamese, 6
  - Bengali, 6
  - Dogri, 6
  - Gujarati, 6
  - Hindi, 6
  - Kashmiri, 6
  - Konkani, 6
  - Marathi, 6
  - Nepali, Oriya, Punjabi, Sanskrit, 7
  - Sindhi and Urdu, 8
- Parent Languages, 10

Indo-French Researchers, 12
Indo-Gangetic
- Plains, 5, 216
- Riverine System, 4

Indo-Greek,120
- Kingdom, 120
- Kings, 120

Indo-Parthians, 122
Indo-Roman Relations, 142
Indo-Sassanid Kushanshahs, 123
Indo-Scythians, 120
- Sakas, 120

Indra, 30, 31
- Prominent God of Rig-Veda, 26

Indus
- And its Tributaries, 5
- Civilisation, 170
- River, 214
- Valley, 15, 25, 27, 87, 118
- Valley
  - Cities, 24
  - Civilisation, 18
  - Region, 26

Industrial
- Programme in India, 236
- Revolution, 110

Industrialisation, 250
Inscriptions, 109, 110, 143
- Of Hathigumpha, 124

Interpretation Act of 1889, 223
Invaders, 216
- Aryans, 216
- Huns, 216
- Kushana, 216
- Yueh-Chis, 216

Invasion of Timur, 182

Iran, 118
Iran Tools and Weapons, 25
Iranian
  Avestha, 29
  Highland, 25
Irish Constitution 277
Irrigation, 5, 224
  Canals, 109, 243
  Works, 110
Isha-Upanishads, 33
  Kena Upanishads with Sama Veda, 33
  With Shukla Yajurveda, 33
Islam, 136
  And Christianity, 247
Islamic Sultanates, 182
Ismail Adil Shah, 188

J

Jagannath Temple Puri Orissa, 134
Jahangir, 210
Jain
  Monks, 45, 149, 192
  Monuments, 145
    Kambadahalli, 145
    Shravanabelagola, 145
  Remains Sites, (JRS), 73
    Chalukyas, 73
    Chandel or Rajputs, 73
    Gupta, 73
    Kalachuris, 73
    Kushana, 73
    Maurya, 73
    Rashtrakutas, 73
    Sunga, 73
  Version of Ramayana, 49
  Versions of Mahabharata, 45
  Writers, 76
    Pampa—Ranna, 76
Jainism, 72-74, 127, 145
  And Buddhism, 142, 144
Jalaluddin Mohammad
  Akbar, 170, 191
  Third Mughal Emperor, 191
Jamshedpur Bengal, 236
Janna's Yashodra Charita, 153
Japan and China, 249
Japanese Constitution, 277
Jarasandha, 85
Java, Malaya, 143
Jazya Tax on Brahmans, 185
Jinnah, Muhammad Ali, 269, 270
  Founder Pakistan, 269
Jivaka Chintamani, 144
Jizya (Jazya), 192
Jnanayoga, 70
Judiciary and Administrative Jobs, 148
Jurassic Period, 2

K

Kabul, 189
  River, 118
Kadambas, 144, 145
Kakatiya
  Dynasty, 151
  Rulers, 150
    Rudra—Pratipendra, II, 150
Kalabhras, 144
Kalachuris, 151
Kalinga, 87, 89, 90, 134, 138, 155
  Country, 111
  War, 109
Kalyani Chalukyas, 149
Kama Sutra, By Vatsyayana, 116
Kamban's Ramavatharam, 144
Kanava Gotras, 113
Kanchipurna, 162

Kannada Literature, 153
Kanva Dynasty, 113
Karma, 79
  Kanda, 33
    Brahmins (Commentaries), 33
    Samhitas, 33
  Theory in Jainism, 74
  Yoga, 52
Karnataka Coastal Rivers, 330
Karur, Capital of Cheras, 141, 143
Kashmir, 121, 280
Katha Upanishads, 52
Kauravas, 49
  Army, 41
Kautilya, 88-91, 171
Kaveri
  Delta, 143
  Poompa Hinam, Chola Town, 143
  River Basin, 330
Kerala Coastal Rivers, 330
Kharvela, King of Kalnga, 124
Khilji Dynasty, 151, 182, 183
Khonde Rao, 197
King
  Amoghavarsha I, 148
  Bhoj, 131
    Ruler of Malwa, 131
      Writings on Philosophy,— Medicine, Yoga and Phonetics, 131
  Dhana Nanda, 86
  Janamejaya, 39
  Kakushtavarma, 144
  Martin Luther Jr., 53
  Narasimha Deva, 134
  Saunaka Kulapati, 39
  Udayan, 83
Kingdom of Chalukyas, 130
Kingdoms of-, 145
  Gujaraths, 145
  Kosala, 145
  Lata, 145
  Malva, 145
Kohinoor Diamond, 151
Kollur Mine, 151
Konarak Sun Temple, World Heritage Site, 134
Krishna, 72
Krishna and Jarasandha, 45
Krishna's Order to Arjuna, 53
Krishnadevaraya, Son of Narasa Nayaka of Tuluva Community, 155
Kshitigarba, 81
Kumaragupta I, 115
Kumaragupta II, 115
Kumaragupta III, 115
Kumara Devi, 113
Kumarapala, Chalukya Ruler, 77
Kuru Panchala Kingdoms, 121
Kurukshetra War, 39, 41, 44
Kushanas (Kushans), 122, 123, 113

L

Labour Government (England), 238
Lahore Fort, 206
Lak Phusi Pass, 21
Lakshdweep, 143
Lal Bagh in Bangalore, 199, 201
Lancashire Clothing, 236
Land System, 107
Language of Supreme Court/ High Courts, 305, 306
Languages, 6
Languages and Literatures, 126
Laurasia, 2
Lawrence, John, 234
Leo Tostoy, 248

Lichchavi Princess, 113
Lingayat or Virashaiva Cult, 152
  Dharma, 168
Linguistic Science, 7
Literacy, 110
  Movement, 2
Literacy, 10
  Languages
    Braj, Avadhi, Mathili, 10
Lodi (Lodhi) Dynasty, 182, 185
Lodi's Army, 190
Lord
  Amherst, Governor General, 238
  Bahubali, 73
  Krishna in Champu Style, 154
  Lytton, 234
  Palmerston, 222
  Vishnu, 114

M

Macaulay, 244
Macedonian(s), 119
  Army, 104
Madagascar and South Africa, 2
Madanpala, Pala King, 133
Madhava Varma, 128
Madhavacharya, 70, 164, 165, 166
  Proponent of Tattvavada (Philosophy of Reality), 164
  Works, 166
    Commentaries on Brahmsutras, 166
    Commentaries on Gita, 166
    Commentaries on Upanishads, 166
    On Vedas, 166
      Related to Tattvavada, 167
Madhva from South Canara, 137
Madhya Pradesh, 122
Madrasas, 184
Magadh Kingdom, 113
Magadha
  Dynasties, 84
  Empire, 83, 84, 85
Magadhan Army, 87
Magadhi (North Bihar), 10
Mahabharata, 38, 39, 40, 49, 56, 85
  Great Story of Bharata Dynasty, 39
  List of Formations, 43
  Major Sanskrit Epic, 39
  Outlne, 41
  Parvas, 40
Maha-Janapadas (Indo-Aryan Kingdoms), 37, 83
Mahanadi River Basin, 329
Maharani Regent, 120
  Vanivilas Sannidhi Pratap Kumari Devi, 130
Maharashtra, 122
  Coastal Rivers, 331
Mahavira, Vardhaman, 73
Mahayana, 80-82
  Buddhism, 120
  Buddhist, 127
Mahayana's Great Vehicle, 81
Mahipala, King of Bengal, 144
Mahmud of Ghazni, 172, 173
  Son of a Turkish Slave, 172
Main Provisions of Bill, 222-223
Maitrakas, 128
  Empire, 128
Maitreya, 81
Maja Masjid Mosque, 194

Major Puranas, 60
Agni—Vishnu, 60-63
Sects, (Jains), 75
Digambaras, 75
Shvetambar, 75
Major Upanishads, 33
Aitareya, 33
Brihadaranyaka, 33
Chhanddgya, 33
Isha, 33
Katha, 33
Kena, 33
Mandukya, 33
Prashna, 33
Shwetashweatara, 33
Taittiriya, 33
Malabar Coast, 141
Malaprabha Basin in Karnataka, 146
Malaya and Singapore, 221
Malaysian Constitution, 277
Male and Female Demons, 31
Malik Ahmad Shah Babri, Govt. of Junnnar, 187
Malik Kafur, 183
General of Alauddin Khilji, 183
Malva, 122
Mamluk (Slave) Dynasties, 182, 183
Mandalay Burma (Myanmar), 270
Mandela, Nelson, 53
Manjusri, 81
Mantras/Hymns, 28
Manufacturing Activity, 16
Maratha
Empire, 213
War II, 198
Maratha's Defensive Strategy, 215
Marco Polo, 141
Maritime Trade, 139
Marshal, John, 110
Maruts, 30
Marwari (Rajasthan), 10
Maurya, Chandragupta, 86, 87, 109
Mauryan Empire, 107, 109, 118, 123, 136, 139
Max Muller, 248
Mayurasharma, King, 145
Medical Practices, 94
Medieval Cholas, 144
Mediterranean and Alpine Sub-Races, 6
Meenakshi Temple Madurai, 141
Megalithic Culture, 25
Megasthenes Greek Historian, 96-100, 109, 137, 140
Hunting the Elephants, 102
Mutilation, 101
On Administration, 108
On Armed Women, 102
On Brahmins, 105, 106
On Hunting, 102
On Manners of Indians, 100
On Other Things, 108
On Palace, 107
On Punishment, 101
Sacrifices, 102
Megasthenes's Indica, 96, 97
Mehrgarh, 18, 27
Mehrgarh Site, 15-17
Mesopotamia, 25
Mesozoic Period, 2
Message—On Rocks and Stones, 111
Metal Workers Furnaces, 21
Metallurgical Seamless Globe, 208
Middle Paleolithic Sites, 14
North Karnataka, 14

Military
Based Society, 26
Defence, 19, 25
Encounters with Pakistan, 280
Expedition to Afghanistan and Tibet, 221
Formations, 42
Organisation, 213
Rockets, 199
Rockets Innovation, 197
Mimamsa, 53
Ministry of Education and Culture, 10
Mlechchha Dynasty Rulers, (MDR), 126
Modern Influence in Northern India, 11
Moghulistan Land of
Mughals, 171
Mohammad Bin Tughlaq, 184
Mohenjo Daro, 20
Moist Deciduous Regions 5
Monasteries, 161
Mongol Invasion, 182
Mongoloid
Hill People, 20
People, 6
Monism, 160, 163
Monotheism, 164
Of Hinduism, 69
Morley-Minto Reforms, 237
Mother
Earth, 59
Goddess, 21, 59
Goddess Kottravai, 142
Mount Abu, 127
Mud-Brick Structures, 16
Mughal
Astronomers, 207
Celestial Seamless Globes, 208
Cuisines, 207
Empire, 170, 218
Observatories, 207
Rule in India, Influence of, 206
Muhammad of Ghur, 181
Assassinated in 1206, 182
Muhammad of Ghor, 183
Muhammad Shah III, 188
Mumtaz Mahal, 194
Music Traditions, 64
Muslim
Community (ies), 157, 185
Conquest, 128
Cultures, 245
Dynasties, 182
Invasions, 129, 151, 152
Muslim Kingdoms Conquered by Aurangzeb, (MKC), 195
Adilshahis of Bijapur, 195
Nizams of Ahmadnagar, 195
Qutub Shahs of Golconda, 195
Mutiny, 222
Muziris in Pandayan Kingdom, 141
Mysore
Chitradurga, 156
Rockets, 197, 198
War II, 200
War III, 200
War IV, 200
Mystical Poems, 132
Mythology
And Functions, 57, 58
Cosmological, 58
Metaphysical, 58
Psychological, 58
Sociological, 58

N

Naga Lineage, 115
Naimisha Forest, 39
Nanda Dynasty, 84
Narmada
Homo, 13

Man, 12, 13
Valley, 13
Nasiru-ud-Din Muhammad Humayun, 190
National
Book Trust, 274
Institutes of Technology, 274
Literacy Academy, 274
Parties of India and Their Symbols, 314-319
Nava Vidhan Religious Movement, 237
Negritos, 6
Nehru, Jawahar Lal (Brief), 273
Autobiography, 274
Discovery of India, 274
Education and Social Reforms, 274
Glimpses of World History, 274
Indian PM, 1, 238, 248, 276-278
Towards Freedom, 274
Neolithic Period, 16
Nepal, 129
New Dominion of Pakistan, 238
Nicobar Islands, 219
Nilgiris Hills, 234
Nimabarka and Vallabha from Andhra Prdesh, 137
Nirvana, 79, 81
Nizam Shahi Dynasty, 187
Noble
Eight Fold Path, 82
Works of Kalachuri Period, 152
Non-Aryan Invasion Theory, 27
Non-Cooperation, 237
Non-Dualistic
Meditation, 237
Philosophy, 160
Nordic Element, 6
North-East India, 14
Northern
Mountain Belt, 4
Pakistan, 118
Nurudin Salim Jahangir, 193
see under Jahangir also
Administration, 193
Jhangir, Art and Architecture, 193
Death in 1627 AD, 194
Paintings, 193
Nyana, 53

O

Oceanic Fossil, 2
Official Language of India, 304, 324
Old
Kingdom of Egypt, 19
Upanishads Details, 34
Oligocene and Miocene Period, 4
Order of Monks, 111
Organisations, 1
Arya Samaj, 2
Brahma Samaj, 1
Organised Industry in Western Asia, 21
Ottomon, 218

P

Pahlavas or the Ancient
Parthians of Iran, 121, 122, 146
Paintings, 116
Pakistan, 15, 190
Department of Arachaeology, 15
Pala
Dynasty, 133
Dynasty of Kamrupa (Assam)
Dynasty Rulers, (PDR), 126, 133

Brahmpala, 126
Gopala, 126
Harshapala, Dharmapala and Jayapala, 126
Indrapala, 126
Ratnapala, 126
Rulers Texts on All Knowledge, 132, 133
School of Sculptural History, 133
Palaces, Tombs or Forts Built by Mughals, 206
Palas, 132
Followers of Mahayana, 132
Followers of Tantric System of Buddhism, 132
Gopala First Ruler, 132
Paleolithic
Sites, 12
Tools, 14
Adamgarh, 14
Belan, 14
Bhimbetka, 14
Central Asia, 14
Gujarat, 14
Rajasthan, 14
Sithwal, 14
Palestine Imports, 156
Copper—Gold and Silver, 156
Pali 9
Pallavas, 141, 146
Pandaia Daughter of Heracles, 140
Pandava Charitra, 45
Pandavas, 45, 49
Pandayan (s), 139, 141
Temple Architecture, 141
Trade and Literature, 141
Queen, 140
Pandya
Kingdom, 140, 141
Kulasekharan, 140
Panini, 7, 121
And Kautilya, 119
Principles, 7
Parliament of World Religions Chicago, 248
Parliamentary Form of Government, 276
Parmaras, 130
Parshavanath, 72
Pathans, 221
Patliputra, 85, 110
Peacock Throne, 194
Pearl Mosque Agra, 194
Pebble Stone Tools, 14
Pegu Islands, 144
Persia and India, 121
Persian
Arabic and Turkish Words, 11
Achaemenid Empire, 119
And Arabic, 10
And Greek Invasions, 119
Cultural Influences, 170
Dynasty, 123
Gulf, 221
Rule, 121
Peshwa, Madhavarao, 214
Peshwas, 214
Phallic Worship, 21
Philosophers, 1
Pillard Hall, 20
Pillars Marking Distances, 110
Plan for Partition (1947), 237
Plato, 106
Plebiscite in Kashmir, 280
Pleistocene
Epoch, 13
Mammals, 13
Period, 18
Pliny, Roman Historian, 142

Plutarch, 119
Poetry and Drama, 8
Poets—Instrumentalists, 206
Policies and Society, 2
Policy of Non-Violence or Ahimsa, 109
Portugal's
  Northern Province, 218
  Settlements of Daman, Diu, Chaul, Goa—Mumbai, 218
Portuguese, 218
  East India Company, 217
Porus, 119
Postal Services (1854), 233
Practice of Sati, 246
Practices, 1
  Sati, 2
  Superstition, 2
  Untouchability, 2
Prakrit
  Dialect, 9
  Languages, 8
Prehistoric
  India, 12
    Skilled in Crafting Stone Tools, 12
    Skilled in Havel Axes, Cleavers, Flakes, 12
  Inhabitants, 6
Primeval Man, 31
Primitive Agriculture, 24
Princely States, 224
Princess
  Of Kadamba of Kuntla Region, 115
  Sugayadevi, 130
  Vijayadevi, 130
Prolaraja, First King of Kakatiyas, 150
Protection of Artisans, 94
Proto-Indo-Iranians Times, 29
Ptolemy, 141
  Astronomer, 143
Pulakesi I, 145
Pulakesi II, 145, 146
Punjab, 121
  Folk Dances, 212
Puranas, 53, 55, 56, 57, 85, 258
  Bhagavata, 55
  Classic Literary Text, 53
  Garuda, 55
  Narada, 55
  Padma, 55
  Stories of Gods, 56
  Varaha, 55
  Vishnu, 55
Puranas/Mythologies, 53
Puranic Hinduism, 255
Puru Gupta, 115
Purushapura (Modern Peshawar), 118
Pushya Varma, 125
Pushyamitra Sunga, 113

Q

Qasim Basid, Founder of Bidar Sultanate, 187
Queen Victoria's Proclamation, 234
Quit India Movement, 237
Quran, 39
Qutub Shahi
  Dynasty, 188
  Rulers, 189
Qutub-ud-Din Aibak, 183

R

Rabab, 211
Radhakrishnan, S, 29
Radio Carbon Dates, 15
  Neolithic—Dam Sadaat, 15
Rai Dynasty, 123
Raigad, Maratha Empire Capital, 213

Raja
  Jaipal, 170, 172
  Wadiyar of Mysore, 197
Rajagopalachari, Chakravarti,
  Brief, 274-275
Rajasthan, 122
  Kucch Zones, 2
Rajendra Chola's Navies, 143
Rajshahi (Bangladesh), 219
Rajya, Rashtra, Desha—
  Avani, 115
Ramagupta, Samudragupta's
  Elder Son, 114
Ramakrishna Mission, 246,
  247
Ramakrishna Paramhansa,
  246, 247, 259
  Mystic, 246
  Nirvikalpa Samadhi
    Experience, 247
  Principles, 247
  Teachings, 248
Ramanuja from Kanchi, 137
Ramanujacharya, 161, 162,
  163
  Philosopher, Spiritual
    Leaders, 161
Ramanujacharya's
  Books, 163
  Theistic Philosophy, 70
  Vishishtadvaita
    Philosophy, 163
Ramayana, 47-49
  And Mahabharata, 38, 83,
    119
Rana Ratan Singh, 183
Ranjit Nagaara, 211
Ranjit Singh, Maharaja, 209,
  210
Rann of Kutch, 280
Rashtrakuta(s), 130, 149
  Empire, 147
  Inscriptions, 148
Rayalaseema (Land of
  Stones), 151
Razia Sultana, 183
Rebellion of 1857, 221, 222
Red Fort, 194
Red Fort Agra, 206
Red Sea Ports, 156
Red Ware, 17
Reform
  Brahmanism's Practices,
    252
  Movement, 223
Reformations, 184
Regional Languages, 9
Regionalism, 137
Religious
  Persecutions (of Sikhs),
    210
  Philosophical Beliefs, 1
  Poets, Kabir, 71
  Proclamation, 111
  Teachings, 1
  Traditions, 142
Renunciation of Money and
  Property, 51
Reservation of Seats, 276
Revolt of 1857, 244
Ribhus, 30
Rig-Veda, 29-31, 34, 56, 60
  Aryan First Great Literary
    Work, 25, 26
  Gods, 29
  Period, 32
Right to Constitutional
Remedies, 299
Rights of Citizenship, 285,
  289
Rishis, 31
  Agirasa, 31
  Atharvana, 31
Ritualism, 164
River
  Bolan, 16
  Brahmputra, 5
  Gandak, 151
  Ganges, 119

Ghaghara, 151
Indus, 5, 214
Kabul, 118
Kortallaiyar North West Chennai, 12
Tungbhadra, 135
Rivers
Andhra Pradesh Coastal-, 330
Flowing in The Arabian Sea, 330
Karnataka Coastal, 330
Kerala Coastal, 330
Of India, 325
Tamil Nadu Coastal, 330
West Bengal Coastal, 328
Rocket
Research, 199
Technology, 197
Rockets, 199
Roman
Coins, 143
Empire, 19, 110, 143, 218
Empire by Greco-Roman Sailors, 216
Gold Coins, 139
Roots and Tubers, 12
Roy, Raja Ram Mohun, 238, 241, 245, 246, 252, 254, 255
Educationalist, 245
Journalist, 245
Philosopher, 245
Politician, 245
Social Reformer, 245
Writer, 245
Royal Woolwich Arsenal, 199
Rudra, 30
Rudrabhatta's Jagannatha Vijay, 154
Rudradeva, 151
Rudraprshnabhashya by Vidyatirtha, 154
Rule of Govind II, 147
Rules of War, 43
Russian Constitution, 277
Russo-Japanese War, 249

S

Sabuktagin, Amir of Ghazni, 170
Sailendra Empire of Java, 133
Sakas, 121, 124
Salvation, 70, 161, 166
Sama
Gana, 64
Veda, 30, 36, 64
Samakhya, 53
Sambara, Dasyus Ruler, 26
Samudragupta, 113
Sangam, 143
Academy, 139
Era, 139
Kingdom, 144
Literature, 139
Sangha, 111
Sankara, 70
From Kerala, 137
Sankara's Philosophy, 70
Sanskrit, 7-9
Classical Language, 8
Literature, 8
System of Education, 239
Satraps, 216
Satvahanas, 126
Dynasty of Andhra Pradesh, 113, 118
Empire, 123,146
Satyagraha, 237
Satyarth Prakash, (Arya Samaj Religious Book), 259
Saurashtra, 122
Savana Type of Vegetation, 12
Savitar, 30
Sayyid Dynasty, 182
Scientific Interactions, 8
Astrology, 8

Linguistics, 8
Mathematics, 8
Scindhias of Gwalior and Ujjain, 214
Sculpture, 116
Scythians and
Kushanas, 120
Parthians Invaders, 121
Sea Level, 4
Second
Council at Vaishali, 80
Set of Six Puranas, (SSS), 55
Bhavishya, 55
Brahma, 55
Brahmananda, 55
Brahmavaivarta, 55
Markandeya, 55
Vamana, 55
Seleukia Empire, of Iraq, 145
Seleukos, 87, 96, 146
Greek Ambassador, 140
Semi Industry, 21
Sen, Amartya, 277
Sen, Hemanta, Founder of Sena Dynasty, 133
Sen, Kesab Chandra, 247, 259, 260
Bengali Religious Preachers, 259
Sen, King Lakshman, 133
Sena Dynasty, 133
Servants of India Society, 267, 268
Settlements, 12
Sites, 19
Shah Jahan, 194
Shah Jahan's Contribution to Architecture, 206
Shahi Dynasties, 123
Shaivite Chola Rulers, 163
Shankaracharya's Advaita Philosophy, 160, 162
Shantineketan, 261
Shell Industry, 17
Shias, 185
Ship Building, 156
Shiva Sutra, 213
Shivaji, 278 see under Chatrapati also
Shivaji Jayanti, 271
Shravanabelagola, 73
Shunga Dynasty, 113
Siberia, 121
Sikander Lodi, 185
Sikh
Architecture, 212
Art and Culture, 212
Culture, 212
Empire, 209, 210, 211
Empire Security Administration, 210
Empire Security, Innovation Military, Eco. and Govt. Reforms, 210
Sikhism, 209, 210
Silk Route, 118
Simla Summer Capital, 234
Sind and Baluchistan, 20
Sindh, 6
Skandagupta, 115
Skinning, 12
Slave Dynasty, 170
Smelting Copper, 17
Social
And Religious Practices, 69
Order, 69
Reform Movement, 254
Reformers, 243
Reforms, 152, 233, 243, 259, 269
System of Dowry and Sati, 259
Untouchability, 259
Women's Education, 259

Security, 32
System, 107
Sogdiana, 121
Sohan Valley near Rawalpindi Pakistan, 14
Soil Under Irrigation, 97
Solankis, 130
Soma, 30, 31
Somapura Mahavira, Built by Dharampala, 132
South Africa, 237
South Asia, 5
Southern Gondwana, 2
Soviet Union, 280
Special Directions, 307
Sri Aurobindo, 248
Sri Gupta, 113
Sri Lanka and India, 141
Sringeri, 154, 161
St. Francis Xavier, Jesuit Missionary, 218
Standardisation of
Development of
Devanagri, 10
Of Hindi Grammar, 10
Steel Exports, 156
Stegoden (Extinct Animal), 13
Stone Implements, 13
Choppers, 13
Cleavers, 13
Hand Axe, 13
Scrappers, 1
Strabo, Historian, 140
Sub-Continent of Indian Region, 2
Suddhi, Purification Ceremony, (Arya Samaj), 255
Sumarians and Persians Gulf Region, 24
Sumatra, 143
Sungas, Kanavas, 124
Supercontinent of Pangaea, 2
Superstitions, 250
Surat Session of Congress, 270
Suri, Acharya Hemachandra, 77
Suri, Sher Shah, 191
Surya, 30
Sutra Period, 53
Sutta Pitaka, 80
Swadeshi Clothes, 236
Swaraj, 270
Swedish East India Company, 217

T

Tagore, Debendranath, 237
Tagore, Dwarkanath, 246
Tagore, Rabindra Nath, 2, 242, 260
Bengali Poert, 260
Gitanjali, 261
List of Poetry—English, 261, 262
Musician, 260
Painter, 260
Playwright, 260
Taj Mahal Agra, 194
World Heritage Site, 206
Tajikistan, 122
Takshashila (Modern Taxila), 118
Tamil
Land, 109
Language, 141
Literature, 143
Tools, 12
Tantra, 258
Tantra and Vaishnava Bhakti, 247
Tantrism, 258
Tanwar Dynasty, 131
Descent of Chandravanshi Pandavas, 131
Tapti River Basin, 331
Taranatha, Tibetan Scholar, 132

Tata Iron and Steel Company, 236
Taxation System, 110
Taxsasila, 110
Teachings, 1
 Buddhist, 1
 Hindu, 1
 Jain, 1
 Of Gita, 53
 Of Vedas, 53
Technical Revolution, 21
Techniques of War, 183
Technological Progress, 110
Technology, 209
Technology of Mehrgarh I, 16
Telegraph Lines, 224
Temple of Augusti, 142
Terracota Beads, 16
Terrorism, 270
Thanjavur Maratha Kingdom, 214
Theism, 71
Theories of Eclipses, 175
Theravada First Council, 80
Third Set of Puranas, 55
Thousand Pillars Temple in Hanumakonda, 151
Tibet, 111, 245
 And Afghanistan, 210
Tilak, Bal Gangadhar, 53, 269
 Books Written by -, 271
 Critic of Western Education System, 270
 Educationalist, 269
 Gita Rahasya, 53
 Indian Nationalist, 269
 Joined Indian National Congress, 270
 Social Reformer, 269
 Swaraj is my Birth Right and I Shall have it, 269
Timurids-Great Cultural Traditions, 206
Tippu Sultan, 198-200, 209
 Death During 4th Mysore War, 200
 Hated Christians, 199
 Son of Hyder Ali, 198
Tirthankaras, 73
 Ajitanatha, 73
 Aristaneme, 73
 Rsabha, 73
 Worship, 75
Togau, 16
Togau/Kechi Beg Period, 17
Tomar Rulers, 131
Tools of Bronze and Copper, 19
Trade, 110
 With Ancient Near East, 19
Trading
 Centres, 219
 Monopoly, 217
Traditional Trade Rules, 218
Tripuri, Capital near Jabalpur, 151
Tropic of Cancer, 6
Trust Deed of 1830, Excerpts, 252
Tughlaq Dynasty, 182, 184, 185
Turko-Afghan Conqueror, 170
Turko-Afghan-Khiljis, 170
Turko-Iranian
 Areas, 206
 Cultures, 206
Turks, 170
Types of Music (TOM), 66
 Bhangra, 66
 Lavani, 67
 Light Classical, 66
 Rabindra Sangeet, 67
 Rajasthani Music, 67
 Uttrakhandi Music, 66

U

Ugrasrava Sauti, 39
Undavalli Caves, 128
United East India Company
of Netherlands, 217
Universal
Society, 171
Suffrage, 276
University of
Calcutta, 235
Nalanda, 127
Upanishadic Teachings, 70
Upanishads, 33, 56, 70, 71,
160, 162
And Darshanas, 38
Defined, 33
Ural Mountains, 29
Urdu, 9
Urdu Language, 207
Urubhanga by Bhasa, 40
USA Constitution, 277
Use of Copper and Bronze, 21
Uzbekistan, 122

V

Vachna Sahitya in Kannada,
168
Vaisampayana, 39
Vaisesika, 53
Vaishnava
Bhakti, 259
Movement, 70
Vakataka
Empire, 126
Rulers, 126
Vindhyasakti—
Harisena, 126
Vallabha Cult, 72
Vallabhacharya, 72
Valley of Indus Valley, 19
Varahamihira, 175, 176
Varahi Cave Temple at
Mahabalipuram, 146
Vardhamana of Jainism, 77
Vardhana, Kubja Vishnu,
147
Varman
Dynasty Ruled by
Kamrupa (Assam), 125
Dynasty Rulers, (VDR),
125, 126
Balavarman, 125
Bhuti Varman, 1125
Chandramukha
Varman, 125
Ganapati Varman, 125
Kalyana Varman, 125
Mahendra Varman, 125
Narayana Varman, 125
Pushya Varman, 125
Samudra Varman, 125
Sthitha Varman, 125
Susthitavu—Bhaskara
Varman, 125
Varuna, 30
Vasco-da-Gama, 216, 217
Portuguese Sailor, 216
Vashisht Advaita, 70
Veda, 33
Vedanta, 53, 70, 258
Philosophy, 70
Vedantic Schools of
Philosophy, 162
Vedantism, 258
Vedas, 8, 26, 28, 39, 127,
160, 161, 164, 255, 259,
257, 258
And Upanishads, 254
Vedic
Chronology, 271
Civilisation, 118
Cosmology, 31
Deities, 29
Agni, 29, 30
Dyaus, God of Heaven
and Earth, 29
Surya, 29
Varuna, 29

Vayu, 29
Hinduism, 255
Hymns, 29, 271
India, 26
Literature, 8, 33
Period, 28
Philosophy, 257
Sacrifices, 160
Schools, 148, 255
Times, 39, 118
Veera Ballala II, 152, 153, 154
Vengi Territory, 149
Venkata Hills, 137
Vidyaranya, A Sage at Sringeri, 151
Vidyasagar, Ishwar Chandra, 248
Brief Bio Sketch, 264-265
Vijayanagar Architecture, 159
Combination of Chalukya—Chola Style, 150
Vijayanagar Empire, 153, 154, 155, 157, 159, 183, 186
Kingdom of Bisnaga referred by the Portuguese, 154
Vikramaditya VI, 149
Vikramarjuna Vijaya, 148
Vikramendra Varma I, 128
Village Hathnora (Madhya Pradesh), 23
Vinaya Pitaka, 80
Vindhya Mountains, 170
Ranges, 135, 136, 138
Virasaiva Movement, 152
Vishayapatis, 115
Vishnu
And Shiva, 30
Pratap, 150
Purana, 154
Vishnukundins, 127
Empire, 127
Great Supporters of Learning, 127
Kings, 128
Ruled Deccan, Orissa, and South India, 127
Visionary Poets, 31
Vivekananda, Swamy, 248, 249, 250, 251
Chief Disciple of Ramakrishan Paramhansa, 246-248
Philosophy, 249
Vocational and Technical Schools, 274
Volcanic Eruptions, 2
Vyasa, 39
Vyuhas, 42

W

Wadiyar,
Kanteerava, Narsimharaja, 130
Krishnaraja, 130
Maharaja, Jayachamaraja, 130
War
Against Muslim Rulers, 153
And Agriculture, Main Occupation of the Times, 26
Drums, 212
Rockets, 197
With Marathas, 198
Way of Celestial Lights, 59
Weaponry, 42
Weights and Measures, 28
Weimer Constitution, 277
Western
Education System, 270
Gangas, 134
Konkans Coastline, 214
Satraps, 122
Wheel Made Vessels, 17

Wilkins, Charles, 7
Wood Working, 12
World
  Economy, 216
  Health Organisation, 278
  War II, 237, 271

X

Xuanzang, Chinese Pilgrim, 127

Y

Yadav Clans, 150
Yadavaprakasha, 162
Yadavas, 149, 150
  Feudatories of Western Chalukyas, 149, 150
Yajur Veda, 30, 34, 73
Yavanas, 121, 122
Yoga, 53
Yoga—Traditions, 56
Yueh-Chis and Huns, 136

Z

Zahi-ud-din Muhammad Babar, 189
Zakaya Caste, 148
Zanzibar, 221
Zoroastrian Iranian, 175